IB Study Guide

Psychology

FOR THE IB DIPLOMA

Jette Hannibal

OXFORD
UNIVERSITY PRESS

OXFORD
UNIVERSITY PRESS

Great Clarendon Street, Oxford OX2 6DP

Oxford University Press is a department of the University of Oxford.
It furthers the University's objective of excellence in research,
scholarship, and education by publishing worldwide in

Oxford   New York

Auckland   Cape Town   Dar es Salaam   Hong Kong   Karachi
Kuala Lumpur   Madrid   Melbourne   Mexico City   Nairobi
New Delhi   Shanghai   Taipei   Toronto

With offices in

Argentina   Austria   Brazil   Chile   Czech Republic   France   Greece
Guatemala   Hungary   Italy   Japan   Poland   Portugal   Singapore
South Korea   Switzerland   Thailand   Turkey   Ukraine   Vietnam

Oxford is a registered trade mark of Oxford University Press
in the UK and in certain other countries

© Oxford University Press 2012

British Library Cataloguing in Publication Data

Data available

ISBN-13: 978-0-19-912830-3

10 9 8 7 6 5 4 3 2 1

Printed in Great Britain by Bell & Bain Ltd, Glasgow

Paper used in the production of this book is a natural, recyclable product made from wood grown
in sustainable forests. The manufacturing process conforms to the environmental regulations of the
country of origin

Acknowledgements
The Publisher would like to thank the following for permission to reproduce photographs:

Cover photo: Brian J.Abela/Shutterstock.com

P29: Patrice Latron/Look At Sciences/Science Photo Library; P104: Mom I Love You! Stop Smoking!
Design by Terrence A. Lynch.

All artwork by HL Studios.

Introduction

This study guide in psychology has been designed to give students the opportunity to study and to revise each of the learning outcomes from the IB psychology guide. The content follows the structure of the guide for the core (HL/SL), the options (HL/SL), and qualitative research methods (HL). An additional section covers how to write papers, including short answer questions and essays. It also includes model answers with examiner's comments. Further chapters covering the Internal Assessment and the Extended Essay can be found on the associated website **www.oxfordsecondary.co.uk/psychsg**

This study guide is organized in boxes with headlines and bullet points to give you a quick overview and facilitate your learning. All learning outcomes are covered with examples. If the learning outcome asks for "examples" or "empirical studies" you have to learn at least two, and this is taken into consideration in the study guide.

This book is intended as a useful supplement to a course book, it can help students to focus and structure the learning process in relation to content and learning outcomes. It is also a support in revision of the material and the skills that are assessed at the exams. You are encouraged to read the **IB Psychology Course Companion**, which develops the various topics more and puts them into perspective.

The fundamental building blocks of psychology are theories, including concepts and empirical studies, combined with critical thinking skills. Many of the key studies and theories are provided here, with guidance on how to evaluate and discuss. One of the main challenges in studying psychology is to learn what psychologists have to say on various topics based on theoretical propositions and empirical research. Academic psychology reflects the complexity of human beings and there are no simple answers to complex questions. Part of the joy of studying psychology is to get an insight into fascinating human beings, how knowledge is created and why it is sometimes necessary to review what we know.

The psychology student is therefore trained in critical thinking and arguing based on evidence. These core skills are important and should always be the focus of learning psychology. Taken together, psychology students have a unique opportunity for becoming knowledgeable, reflective thinkers, and skilled communicators.

General learning outcomes

General learning outcomes

There are general learning outcomes for the levels of analysis and the options. They are stated at the beginning of each level of analysis and option in the description of the content, and they apply to all parts of the content.

Levels of analysis

You may be asked questions in the general learning outcomes in all levels of analysis, either alone or integrated with the content.

- Discuss how and why particular research methods are used at the biological/cognitive/sociocultural level of analysis.

This learning outcome is focused on research methods (e.g. the experiment, the observation, the case study, scanning techniques). Characteristics, strengths and limitations of various research methods are outlined in chapter 1. Apply this knowledge of methodology to particular studies where appropriate.

- Discuss ethical considerations related to research studies at the biological/cognitive/sociocultural level of analysis.

General ethical considerations are explained in unit 1.4. Some of these considerations may apply to research studies within all the levels of analysis. You need to look at a particular study and ask yourself which ethical considerations could be relevant for the study you use.

Options

The general learning outcomes apply to all the options, i.e. abnormal psychology, developmental psychology, health and human relationships, and sport psychology. So you could replace "behaviour" with the title of each options.

You may be asked questions in the general learning outcomes in all levels of analysis, either alone or integrated with the content. Since critical thinking (e.g. analysis, evaluation) is assessed in the options you should consider where it could be relevant to apply these learning outcomes (e.g. if it is relevant to evaluate the methodology of a research study).

- To what extent do biological, cognitive and sociocultural factors influence behaviour?

This means that you should consider the extent to which these factors could influence behaviour and integrate research in your answer.

- Evaluate psychological research (i.e. theories and/or studies) relevant to the study of behaviour.

This means that you should be able to evaluate particular theories and studies (i.e. focus on strengths and limitations) when relevant.

Contents

- Psychology is the scientific study of human behaviour and mental processes. In the IB Psychology programme, the focus is on the biological, cognitive and sociocultural levels of analysis when trying to explain psychological phenomena.
- Scientific means that data collection is done in a systematic way, and that the research is conducted using quantitative or qualitative methods.
- Psychologists use various research methods depending on the purpose of the study. Traditionally, quantitive methods have been considered to be the most scientific but there is an increasing use of qualitative methods in psychology. Sometimes qualitative and quantitative methods are used within the same study.
- Psychologists formulate theories to try to explain psychological phenomena. Psychological theories are based on certain assumptions and each theory includes concepts.
- Empirical research is often based on a research hypothesis. Sometimes the research hypothesis is based on a theory but sometimes the research study generates a theory.

What is a research hypothesis?

A research hypothesis is a precise and testable statement that predicts what is expected to happen to the variables in a research study. The research hypothesis may be based upon the predictions of a theory but this is not always the case. The research hypothesis is either accepted or rejected on the basis of the findings of an empirical study.

What is an empirical research study?

Empirical research is any activity that includes the organized collection and analysis of empirical data.

The researcher decides on which methodology to use for data collection in the research study depending on the aim of the study (for example quantitative or qualitative methods).

What is a research method?

A research method is the way the researchers collect and analyse data. The data of a research study is analysed and interpreted.

The method may be quantitative or qualitative.

Quantitative

- The information is numerical (e.g. experiments or surveys).
- Data analysis is in the form of statistics (e.g. mean, standard deviation, or percentages).

Qualitative

- The information is in the *meaning* of the data (e.g. diary entries or interview data).
- Data analysis is in the form of interpretation of the data to see what the data reveals.

The research process in experimental research

Observation of and theorizing about a phenomenon
↓
Formulation of a research hypothesis
↓
Collection of empirical data using a scientific method
↓
Analysis of the data and discussion of results
↓
Acceptance or rejection of the research hypothesis

Data means "information". Data is often measurable but not always. For example, qualitative research data is not usually measurable.

Evaluating empirical research studies

The way an empirical study has been conducted is evaluated because a number of considerations can affect the interpretation of the data, such as:
- methodological considerations
- ethical considerations
- cultural considerations
- gender considerations.

There are special ethical rules in relation to animal research, but the most important is that animals should not suffer unnecessary harm.

Consider some of these questions when evaluating research studies:

- **Has the study been conducted in an ethical way?** Have participants been put at risk? The British Psychological Society (BPS) and American Psychological Association (APA) have codes of ethics for psychological research.

- **Has participants' privacy been invaded or have their rights been violated?**

- **Did the animals suffer unnecessarily?** Was the research justified, that is, were the results so important that they justified the use of animals?

- **Did the study use a representative group of people as participants?** Is there a sampling bias? It could be that only males or only females participated in the study or there could be a cultural bias, for example only American college students participated.

- **Was the study carried out in a natural environment** (e.g. in a school) **or in an artificial environment** (e.g. in a research laboratory)?

- **Were the tasks given to participants similar to those they would encounter in real life?** Laboratory experiments often ask participants to do things they would not do in real life (e.g. giving electrical shocks to another participant).

- **Are the findings of a study supported or challenged by those of other studies?** If two studies investigate the same phenomenon and get very different results then we should consider why that is.

- **Are the findings socially sensitive?** If the research topic is controversial (e.g. deprivation studies, homosexuality, genetic research, or intelligence) special attention must be given to how the data is used. Some topics are controversial and research can be misused.

What is a psychological theory?
A psychological theory is a statement about a possible relationship between psychological variables.

The aim of psychological theories is to:

- summarize, simplify, and explain psychological phenomena
- make predictions about the possible relationship between psychological variables
- enable application to real-life issues (e.g. treatment programmes or educational schemes).

Psychological theories are *principles* and *not laws* like in some scientific theories.
Psychological theories should be seen as statements that are probable rather than certain.
Psychological theories are always open to some degree of probability or improbability.

Evaluating psychological theories
A psychological theory can give insight into psychological phenomena which cannot be observed (e.g. memory processes) or offer some order by describing and explaining psychological phenomena in the social world (e.g. prejudice) in a precise and coherent way with the use of psychological concepts.

Some criteria for evaluating a psychological theory:

- **Does the theory reflect the facts?** Is the theory validated through empirical research and observations?

- **Is the theory clear and understandable?** Are the predictions possible to grasp?

- **Is the theory useful for explaining as well as predicting?** Does the explanation offered make sense in relation to what is observed?

- **Is the theory practically useful?** Can it be used in real-life situations, such as predicting under what circumstances people will quit smoking? Or can it be applied to create strategies for behavioural change, such as educational soap-operas based on social learning theory?

- **Is it possible to test the theory in a scientific way?** Can the theory be supported in empirical studies?

What is a model?
A model is a physical representation of what a psychological phenomenon could look like. A model is mostly based on a theory. It is a hypothetical construct and it should not be mistaken for the real thing.

An example of a model is the multi-store model of memory suggested by **Atkinson and Shiffrin (1968)** which described the memory system as having several stores.

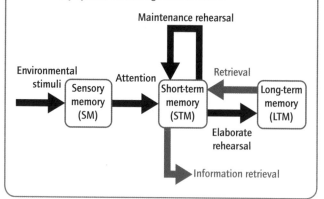

Types	Laboratory experiment (true experiment)	Field experiment (quasi experiment)	Natural experiment (quasi experiment)
Characteristics	■ It takes place in a laboratory (artificial environment). ■ The researcher manipulates the IV and controls all other variables (to avoid confounding variables). ■ There is a controlled environment and standardized procedures.	■ It takes place in a natural environment. ■ Impossible to obtain total control so there may be confounding variables. ■ The researcher manipulates the independent variable (IV).	■ The independent variable (IV) is naturally occurring. ■ The researcher does not manipulate the variables but records possible effects of a variable (IV) on another (the dependent variable or DV).
Strengths	■ It can establish **cause-effect** relationships. ■ There is variable control and accuracy of measurements → **objectivity**. ■ It is easy to **replicate** (increase reliability of results).	■ It has more ecological validity than laboratory experiments because behaviour occurs in a natural environment. ■ There are fewer demand characteristics (especially if participants do not know that they are being studied).	■ It has ecological validity – the focus is on natural behaviour in a natural environment. ■ There is very little bias from demand characteristics, especially if participants do not know they are being investigated.
Limitations	■ Artificiality may result in lack of ecological validity. ■ Results may be biased because of demand characteristics and experimenter effects. ■ Sometimes deception is necessary (ethical issue).	■ There is a risk of bias from confounding variables because there is less control. ■ It is nearly impossible to replicate exactly. ■ It is more difficult to record data accurately. ■ Possible ethical issues, for example problems with informed consent, exposure to unpleasant situations, invasion of privacy.	■ It is impossible to establish cause-effect relationship. ■ The research is impossible to replicate exactly – often case studies. ■ There are ethical issues of consent, deception, invasion of privacy.
Examples from the sociocultural level of analysis	Investigating the reaction of children after watching either an adult model acting aggressively towards a Bobo doll or not acting aggressively towards the Bobo doll (**Bandura et al. 1961**).	Investigating whether creating in-group/out-group attitudes in two groups of 11-year-old boys would result in intergroup aggression or not. Similarly, investigating whether cooperation could eliminate aggression (**Sheriff et al. 1956, 1961**).	Investigating levels of aggression in children in a small community on Saint Helena Island before and after the introduction of television (**Charlton et al. 1997**).

> **True experiment**: there is control over variables and the possibility for random allocation to experimental conditions.
> **Quasi experiment**: there is no control over variables (e.g. if they are naturally occurring such as gender, ethnicity, age) and no possibility of random allocation to conditions.

1.3 Non-experimental methods

Interviews	▪ Collection of data from individuals by asking them (self-report method) – mostly in a face-to-face situation (but can also take place by telephone or email).
	▪ Qualitative approach to research (mostly) – collecting subjective data, interpreted by the researcher.
	▪ No cause-effect relationships but rather "perception" and "subjective understanding" of situations and events.
Structured interviews	▪ Very structured approach – interview schedule states questions and the order they will be asked, but possible for interviewer to be flexible. Often closed questions.
	◘ **Strength**: easy to analyse data.
	◘ **Limitation**: somewhat artificial as the structure imposes many limitations to understanding participants.
Unstructured interviews	▪ Specification of topics and allocation of time (somewhat like a conversational interview).
	◘ **Strength**: open to the respondents' own ideas
	◘ **Limitation**: may be difficult to analyse data since the interview may take many different directions.
Semi-structured interviews	▪ Interview schedule with specified questions but more informal and flexible.
	◘ **Strength**: possible to maintain focus of interview (because of the interview schedule) but flexible and gives opportunity for respondents to talk more freely.
	◘ **Limitation**: data analysis very time consuming.
Ethics in interviews	▪ Ethical issues when interview topic is socially or personally sensitive.
	▪ Professional competence important so that interviewer can avoid making respondents feel uncomfortable.
	▪ Inform respondents about right to withdraw.
	▪ Avoid abuse of information.
Survey	▪ Often used to collect data from larger groups (small-scale surveys under 300, large-scale surveys over 300).
	▪ Questionnaires – or interviews (self-report data).
	▪ Use of closed or open-ended questions.
	◘ **Strength**: possible to collect data in a relatively quick and easy way.
	◘ **Limitation**: self-report data may be affected by response bias.
Questionnaire	▪ Data is collected through the use of written questions – surveys:
	◘ open-ended questions
	◘ closed questions
	◘ quantitative and qualitative data.
Qualitative data – qualitative analysis	▪ Data which express what people think and feel and which are not numerical. Qualitative data can be turned into quantitative if they are categorized.
	▪ Qualitative analysis: a kind of analyis that focuses on the *meaning* of what participants say and the way they experience an event, rather than individual words.
	▪ Qualitative analysis involves interpretation (often related to a theoretical framework, such as thematic analysis or grounded theory).
Quantitative data – quantitative analysis	▪ Numerical data (numbers) express amount, length etc., and the data can be measured in numbers or quantity.
	▪ Quantitative analysis uses the numerical data for analysis and interpretation. This takes place in the form of descriptive statistics (e.g. mean and standard deviation) and inferential statistics (any statistical test) which is used to make inferences about the data.

1.4 Ethics in research

<table>
<tr><th>General ethical principles in research with humans</th><th>General ethical principles in research with animals</th></tr>
<tr><td>

- **Informed consent**: Researchers must inform participants about the nature of the research study (briefing). The participants must know what the research is about and what will happen in the study so that they can consider whether they will participate or not. If children participate in research it is mandatory to obtain parental consent.

- **Deception should be avoided**: Researchers must not deceive participants deliberately without a valid justification. Slight deception could be used if it can be justified and it does not harm participants.

- **Protection of participants**: As a rule, participants should suffer no physical or psychological harm in the research. Researchers should avoid invasion of privacy in covert observational studies unless it is justified.

- **Debriefing**: Researchers must inform participants about the results of the research and assure them that they have not been harmed in any way, especially if deception was used.

- **Right to withdraw**: Participants have the right to withdraw at any moment in the research process. They also have the right to withdraw their data from the study when it is finished if they are not satisfied with the development of the research.

- **Confidentiality**: Researchers must assure that all data remain anonymous so that participants will not be recognized.

</td><td>

- **Stress and pain**: Researchers should take measures to minimize stress and pain.

- **Consider alternative ways**: Researchers should consider whether there are alternatives to animal research.

- **Approval of research projects by ethical committee**: Researchers must ask for permission to conduct research with animals. The application must include details of the study including potential harm to animals and possible benefits of that research.

- **Researcher competence**: The researcher must have skills and experience in doing research with animals.

It is only recently that ethical guidelines for animal research have been formulated. Much of the research conducted before the 1970s did not consider animal suffering a major problem. Animals are used in research because (1) they are easy to control, (2) they can be used where it is not possible to use humans for ethical reasons, (3) there is some similarity between animal and human physiology.

</td></tr>
</table>

Ethical considerations to include in evaluation of research

- Did the researchers get informed consent from participants?
- Were participants harmed in any way?
- Was the study justified? If participants or animals have been subjected to unpleasant experiences it is important to consider if the results made it worthwhile.
- Were there ethical guidelines when the study was conducted?
- Were the results important and have they benefited humans?
- Could the study have been conducted in alternative ways?

2.1 Outline principles that define the biological level of analysis

Principle 1: There are biological correlates of behaviour.
This means that there are physiological origins of behaviour such as neurotransmitters, hormones, specialized brain areas, and genes. The biological level of analysis is based on reductionism, which is the attempt to explain complex behaviour in terms of simple causes.

Principle 1 demonstrated in:

Newcomer et al. (1999) performed an experiment on the role of the stress hormone cortisol on verbal declarative memory. Group 1 (high dose cortisol) had tablets containing 160 mg of cortisol for four days. Group 2 (low dose cortisol) had tablets with 40 mg of cortisol for four days. Group 3 (control) had placebo tablets. Participants listened to a prose paragraph and had to recall it as a test of verbal declarative memory. This memory system is often negatively affected by the increased level of cortisol under long-term stress. The results showed that group 1 showed the worst performance on the memory test compared to group 2 and 3. The experiment shows that an increase in cortisol over a period has a negative effect on memory.

Principle 2: Animal research can provide insight into human behaviour.
This means that researchers use animals to study physiological processes because it is assumed that most biological processes in non-human animals are the same as in humans. One important reason for using animals is that there is a lot of research where humans cannot be used for ethical reasons.

Principle 2 demonstrated in:

Rosenzweig and Bennet (1972) performed an experiment to study the role of environmental factors on brain plasticity using rats as participants. Group 1 was placed in an enriched environment with lots of toys. Group 2 was placed in a deprived environment with no toys. The rats spent 30 or 60 days in their respective environments before being killed. The brains of the rats in group 1 showed a thicker layer of neurons in the cortex compared to the deprived group. The study shows that the brain grows more neurons if stimulated.

Principle 3: Human behaviour is, to some extent, genetically based.
This means that behaviour can, to some extent, be explained by genetic inheritance, although this is rarely the full explanation since genetic inheritance should be seen as genetic predisposition which can be affected by environmental factors.

- Researchers interested in the genetic origin of behaviour often use twins so that they can compare one twin with the other on a variable such as intelligence, depression or anorexia nervosa.

- Identical twins (monozygotic twins – MZ) are 100% genetically identical as they have developed from the same egg. They therefore act as a control for each other. Fraternal twins (dizygotic twins – DZ) have developed from two different eggs. They share around 50% of their genes so they are no more similar than siblings.

- Twin research never shows a 100% concordance rate so it is believed that genes are a predisposing factor rather than the cause of behaviour. Therefore it is also important to consider what environmental factors could influence the expression of the genetic predisposition.

Principle 3 demonstrated in:

Bouchard et al. (1990) performed the Minnesota twin study, a longitudinal study investigating the relative role of genes in IQ. The participants were MZ reared apart (MZA) and MZ reared together (MZT). The researchers found that MZT had a concordance rate of IQ of 86% compared to MZA with a concordance rate of IQ of 76%. This shows a link between genetic inheritance and intelligence but it does not rule out the role of the environment.

Examine one study related to localization of function in the brain

The case study of H.M.

- This case study is important because it provided evidence that there are different memory systems in the brain (see unit 3.3).
- **Milner (1957)** was the first to report the case of H.M. and the profound effects on memory functioning, following an operation which removed the hippocampus and adjacent areas in H.M.'s brain.
- **Corkin et al. (1997)** did a MRI scan of H.M's brain. Brain imaging was used because it allowed the researchers to get a precise picture of the brain damage. They discovered that parts of the temporal lobe, including the hippocampus and the amygdala, were missing, but also that the damage was not as extensive as previously believed.

H.M. suffered from epileptic seizures after he fell off a bike, aged seven. It was assumed that the seizures were connected to the accident and he became increasingly incapacitated.

When H.M. was 27, the neurosurgeon William Scoville, performed experimental surgery in order to stop the seizures. Tissue from the medial temporal lobe, including the hippocampus, was removed on both sides of his brain.

After the operation H.M. suffered from amnesia. He could not create new episodic and semantic memories, but he was able to learn a few procedural memories. His personality remained unchanged and there was no general intellectual impairment.

This case study shows that the hippocampus is important in memory processing and particularly in the storage of new memories.

H.M. participated in research studies until his death in 2008, and his brain was donated to science.

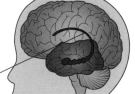

The hippocampus

What can be learned about localization of function in the brain in relation to memory from the case study of H.M?

- The hippocampus and the areas around the hippocampus play a critical role in converting memories of experiences from short-term memory (contemporary store) to long-term memory (permanent store).
- H.M. could retain memories of what had happened before the surgery. This indicates that the hippocampus is a temporary rather than a permanent memory store.

- H.M. could learn a few new procedural memories so this indicates that such memories are not stored via the hippocampus.
- The fact that H.M. (and other people with amnesia) had deficits in one part of the memory system but not in others is evidence that the brain has several memory systems and that these are supported by distinct brain regions.
- The study shows that memory processes are much more complex than originally believed. Although the hippocampus is very important in the storage of new memories it is not the only structure involved in the process.

Evaluation of the case study of H.M.

- The operation was based on the assumption that H.M's seizures would stop and it was successful in this respect, but the brain damage caused memory problems that had not been anticipated.
- H.M. participated in research for more than 50 years. He participated in many kinds of tests (e.g. cognitive tests, observations, and neuroimaging studies).
- This longitudinal case study has contributed enormously to the knowledge of how memory processes are related to specific brain areas, for example:
  - The medial temporal lobes are important for the forming, organization, consolidation, and retrieval of memories.

  - Cortical areas are important for long-term memory, for facts and events (semantic and episodic memories), and the use of that information in daily life.
  - Procedural memories are not processed by the hippocampus.
- There are ethical considerations in this case study. Since H.M. was not able to remember all the times he participated in research it could be argued that it was unethical. However, the findings of the study are very important and this justifies it.
- It is not usually possible to use the findings from a single case study to generalize about a larger population, but since the findings from other case studies of people with brain damage like H.M. tend to support those from this case study, it may be possible to generalize to some extent.

Explain, using one or more examples, the effects of neurotransmission on human behaviour

- When a nerve impulse reaches the end of the neuron, the neuron fires and neurotransmitters are released into the synaptic gap where they travel to the neuron at the other side of the synaptic gap.

- If the neurotransmitter is not absorbed it can be re-uptaken, diffused out or destroyed. The neurotransmitter then binds to specific receptors at the other side. If a neurotransmitter is blocked or replaced (e.g. because another chemical interferes) then the messages change. This affects the physiological system, cognition, mood, or behaviour.

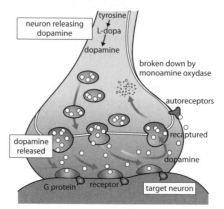

Synaptic transmission

Dopamine

Dopamine is a neurotransmitter involved in goal-directed behaviour (motivation) such as pleasure seeking, control of movement, emotional response, and addictive behaviour. Dopamine is released in the brain's reward system.

Dopamine and addictive behaviour

- Dopamine is released in the brain's reward system and has been associated with pleasure seeking and addictive behaviour. Addictive drugs or substances increase the amount of dopamine in the reward system.

- Dopamine can be relesed by environmental triggers (e.g. the sight of a cigarette package, food, or a gambling machine) because this is associated with pleasure (reward).

- Nicotine is the psychoactive ingredient in tobacco, which increases the level of dopamine in the brain's reward circuit causing feelings of pleasure and relaxation.

Berridge and Kringelbach (2009) on dopamine in pleasure seeking

fMRI scans were used to study brain areas involved in the subjective experience of pleasure. They found that the orbitofrontal cortex was active when people reported feeling pleasure.

The researchers concluded that: dopamine and the nucleus accumbens is perhaps rather involved in *pleasure seeking*. This could explain addictive behaviour (e.g. nicotine addiction leads to craving).

The orbitofrontal cortex and natural opiods (endorphins) are perhaps linked to the subjective experience of pleasure.

Fisher (2004) on dopamine in "addiction to love"

This is an evolutionary explanation of behaviour. "Being in love" has similarities with "being addicted" according to Fisher.

- Dopamine increases desire and reward by triggering the same emotional rush of pleasure when you see or think of the loved one as if you were taking a drug like cocaine.

- Dopamine can explain the highs of romantic passion (high levels of dopamine) and the lows of rejection (low levels of dopamine).

Acetylcholine (ACh) on memory

- ACh is a neurotransmitter which has been linked to synaptic plasticity in the hippocampus and it seems to play an important role in learning and short-term memory via the cholinergic system (Shinoe et al. 2005).

- The cholinergic system is a system of nerve cells that uses acetylcholine in transmitting nerve signals. Memory processing and higher cognitive functioning are dependent on the cholinergic system.

Martinez and Kesner (1991) ACh in memory formation

Aim To investigate the role of ACh in memory formation
Procedure Experimental study using rats. They were trained to run a maze. They were divided into three groups.

- *Group 1:* received injection with scopolamine (blocks ACh receptor sites, reducing available ACh).

- *Group 2:* received injection with physostigmine (blocks production of cholinesterase (enzyme) which cleans up ACh from the synapses) leading to more available ACh.

- *Group 3:* The control group.

Results

- *Group 1* had problems finding their way through the maze and made more mistakes.

- *Group 2* ran quickly through the maze and made few mistakes. The group was quicker than the control group.

Evaluation

The study shows that ACh is important in memory since the rats showed different memory capacity depending on ACh level. Since this was a controlled laboratory experiment, it can be concluded that the level of ACh is one factor that affects memory but the neurobiology of memory is very complex.

2.4 Explain, using examples, the function of two hormones on human behaviour

Cortisol and memory

Cortisol is a hormone produced by the adrenal cortex in response to stress and to restore homeostasis (the body's normal balance). Chronic stress may result in prolonged cortisol secretion and this can lead to physiological changes such as damaged immune system and impairment of learning and memory. This is because high amounts of cortisol results in atrophy of the hippocampus (Sapolsky, 1996).

Newcomer et al. (1999) Experiment on cortisol and memory

Aim To investigate how levels of cortisol interfere with verbal declarative memory.

Procedure A self-selected sample (recruited through advertisement) of 51 normal and healthy people aged 18–30 was used. It was a randomized, controlled, double-blind experiment running for four days. All participants gave informed consent. There were three experimental conditions: **1.** A high level of cortisol (tablet of 160 mg per day), equivalent to cortisol levels in the blood as a consequence of a major stressful event. **2.** A low level of cortisol (tablet of 40 mg per day), equivalent to cortisol levels in the blood as a consequence of a minor stressful event. **3.** A placebo (tablet of no active ingredient).

Results The high-level group performed worse on the verbal declarative memory test than the low-level group. They performed below placebo levels after day 1. The low-level group (mild stress) showed no memory decrease.

Evaluation This was a controlled randomized experiment so it was possible to establish a cause-effect relationship between levels of cortisol and scores on a verbal declarative memory test. Ethical issues were observed with informed consent. The negative effect of taking high dosages of cortisol was reversible so no harm was done.

Oxytocin and trust

- The hormone oxytocin is secreted by the hypothalamus and released (1) into the blood stream via the pituitary gland or (2) into the brain and spinal cord where it binds to oxytocin receptors. Oxytocin acts primarily as a neurotransmitter in the brain.

- Oxytocin has been linked to trusting other people. Experimental manipulation of oxytocin levels has shown increase in trust.

- According to evolutionary psychologists, trust is an important social tool in the relationship between humans.

Trust is an adaptive mechanism as it helps humans to form meaningful relationships at a personal and professional level. Betrayal disrupts bonds of trust and may result in avoidance of the person who has betrayed you.

- Learning who to trust and who to avoid is important for survival and the well-being of an individual. Humans should also be able to move on after experiences of breaching trust if long-term relationships and mental well-being are to be preserved.

- Oxytocin could play a role in reducing fear reactions via the amygdala that may arise as a consequence of betrayal.

Baumgartner et al. (2008) The role of oxytocin in trust in economic behaviour

Aim To investigate the role of oxytocin after breaches of trust in a trust game.

Procedure

- The participants played a trust game used by economists and neuroscientists to study social interaction.
  The "investor" (player 1) receives a sum of money and must decide whether to keep it or share it with a "trustee" (player 2). If the sum is shared the sum is tripled. Then player 2 must decide if this sum should be shared (trust) or kept (violation of trust).

- fMRI scans were carried out on 49 participants. They received either oxytocin or placebo via a nasal spray.

- Participants played against different trustees in the trust game and against a computer in a risk game. In 50% of the games their trust was broken. They received feedback on this from the experimenters during the games.

Results

- Participants in the placebo group were likely to show less trust after feedback on betrayal. They invested less.
  Participants in the oxytocin group continued to invest at similar rates after receiving feedback on a breach of trust.

- The fMRI scans showed decreases in responses in the amygdala and the caudate nucleus. The amygdala is involved in emotional processing and has many oxytocin receptors. The caudate nucleus is associated with learning and memory and plays a role in reward-related responses and learning to trust.

Evaluation

- Oxytocin could explain why people are able to restore trust and forgive in long-term relationships.

- Scanner research is merely mapping brain activity but nothing definite can be said about what it really means at this point in science.

- Giving oxytocin like this in an experiment may not reflect natural physiological processes. The function of oxytocin is very complex and it is too simplistic to say that it is "the trust hormone".

Effect 1: Environmental effects on dendritic branching (brain plasticity)

- Environmental stimulation refers to the way the environment provides stimulation in the form of social interaction and learning opportunities for animals and humans. Experiences are processed in the brain's nervous system, and stimulating environments will result in increased numbers of synapses (brain plasticity). Gopnick et al. (1999) describe neurons as growing telephone wires that communicate with each other.

- An enriched environment is characterized by multiple opportunities to learn new things. Researchers have used animal models to study synaptic changes in the brain because it is not possible to use humans in deprivation experiments.

- Instead researchers use case studies of children who have grown up in total neglect, i.e. with little or no experience of language, touch and interaction with other humans. The brains of neglected children are often smaller and there is scientific evidence of altered brain function (e.g. in intelligence and emotions)

Three-year-old children

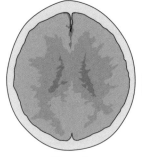 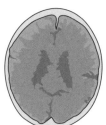

Normal   Extreme neglect

Brain scans of brains of three-year-old children: normal brain and brain with signs of extreme neglect in a child (Perry, 1997).

Rosenzweig, Bennet and Diamond (1972) The role of environmental stimulation on brain plasticity

Aim To investigate whether environmental factors such as a rich or an impoverished environment affect development of neurons in the cerebral cortex.

Procedure

- Rats were placed in either an enriched environment (EC) or an impoverished condition (IC).

- EC: 10–12 rats in a cage provided with different stimulus objects to explore and play with. This group also received maze training.

- IC: each rat in an individual cage (isolation and no stimulation).

- The rats typically spent 30 to 60 days in their respective environments before they were killed so the researchers could study changes in brain anatomy.

Results

- The anatomy of the brain was different for rats in the EC and the IC.

- The brains of EC rats had increased thickness and higher weight of the cortex. EC rats had developed more acetylcholine receptors in the cerebral cortex (important neurotransmiter in learning and memory).

Evaluation

- The experiment was a rigorously controlled laboratory experiment so it was possible to establish a cause-effect relationship.

- The experiment used animal models and therefore it may be difficult to generalize to humans unless research with humans provides the same results.

- Follow-up of this research indicated that just 2 hours a day in an enriched environment produced the same plastic changes in the brain as in rats that had been constantly in the EC condition. This shows that the brain can change and adapt to new situations.

- Since brain plasticity is assumed to follow the same pattern in animals and humans the implications of the study are that the human brain will also be affected by environmental factors such as intellectual and social stimulation.

- The research challenged the belief that brain weight cannot change. This was an important finding.

There are ethical issues in the use of animals in research like this. Since the results contributed to a much better understanding of the role of environmental factors in brain plasticity it can be argued that the research was justified in spite of the ethical issues.

Reference: Rosenzweig, M.R., Bennet, E.L., and Diamond, M.C. (1972) 'Brain changes in response to experience', Scientific American, 226 (2) 22–29.

Effect 2: Environmental stressors and hippocampal damage in PTSD patients

- A stressor is any event that threatens to disrupt the body's normal balance and starts a stress response such as secretion of stress hormones and activation of the 'fear sensor' in the brain, the amygdala.

- A stressor may be an acute stressor (e.g. being assaulted, having an accident) or it could be a chronic stressor (e.g. anticipation of violence or worrying).

- The fight or flight response (coping mechanism) is a pattern of physiological responses that prepares the body to deal with emergency. Sapolsky (1996) has shown in animal studies that long-term stress and a prolonged flow of cortisol can influence the size of the hippocampus, which plays a major role in memory.

Trauma and PTSD

- Traumatic episodes (i.e. frightening situations from which a person cannot escape) produce intense fear. In about 5% of the population this may lead to PTSD (post-traumatic stress disorder) with effects that can last for a brief period or a lifetime.

- Combat veterans and survivors of childhood sexual abuse who suffer from PTSD tend to have a number of stress related problems such as forgetfulness and difficulty learning. In such patients stress–related physiological changes have been observed in the brain, especially in the hippocampus, which play an important role in integrating different aspects of a memory at the time of recollection.

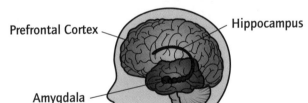

Prefrontal Cortex · Hippocampus · Amygdala

Bremner et al. (2003) Stress, PTSD and memory problems related to reduction of hippocampal volume.

Aim To measure the volume of the hippocampus based on the theory that prolonged stress may reduce the volume of the hippocampus due to increased cortisol levels.

Procedure

- MRI scans were made of the brains of the participants and participants completed memory tests (e.g. remembering a story or a list of words).

- The participants were veterans and female adults who had experienced early childhood sexual abuse. Some had developed PTSD, but not all.

Results

- The researchers found that there were deficits in short-term memory and then performed MRI scans of the participants' brains.

- They found that the hippocampus was smaller in PTSD patients than in a control group. The veterans with most memory problems also had the smallest hippocampus.

- The findings showed a clear correlation between number of years of abuse as measured by a trauma test, memory problems and hippocampal volume.

- People suffering from PTSD often suffer from other psychological disorders (e.g. depression) which could perhaps also play a role in the observed changes in the brain.

Evaluation

- The sample was very small so it is difficult to say anything definite about the relationship between trauma and hippocampal volume.

- There could be alternative explanations to differences in hippocampal volume (e.g. that people who suffer from PTSD often suffer from depression as well). Depression is also associated with reduction of the hippocampus. However, the findings of a large reduction of hippocampal volume in combat-related PTSD has been replicated many times.

- Cognitive neuroscience is the scientific study of biological correlates of mental processes (cognition). This area of research investigates how various brain areas are involved in cognitive processes (e.g. how brain damage affects memory), but in recent years researchers have also investigated how cognition and physiological processes may interact in people who meditate.

- A number of neuroscientists are examining how meditation or mindfulness-based stress reduction (MBSR) may influence brain functions (e.g. the effect of meditation on attention, emotional reactivity and stress).

- Interaction of cognition and physiology can be seen in the self-regulation of attention (MBSR) which seems to have physiological benefits (e.g. stress reduction).

- Interaction of cognition and physiology can be seen in the self-regulation of attention (MBSR) which seems to have physiological benefits (e.g. stress reduction).

Davidson et al. (2004) Brain waves and compassion meditation

Aim To investigate whether meditation can change brain activity.

- Eight monks who had practised meditation for many years and a control group of 10 students who had one week of training participated in the study. Cognitive activities (including meditation) produce electrical activity when the neurons fire. This was recorded by the EEG (electroencephalograph which records electrical activity as brain waves).

- Participants were asked to meditate on 'unconditional compassion', i.e. open the mind for feelings of love and compassion for short periods.

- The control group participated in a training session where they were asked to think of someone they cared about and to let their mind be invaded by love and compassion.

- After initial training the participants were asked to generate an objective feeling of compassion without focusing on anyone in particular.

- The EEG of the monks' brains showed greater activation as well as better organization and coordination of gamma waves. There was a positive correlation between hours of practice and level of gamma waves.

Evaluation

- The results support the idea that attention and affective processes are skills that can be trained but more research is needed to establish if the change in brain waves is caused by hours of training and not individual differences before training.

Vestergaard-Poulsen et al. (2009) found that extensive practice of meditation involving sustained attention could lead to changes in brain structure. They found structural changes in the lower brain stem of participants engaged in long-term practice of meditation compared with age-matched non-meditators.

- MRI scans of two groups of participants – meditators and non-mediators.

- The study found structural changes in brain stem regions concerned with control of respiration and cardiac rhythm (autonomic nervous system). The connection of neurons in this area seemed more complex in people who meditated.

- This could explain some of the beneficial effects found in research on stress reduction techniques such as MBSR because cortisol levels are reduced and the cardiac and breathing rhythm slow down.

- Meditative practices have already been applied in health psychology, for example Davidson et al. (2003) found that Mindfulness meditation could increase positive emotion and immune responses.

- MBSR has also been found to alleviate pain (Grant et al. 2010).

See more on the application of MBSR in unit 7.5.

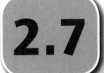

2.7 Discuss the use of brain-imaging technologies in investigating the relationship between biological factors and behaviour

- Brain-imaging techniques are used in neuroscience to investigate the relationship between behaviour and brain structures, for example after brain damage or to find out which areas of the brain are involved in which cognitive activities (cognitive neuroscience).

- Brain-imaging technology is a promising way to investigate the possible relationship between biological factors and behaviour, but so far scanning can merely register structures and activity in the brain. It is not possible to determine cause-effect relationships at this point.

MRI scan: magnetic resonance imaging

MRI scans can give detailed pictures of internal structures in the body. The body consists, to a large extent, of water molecules. In the MRI scanner a radio frequency transmitter is turned on and it produces an electromagnetic field.

Strengths of MRI	Limitations of MRI
■ MRI scans are particularly to show how the blood flows in the brain and can be used to identify problems with blood circulation. They can be used for the early detection of Alzheimers' disease. ■ They are safe to use since no radioactive material is used.	■ They are very expensive. ■ Movement may affect the pictures. ■ They cannot say anything about cause-effect relationships.

Ashtari et al (2009) used MRI to investigate whether substance abuse (marijuana) can damage the developing brain in adolescents and young adults.

- The researchers scanned the brains of 14 young men with a history of heavy marijuana abuse over a long period. The control group consisted of 14 young men who had not used marijuana.

- The results of the scan indicated that there were brain abnormalities in the frontal, parietal and temporal regions of the brains of the marijuana users. The development of white matter (myelin) was affected and this could explain slow information processing in the brain.

- The researchers concluded that early marijuana use can affect brain development negatively but since the study gave correlational data more research is needed.

fMRI scan: functional magnetic resonance imaging

The fMRI scanner measures changes in blood flow in the active brain. This is associated with use of oxygen and linked to neural activity during information processing. When participants are asked to perform a task, the scientists can observe the part of the brain that corresponds to that function. fMRI scanning is widely used by cognitive neuroscientists and other researchers and its use has increased enormously over the last 10 years.

Strengths of fMRI	Limitations of fMRI
■ It does not use radioactive substances. ■ It can record activity in all regions of the brain.	■ The focus is mostly on localized functioning in the brain and does not take into account the distributed nature of processing in neural networks. ■ The results are correlational so it is not possible to establish cause-effect relationships.

Harris and Fiske (2006) used fMRI scans to study students' brain processes as a response to being presented with pictures of extreme outgroups. This study in social cognition aimed to find the biological correlates of stereotypes and prejudice.

- The researchers scanned students while they were watching either pictures of different humans or objects. It was predicted that the medial prefrontal cortex would be active when participants looked at humans but not when they looked at objects.

- This was found except when participants looked at pictures of people from extreme outgroups such as the homeless and addicts. Brain regions related to 'disgust' were activated and there was no activity in the prefrontal cortex.

- The researchers concluded that this indicated a dehumanization of the outgroups. These groups were apparently viewed as 'disgusting objects' and not people.

13

General issues in brain imaging to consider in a discussion

- Brain imaging is mainly about mapping brain structures and activity in the brain.

- Another limitation deals with localization of function. It may be possible to identify brain structures that are active during a task but, since most structures are linked to other structures in networks, it is not possible at this point to say definitely where things happen in the brain.

Exam Tip If you are asked discuss the use of brain-imaging technologies you need to include at least two examples. If you are asked to discuss one, then don't mention more than one since you will receive no credit for mentioning more.

You can address "how and why specific technologies are used" and "strengths/limitations of using them" including research studies to support your argument. Although brain imaging is exciting as it offers a view into the living brain, it is still too soon to conclude anything definite about which areas are involved in what cognitive processes. The human brain is very complex and, at this point, brain imaging is perhaps best used in diagnosis of brain abnormalities.

2.8 Discuss the extent to which genetics influences behaviour

Gene mapping

Attempt to determine the effect of a particular gene on behaviour such as psychological traits (temperament), psychological disorders (e.g. depression or schizophrenia) or various physiological conditions.

Caspi et al. (2003) Longitudinal study on the possible role of the 5-HTT gene in depression after experiences of stressful events

- The 5-HTT gene influences the level of serotonin, which is known to play a role in controlling mood.

- The researchers compared participants with a normal 5-HTT gene and a mutation of the 5-HTT gene with shorter alleles. Both types are quite frequent in humans but the long allele is slightly more frequent (57%).

- The researchers found that participants who carried a mutation of the 5-HTT gene and who had experienced many stressful events were more likely to become depressed after stressful events than those participants who carried the normal 5-HTT gene.

- The 5-HTT gene could indicate a vulnerability to depression after stress and the researchers speculated whether the gene could moderate individual responses to environmental factors.

Evaluation

- Since a large proportion of the population carries the mutation of the 5-HTT gene that makes them susceptible to depression after traumatic events, it can be difficult to conclude that the gene is a major contribution to depression. People who did not carry the mutation also became depressed.

- The study showed a correlation between the presence of a 5-HTT short allele and depression but it is not possible to establish a cause-effect relationship.

- Genes contribute to some extent to behavioural traits and disorders but it is not clear how environmental factors influence genes. Environmental factors were included in the study (stressful events) but there is no evidence against the idea that it could be the stressful events (environmental factors) that made people depressed.

- Much more research is needed before a clear relationship between a gene and a behavioural trait can be established..

You could also use this study in unit 5.5 to discuss etiologies of abnormal behaviour. In this case a possible explanation of depression which could relate to the diathesis-stress model.

Twin studies

- Monozygotic twins (MZ or identical twins) come from the same egg and share 100% of their genes. Dizygotic twins (DZ or fraternal twins) come from two different eggs and share around 50% of their genes. Siblings share 50% of their genes.

- The researchers calculate concordance rate (the likelihood or probability that if one individual has the trait the other will also have it). The concordance rate is assumed to establish if or to what extent a certain trait is inherited.

- In twin studies, one twin acts as control for the other twin. The classic twin study only studied concordance rates and did not include environmental factors. In some cases MZ twins were raised apart and in these cases it was assumed that differences were due to environmental factors.

- In twin research, sets of MZ are compared with sets of DZ twins for a particular trait or disorder. High concordance rates in MZ twins and lower concordance rates in DZ twins for the same behaviour indicate that the trait or disease is linked to genes (inherited). Differences within pairs of identical twins are attributed to environmental factors.

Bouchard et al. (1990) Twin study investigating genetic inheritance in intelligence

- This study used a self-selected sample of MZ twins who had been reared together (MZT) and MZ twins who had been reared apart (MZA) to investigate concordance rates for a number of variables such as IQ.

- The results showed that for IQ (measured by a standardized intelligence test called WAIS) the concordance rate was 69% for MZA and 88% for MZT.

- The researchers concluded that environmental factors do play a role in development of intelligence but IQ is to a large extent inherited and that 70% of the observed variation in the sample could be attributed to genetic variation.

- They claim that the results indicate that in a sample like the one in the study (white, middle-class in an industrialized nation) genetic inheritance in IQ accounts for around two-thirds of the observed variance of IQ.

- They also said that their findings do not indicate that IQ cannot be increased, that is influenced by environmental factor.

Evaluation

- Correlational data cannot establish cause-effect relationships.

- Concordance rates were high in the study but far from 100% so it was difficult to determine the relative influence of genes. Calculation of concordance rates is not always reliable.

- There was no control for the effect of environmental variables in the study and this affects accurate estimations of a genetic contribution to intelligence.

- The findings from this self-selected sample make it difficult to generalize findings.

Problems in genetic research

Genetic research cannot at this point determine the extent to which genetic inheritance influence behaviour because:

- Genes interact with environmental factors in complex ways. It is difficult to measure relative influence of genes and environmental factors.

- Knowledge about genes is still limited.

- There are problems in genetic research (e.g. concordance rates in twin studies cannot say anything about cause-effect relationships). MZ twins being treated in the same way as DZ twins may be wrong (the "equal environment assumption" may be flawed) and this limits the possibility of drawing meaningful conclusions from twin studies.

2.9 Examine one evolutionary explanation of behaviour

- The theory of evolution, suggested by Charles Darwin, is based on the assumption that living organisms face environmental challenges. Organisms that adapt the best have a greater chance of passing on their genes to the next generations.

- Organisms with specific genetic traits that enhance survival are said to be naturally selected. Natural selection is a crucial evolutionary process in Darwin's theory.

One evolutionary explanation of behaviour: disgust in pregnant women

- Nausea and loss of appetite during pregnancy may have been evolved as a way to protect the mother and the fetus against diseases which could threaten the fetus. Disgust has evolved as a food-rejection response to prevent contamination and the spread of illness.

- The theory under investigation is whether disgust has evolved to compensate for the mother and the baby's vulnerability to disease during the first few months of pregnancy.

Fessler et al (2005) Elevated disgust sensitivity in the first trimester of pregnancy

Aim To investigate if disgust sensitivity in the first trimester of pregnancy was elevated as predicted.

Procedure

- A Web-based survey was completed by 691 women recruited through pregnancy-related Web sites. No compensation was offered for participation. The women's mean age was 28.1 years.

- On the Web-based questionnaire, the participants (1) indicated their current level of nausea using a 16-point scale and (2) answered questions to test their disgust sensitivity in eight different areas (e.g. food; contact with animals, body products, and dead animals; hygiene; contact with toilets).

Results

- Overall, disgust sensitivity related to food and body products in women in the first trimester was higher compared to those in the second and third trimesters.

- Disgust was particularly elevated in relation to food, which was exactly what the researchers had predicted.

- Food-borne diseases are particularly dangerous to women in the first trimester and therefore it was predicted that disgust sensitivity related to food would be high. This was supported by the results.

- The results may indicate that nausea and vomiting are evolved behaviour because they limit the likelihood that pregnant women will eat dangerous food.

Evaluation

- The data was collected through questionnaires. Self-reports may not be reliable. This is not an effective way of measuring disgust. It would have been more reliable to confront participants with real disgust-eliciting objects.

- The effect sizes were not big but significant. The findings are supported by other studies (e.g. Curtiss et al. 2004) showing that images that threaten the immune system are judged as more disgusting.

Evaluation of evolutionary explanations

- It is difficult to test evolutionary theories and not much is known about the life of early humans.

- Evolutionary explanations tend to focus on biological factors and underestimate cultural influences.

- According to Davey (1974) disgust for spiders may be explained by people's need to find tangible causes of illness and disease when the causes were unclear.

See also the evolutionary explanation of the role of oxytocin in trust in unit 2.4.

Exam Tip "Examine" means that you should consider whether this evolutionary theory can be supported or not. You should also explain general problems in evolutionary explanations.

Discuss ethical considerations in research into genetic influences on behaviour

Ethical considerations in genetic research

There are specific issues of concern in genetic research within the biological level of analysis. This is particularly true in the search for genes involved in abnormal behaviour, but it is also relevant in research on genetic influence on disease, intelligence, personality, or health. The main reasons for concerns are:

- Knowledge about the role of specific genes in behaviour is still limited so researchers should be careful about making definite conclusions. Genetic research is often reductionist as it does not include environmental factors.

- Genetic research is correlational by nature so one should be careful to make definite conclusions about the risk of developing a disease.

- It is not certain that genetic research, like the Human Genome Project, is ethically neutral. There are historical examples of misuse of ethically sensible data (e.g. eugenics in Nazi Germany) and it is not guaranteed that data could not be misused again (Wallace 2004).

- Genetic research into complex behaviour such as homosexuality is controversial because of the social meaning and significance of homosexuality. Genetic research could result in stigmatization and discrimination as many societies are homophobic. The search for the "gay gene" has generally raised controversy.

Caspi et al. (2003) Longitudinal study on the possible role of the 5-HTT gene in depression after experiences of stressful events

- The researchers compared participants with a normal 5-HTT and a mutation of the 5-HTT gene with shorter alleles. Both types are quite frequent in the human population but the long allele is slightly more frequent (57%).

- The researchers found that participants who carried a mutation of the 5-HTT gene and who had experienced many stressful events were more likely to become depressed after stressful events than those participants who carried the normal 5-HTT gene.

Conclusion

It is not clear what to do with knowledge from genetic research and genetic screening at this point – both at an individual level and in society. For example, being genetically predisposed to depression does not mean that a person will develop depression. The results of genetic screening for depression could cause personal distress and have a negative impact on someone's life (e.g. if based on this they decided not to have children).

Ethical considerations in all genetic research

The DNA profile of each human is unique, except for MZ twins who are 100% genetically similar. The fact that one twin acts as a control in genetic research is the major reason why twins are often used to determine heritability. Genetic information is often seen as special because it is assumed that genes determine behaviour and genes are associated with personal identity. In reality, genetic information can only reveal a potential risk.

Anonymity and confidentiality

- Participants in a genetic study must be sure that their anonymity and confidentiality is protected but in family and twin studies it can be difficult to ensure this fully. This is also the case in the research of rare disorders.

- Participants have a right to know who owns the genetic information and how it will be used in the future (e.g. if their access to insurance or employment could be compromised because of the genetic data).

Informed consent and the right to refuse or withdraw

- Participants have a right to be fully informed about what the research is about, the procedures, what could be the result of the study and how the information will be used.

- Research into genetic influences on behaviour could potentially pose risks to participants and the genetic information could be misused.

- Genetic research can reveal information that is unexpected or a source of distress to participants (e.g. when a participant has no sign of a disorder but the data shows a genetic predisposition).

3.1 Outline principles that define the cognitive level of analysis and explain how these principles may be demonstrated in research

Principle 1: Human beings are information processors and mental processes guide behaviour.

People are active information processors. They perceive and interpret what is going on around them. This is often based on what they already know. There is a relationship between people's mental representation and the way people perceive and think about the world.

Principle 2: The mind can be studied scientifically.

Cognitive researchers use a number of scientific methods to study the mind (e.g. laboratory experiments, neuroimaging, case studies, interviews, and archival research). The most used research method was, for a long time, the laboratory experiment, because it was considered to be the most scientific.

Principle 1 demonstrated in:

Schema theory defines cognitive schemas as mental representations of knowledge. Mental representations (schemas) are stored in categories (concepts) in memory. These schemas provide guidelines for interpretation of incoming information when people try to make sense of the world. Schemas influence cognition in that schemas create expectations about what will happen in specific situations (e.g. what a "teacher" is like or what to expect when you go to a rock concert). Schema theory can, to a large extent, explain reconstructive memory and stereotyping.

Darley and Gross (1983) performed an experiment in which they showed participants videos of a girl playing in a poor environment, then in a wealthy environment. Then they saw a video of the girl in what could be an intelligence test. When the participants were asked to judge the future of the girl they all said that the "poor" girl would do worse than the "wealthy" girl. The study demonstrated how human beings actively process information based on a few salient details to form an overall impression that may not necessarily be correct.

Principle 2 demonstrated in:

Loftus and Palmer (1974) performed an experiment to test reconstructive memory in relation to eyewitness testimony. The aim was to see whether misleading questions could distort memory. Participants saw a picture of a car crash and were asked to estimate the speed of the car based on questions such as "How fast was the car going when it smashed/hit/bumped into the other car?" Words such as "smashed" elicited higher speed estimations. Because the experimental method was used it was possible to establish a cause-effect relationship between the use of specific words and estimation of speed. Experimental research on memory has been criticized for lacking ecological validity.

Corkin et al. (1999) used MRI scans to observe the exact damage to H.M.'s brain. H.M. suffered from amnesia due to a brain operation where the hippocampus and adjacent areas had been removed to eliminate his epilepsy. The scans confirmed damage to these areas. Although a small part of the hippocampus had been spared it was not enough to support storage of new explicit memories.

Principle 3: Cognitive processes are influenced by social and cultural factors.

Research has shown that cognitive processes such as perception, memory, and thinking are influenced by sociocultural factors. **Bartlett (1932)** introduced the concept of "cultural schema" in memory research. He suggested that schemas influence memory in that they lead to distortion or "reconstructive memory". Other researchers suggest that the environment in which people live leads to specific cultural and social demands that influence the way they process information.

DiMaggio (1997) suggests that schemas are (1) representations of knowledge (e.g. stereotypes and social roles) and (2) mechanisms that simplify cognition in the form of "cognitive shortcuts" that are shaped by culture. Schematic cognition is shaped and biased by culture (e.g. culturally based stereotypes).

Principle 3 demonstrated in:

Bartlett (1932) suggested that memory is guided by schemas and that culture can influence schemas. Previous knowledge determines the way people interpret incoming information and memory (memory distortion). He asked British participants to read an unfamiliar Native American story and reproduce it. The participants changed details of the story to fit with their own cultural schemas.

Cole and Scribner (1974) investigated how memory strategies were influenced by culture. The study asked children from a rural area in Liberia and children from the USA to memorize items from four different categories: utensils, clothes, tools, and vegetables. Children from the US improved performance after practice but the Liberian children did not unless they had attended school. Learning memory strategies, like "chunking", appears to be dependent on schooling and the illiterate children in the study did not use these strategies. The researchers concluded that the way cognitive psychologists study memory processes does not always reflect the way people learn to remember in real life.

- A cognitive schema can be defined as a mental representation of knowledge stored in the brain. A schema can be seen as a network of knowledge, beliefs, and expectations about particular aspects of the world.

- Schema processing is to a large extent automatic, i.e. processed with little attention. It involves information from two sources: Input from the sensory system (bottom-up processes) and information stored in memory (top-down processes), which is used to interpret the incoming information (pattern recognition, interpretation).

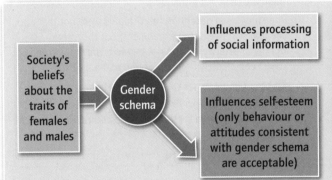

Bartlett (1932) suggests that schemas are active recognition devices representing an effort after meaning. Schemas help people make sense of the world, make predictions about it and what to expect, and provide guidance on how to behave.

DiMaggio (1997) suggests that schemas are (1) representations of knowledge (e.g. stereotypes and social roles) and (2) mechanisms that simplify cognition in the form of "cognitive shortcuts". Schematic cognition is shaped and biased by culture (e.g. in culturally based stereotypes). Gender schemas are examples of cognitive schemas shaped by sociocultural ideas about what is appropriate for men and women (i.e. norms).

Darley and Gross (1983) carried out a laboratory experiment on schema processing in the social world.

- In this laboratory experiment, the participants saw two videos of a girl. In video 1 a girl was playing in a poor environment; in video 2 a girl was playing in a rich environment. Then they saw a video of the girl in what could be an intelligence test.

- When the participants were asked to judge the future of the girls they all said that the "rich" girl would do well and the "poor" girl would do less well.

- The study demonstrates that participants probably used pre-stored schemas of what it means to be poor and rich and interpreted the ambiguous information accordingly. Participants processed information based on a few salient details to form an overall impression that may not necessarily be correct.

Possible ways in which schemas affect memory

- People tend to remember the meaning (gist) of something, not the actual wording.

- People use stored knowledge to make sense of incoming information. If the information is unclear or incomplete, they fill in the blanks or interpret using their schemas. This is called "reconstructive memory" and results in distortion.

- People tend to ignore information that is not in line with their schemas (aschematic information). This may lead to bias in information processing (e.g. in stereotyping where people ignore information that is not in line with their schema).

- People tend to focus on information that is in line with their schemas (schematic information). This may result in "confirmation bias".

Bartlett (1932) "The War of the Ghosts"

Aim To investigate whether people's memory for a story is affected by previous knowledge (schemas) and the extent to which memory is reconstructive.

Procedure Bartlett asked British participants to hear a story and reproduce it after a short time and then repeatedly over a period of months or years (serial reproduction). The story was an unfamiliar Native American legend called "The War of the Ghosts".

Results The participants remembered the main idea of the story (the gist) but they changed unfamiliar elements to make sense of the story by using terms more familiar to their own cultural expectations. The story remained a coherent whole although it was changed. It became noticeably shorter for each reproduction. Bartlett concluded that remembering is an active process. Memories are not copies of experience but rather "reconstructions".

Evaluation

- The results of the study confirm schema theory (and reconstructive memory), but it was performed in a laboratory and can be criticized for lack of ecological validity.

- Participants did not receive standardized instructions and some of the memory distortions may be due to participants' guessing (demand characteristics).

- In spite of these methodological limitations, the study is one of the most important in the study of memory.

Bartlett, F. (1932) *Remembering: A study in Experimental and Social Psychology*. Cambridge: Cambridge University Press.

Brewer and Treyens (1981) Experiment on memory of objects in a room

Aim To investigate whether people's memory for objects in a room (an office) is influenced by existing schemas about what to expect in an office.

Procedure

- Participants were 30 university students, who arrived individually to the laboratory and were asked to wait in an office containing objects (e.g. desk, typewriter, coffee-pot, calendar). There were also other objects that did not conform to the office schema (a skull, a piece of bark, a pair of pliers).

- After waiting for some time, participants were taken out of the office and asked to write down everything they could remember from the room.

Results

- Most participants recalled the schematic objects (e.g. desk, typewriter).

- Some participants reported things that would be expected in a typical office but were not present in this one (e.g. telephone, books).

- Many participants also recalled the skull (unexpected object). The very unusual object resulted in better recall than predicted by schema theory.

Evaluation

- The study confirms schema theory (and reconstructive memory), but it was a controlled laboratory experiment so there are issues of artificiality.

- The study used deception (participants were not told about the real purpose of the experiment) but they were debriefed afterwards and not harmed. The study could not have been made without deception so it was justified.

- There is sample bias. University students were used as participants so it may be difficult to generalize the results.

Brewer, W.F. and Treyens, J.C. (1981) "Role of schemata in memory for places", *Cognitive Psychology*, 13, pp. 207-30.

Strengths of schema theory	Limitations of schema theory
- Schema theory has proven extremely useful in explaining many cognitive processes (e.g. perception, memory, and reasoning). - Schema theory can be used to explain the reconstructive nature of memory, for example in eye witness testimony, stereotyping, gender identity (gender schema) and cultural differences (cultural schemas).	- Cohen (1993) argued that: the concept of schema is too vague to be useful and it is not clear how schemas are acquired in the first place. - Schema theory may focus too much on the inaccuracies of memory but most of the time people remember accurately.

3.3 Evaluate two models or theories of one cognitive process with reference to research studies

Model 1: The multi-store model of memory (Atkinson and Shiffrin, 1968)

This model was one of the first to give an overview of the basic structure or architecture of memory and it was inspired by computer science. The model seems rather simplistic, but it did spark off the idea of humans as information processors and it has been one of the most influential models attempting to describe the memory system.

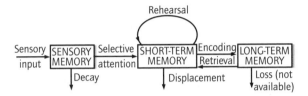

Atkinson and Shiffrin (1968)

- The multi-store model is based on the assumption that memory consists of a number of separate stores and that memory processes are sequential.

- The memory stores in the model are **structural components** that include **control processes** (e.g. attention, coding, and rehearsal). Rehearsal ensures the transfer of information from short-term memory (working memory) to long-term memory.

- **Sensory memory** registers sensory information and stores it for around 1–4 seconds. Information in the sensory memory is modality specific (i.e. related to different senses). Only a small amount of the sensory information will be transferred into the short-term memory (STM) store (depending on whether or not it is attended to).

- **STM** has limited capacity (around seven items) and limited duration (around 6–12 seconds). Information processed in STM is transferred into LTM if it is rehearsed. If not, it is lost.

- **LTM** is believed to be of indefinite duration and of potentially unlimited capacity.

Evidence of the multi-store model of memory: the serial position effect

The serial position effect is believed to be linked to rehearsal, i.e. people repeat things in order to remember. The serial position effect suggests that people remember things better if they are either the first (primacy effect) or last (recency effect) item in a list of things to remember.

Glanzer and Cunitz (1966)

Aim To investigate recency effect in free recall (i.e. in any order).

Procedure This was a laboratory experiment where participants first heard a list of items and then immediately had to recall them in any order.

Results Participants recalled words from the beginning of the list (primacy effect) and the end of the list (the recency effect) best. The results showed a U-shaped curve. If participants were given a filler task just after hearing the last words, the primacy effect disappeared but the recency effect remained.

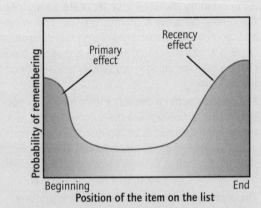

The recency effect could be due to the words still being active in STM (working memory). Rehearsal could be a factor in transfer of information into LTM.

Evaluation The study supports the idea of multiple stores (STM and LTM). This is a controlled laboratory study with highly controlled variables, but there is no random allocation of participants to experimental conditions so it is not a true experiment. There may be problems with ecological validity.

Evidence of the multi-store model of memory: case studies of individuals with amnesia due to brain damage

- Amnesia is caused by damage to the hippocampus and related networks involved in storage of new memories.

- MRI scans shows that H.M. had severe damage to the hippocampus which is critical in the storage of information into LTM.

- H.M. could store new procedural memories (implicit memory) but he was not able to store new explicit memories (semantic or episodic). This shows that the memory system contains different systems.

Strengths of the multi-store model of memory	Limitations of the multi-store model of memory
■ The model pioneered the new approach to memory where humans are seen as information processors. ■ The model's conceptualization of memory as multi-stored is supported by research. ■ It has been possible to make predictions based on the model and to design experiments. ■ The overall model has been modified, for example by **Baddeley and Hitch (1974)** with their new version of short-term memory, the "working memory" model.	■ The model is very simplistic and it cannot account for how interaction between the different stores takes place (e.g. how information from LTM may indicate what is important and relevant to pay attention to in sensory memory). ■ Research into the encoding of LTM has challenged the single-store version of LTM. It is now accepted that LTM contains several stores (e.g. semantic, episodic, procedural).

Model 2: The working memory model (Baddeley and Hitch, 1974)

- Baddeley and Hitch suggested the working memory model as an alternative to STM.
- This model challenged the view that STM is unitary and that information processing is passive.
- Working memory is seen as an active store used to hold and manipulate information. The model has been developed over the years to include findings from research (e.g. a fourth component, the episodic buffer, has been added).

Working memory includes four separate components:
- **The central executive** A *controlling system* that monitors and coordinates the operations of the other components (slave systems). The central executive is *modality free* so it can process information in any sensory modality but it has limited capacity.
- **The episodic buffer** A limited-capacity temporary storage system or *interface* between the other systems in working memory. It is assumed to be controlled by the central executive through *conscious awareness*. The episodic buffer handles information in various modalities. The episodic buffer resembles the concept of episodic memory.
- **The phonological loop** handles *verbal and auditory information*. It is divided into two components:

   1 **The articulatory control system**: the "inner voice".

2 **The phonological store**: the "inner ear". This can hold speech-based material active in a phonological form. It is assumed that a memory trace can only last from 1.5 to 2 seconds if it is not refreshed by the articulatory control system.

- **The visuo-spatial sketchpad**: the "inner eye". This handles visual and spatial information from either sensory memory (visual information) or from LTM (images).

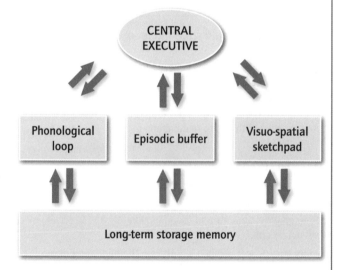

Evidence of the working model of memory
- There is evidence of working memory in the so-called dual tasks experiments. The model assumes that there is a division of tasks between the different slave systems according to modality.
- If two tasks are done simultaneously (e.g. in dual tasks experiments or in multi-tasking) it is possible to perform well if separate systems are used. If concurrent tasks use the same system, it will affect performance negatively.
- **Baddeley and Hitch (1974)** asked participants to answer increasingly difficult questions about simple letter combinations that were shown at the same time. Reaction time increased as the questions became more difficult. The participants were then asked to do an articulatory suppression task (e.g. repeating "the" all the time, repeating numbers from 1 to 6, or repeating random numbers) while they answered the question. There was no significant difference in reaction time between the group

who was asked to repeat "the" or to repeat numbers from 1 to 6. The group who was asked to repeat random numbers had the worst performance. This was interpreted as overload problems for the central executive.

- **Quinn and McConnel (1996)** asked participants to learn a list of words by using either imagery or rehearsal. The task was performed on its own or in the presence of a concurrent visual noise (changing patterns of dots) or a concurrent verbal noise (speech in a foreign language). The results showed that learning words by imagery was not affected by a concurrent verbal task but it was disturbed by a concurrent visual task. The opposite was found in the rehearsal condition. This indicates that imagery processing uses the visuo-spatial sketchpad whereas verbal processing uses the phonological loop. If two tasks used the same component, performance deteriorated. The study thus lends support to different modality-specific slave systems and the idea of limited processing capacity.

Strengths of working memory	Limitations of working memory
■ The model has been useful in understanding which parts of the memory system may be linked to underlying problems in reading and mathematical skills. ■ The model focuses on the processes of integrating information, rather than on the isolation of the sub-systems. This provides a much better basis for understanding the more complex aspects of executive control in working memory.	■ The major criticism of the first models of working memory was the unclear role of the central executive. This has been dealt with by including the episodic buffer in the revised model. ■ The model has been critizised for its emphasis on structure rather than processing.

Compare and contrast the two models

	Multi-store model	Working memory model
Comparison (similarities)	■ Provides possible architecture of the memory system (several stores) ■ STM temporary storage, limited capacity and duration	■ Provides possible architecture of the memory system (several stores) ■ STM temporary storage, limited capacity and duration
Contrast (differences)	■ Focus on the entire memory system ■ Simplistic model of STM – not much focus on interaction between stores. ■ STM temporary storage and gateway to LTM ■ No specifications of content of STM	■ Focus primarily on STM ■ Much more complex idea of STM suggesting possible interactions between the stores, and especially modality-based functions of short-term memory (visuo-spatial sketchpad and phonological loop). The addition of a governing system (central executive) is a strength, although how it works is not yet well documented.
Evaluation	■ STM and LTM are more complex than the model assumes. ■ There is not enough focus on the interaction between the stores (e.g. how information from LTM is used to deal with chunking in STM). ■ Rehearsal is not enough to explain transfer of information to LTM. The model cannot explain why memory strategies and elaborate rehearsal is efficient.	■ Provides a better explanation of storage and processing than the multi-store model in that it can be applied to understanding, reading and mental calculations. ■ Early versions of the model are vague on the role of the central executive, but later development of the model suggests that central executive guides attention via two systems (automatic and supervisory attentional system). ■ The model is broadly accepted and considered important for understanding not only memory processes, but also cognitive processes such as thinking and problem solving (functional approach).

Damage to the hippocampus and amnesia

Scoville and Milner (1957) The case study of H.M.

- Scoville and Milner (1957) described the case of H.M. who fell off his bicycle when he was 7 years old, injuring his head. He began to have epileptic seizures when he was 10. By the age of 27 the epileptic attacks prevented him from living a normal life.
- Scoville performed an experimental surgery on H.M.'s brain to stop the seizures. The seizures stopped but H.M. suffered from amnesia for the rest of his life.
- The case study of H.M. provides information on how particular brain areas and networks are involved in memory processing. This helped scientists to formulate new theories about memory functioning.

H.M.'s memory

- H.M. could no longer store new memories (anterograde amnesia). Most of his memories from before the operation remained intact (partial retrograde amnesia).
- He could not transfer new semantic and episodic memories (explicit memories) into LTM.
- He could form new long-term procedural memories (implicit memories).
- He was able to carry on normal conversations (i.e. had some capacity for working memory) but he would forget what the conversation was about immediately.

What can be learned about the relationship between the brain and memory from the case study of H.M.?

- The memory systems in the brain constitute a highly specialized and complex system.
- The hippocampus play a critical role in converting memories of experiences from STM to LTM (the permanent store).
- H.M. was able to retain some memories for events that happened long before his surgery. This indicates that the medial temporal region with the hippocampus is not the site of permanent storage in itself. It rather seems to play a role in how memories are organized and then stored elsewhere in the brain.
- The medial temporal region with the hippocampus is important for forming, organizing, consolidating, and retrieving memory. Cortical areas are important for long-term storage of knowledge and how to use this knowledge in everyday situations.
- The fact that H.M. and other people with amnesia have deficits in some types of memories but not in others is taken as evidence that the brain has multiple memory systems that are supported by distinct brain regions.

Explanation of the relationship between H.M.'s brain damage and his memory deficits

Corkin (1997) used MRI scans and analysed the extent of the damage to H.M.'s brain to find out. The scans showed that:

- Parts of the temporal lobes including the hippocampus and related structures on both sides were missing. This part of the brain's memory system plays a critical role in transforming short-term memories into long-term memories.
- These areas are involved in specific neurotransmitter pathways in memory (e.g. acetylcholine is believed to play an important role in learning and episodic memories).

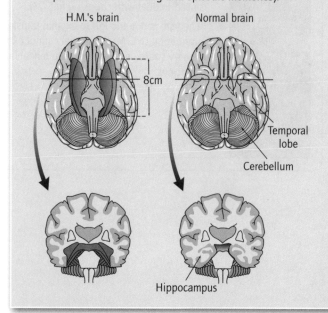

High levels of cortisol and memory deficits

Cortisol is a stress hormone secreted by the adrenal glands in response to physiological or psychological stress. During long-term stress too much cortisol is released and this may affect not only immune functioning, but also memory processes. Chronic over-secretion of cortisol may hinder the brain in forming new memories or accessing already existing memories.

Sapolsky (1968) demonstrated that prolonged stress can damage the neurons in the hippocampus but this can be reversed if normal levels of cortisol are restored. Long-term stress could cause irreversible damage.

Lupien et al. (1998) followed a group of elderly people for five years to study the role of cortisol on memory. They found that cortisol secretion was too high in about 30% of the elderly population. Those who were exposed to excessive cortisol secretion for five years showed memory impairment and atrophy (shrinking) of the hippocampus. They also found that memory impairment can be reversed if the damage had not progressed to "a point of no return".

Lupien et al. (2002) Experiment on cortisol level and memory

Aim The experiment was a follow-up with two groups of the elderly people from the five-year study. The aim of the experiment was to see whether it was possible to reverse memory problems with a drug.

Procedure

- Participants were divided into two groups: group 1 had a moderate level of cortisol at baseline, and group 2 had a high level of cortisol and signs of impaired memory at baseline.

- Both groups were first given a drug preventing secretion of cortisol (metyrapone). Then they had to do a memory test. After this, both groups were given another drug (hydrocortisone) to restore their level of cortisol to previous levels. Results were compared with levels in a placebo group.

Results The results showed that participants with a moderate level of cortisol who were given metyrapone had no problem restoring normal memory function. Participants who, from the start, had a high level of cortisol had no memory improvement. Hydrocortisone caused even greater memory loss.

Exam Tip The learning outcome "explain" requires you to show how biological factors influence a cognitive process. You are supposed to know two biological factors.
You could also use acethylcholine and explain how this biological factor influences memory processes (see more on this in unit 2.3).

3.5 Discuss how social or cultural factors affect one cognitive process

Cultural and methodological considerations in cross-cultural research on memory

- **Wang and Ross (2007)** Culture is both a *system* (values, schemas, models, artifacts) and a *process* (rituals, daily routines, and practices). Culture affects why people remember, how they remember, when they remember, what they remember and whether they find it necessary to remember at all.

- When researchers conduct cross-cultural memory research with participants from Western and non-Western cultures they often use tasks developed in psychology laboratories, such as free recall of lists of unrelated words. In such tasks, the people from Western cultures generally do better. This could be because such tasks are meaningless to non-Western people.

Cultural and social demands determine memory

- **Bartlett (1932)** claims that cultural and social demands can explain the extraordinary ability of Swazi herdsmen to recall individual characteristics of their cattle. The Swazi culture revolves around the possession and care of cattle and it is important for people to recognize their animals.

- **Misty and Rogoff (1994)** argue that culture and memory are enmeshed skills. Remembering is an activity, which is determined by the demands of the social and cultural context in which it takes place. Remembering may be a means of achieving an important social or cultural goal. For example, the Itamul elders in New Guinea have an extraordinary memory for lines of descent and history. This kind of knowledge is important to them because it can help resolve property disputes with conflicting clans.

Cole and Scribner (1974) Cross-cultural study of memory

Aim To investigate free recall in two different cultures, the USA and the Kpelle people in Liberia.

Procedure For the test in Liberia, the researchers used objects that would be familiar to the Liberian children. The list of words belonged to four distinct categories. American children were given free recall tests matching their culture. The researchers presented the words to the participants and asked them to remember as many of them as possible in any order (free recall). In the second part of the experiment, the researchers presented the same objects in a meaningful way as part of a story.

Results

- In the free recall test, the non-schooled participants hardly improved their performance after the age of 9 or 10. They remembered around 10 items on the first trial, and around two more after 15 practice trials. Liberian school children performed as school children of the same age did in the USA. They also used similar memory strategies.

- In the second part of the experiment, the non-schooled Liberian participants recalled objects well because they grouped them according to the roles they played in the story.

- School children in Liberia and the USA used chunking and recalled items according to categories. The non-schooled Liberian children did not use the categorical structure of the list to help them remember. This indicates possible cultural differences in cognitive processes such as categorization and memory.

Evaluation The extent to which it is culture or schooling (or both) that influenced memory and categorization in the study is not entirely clear. The experimental method was used and it can help to establish cause-effect relationship, but since the independent variable was culture (or schooling) it may be difficult to say anything definite about cause-effect relationships.

More research on culture and memory

Rogoff and Waddel (1982) found that Mayan children did better in a memory task if they were given one that was meaningful to them in local terms. The researchers constructed a miniature model of a Mayan village, which resembled the children's own village. The researcher then selected 20 miniature objects from a set of 80 (e.g. animals, furniture, people) and placed them in the model. Then the objects were taken out of the model and replaced among the 60 objects. After a few minutes, the experimenter asked the children to reconstruct the scene they had been shown. Under these conditions, the Mayan children did slightly better than the children from the USA.

The study shows that the content and context of a memory task are important and that useful memory strategies are learned in a sociocultural context.

Culture and memory summing up

- The implication of many cross-cultural memory studies is that, although the ability to remember is universal (hardware), specific forms of remembering (software) are not universal but rather context-bound.

- A methodological problem exists as most memory research is conducted in cultures with formal schooling systems. This makes it difficult to generalize findings to cultures with no formal schooling.

- Memory is not a "tape recorder" or an exact replica of what happened, but rather a "reconstruction". Schema theory can explain why this happens. Reconstructive memory indicates that memory is only reliable to some extent.

- Cognitive researchers have found that memories are not fixed and can be lost, changed, or even created. Memories may also be scrambled in the process of retrieving them and they can be manipulated (**Loftus, 2003**). Eyewitness testimony has been found to be incorrect on numerous occasions where DNA has revealed that the wrong person was convicted. All this indicates that memory is not always reliable.

- We tend to remember the overall meaning (gist) of something and we reconstruct the information to some extent when we retrieve it.

- Sometimes memory is distorted for personal reasons, for example to enhance our own importance (self-serving bias).

Reasons for inaccuracies in memory could be:

- Memory is reconstructive (e.g. **Bartlett, 1932**) and information processing is schema driven (see unit 3.2).

- Memories are constructed after the fact and they are susceptible to post-event information and manipulations (e.g. **Loftus and Palmer, 1974**).

- There is no relationship between people's belief that their memory is accurate and the memory's accuracy (e.g. **Neisser and Harsch, 1992**). (See more on "flashbulb memories" in unit 3.9).

Barlett (1932) The theory of reconstructive memory

This theory assumes that humans are active information processors who construct memories as they try to make sense of what happens based on what they already know. Schemas stored in LTM help people make sense of the world around them. Bartlett called this "effort after meaning". People do not simply remember information because the prestored schemas determine what to remember. He suggested that the reconstructive nature of memory based on schema processing could explain memory distortions (see Bartlett's study in unit 3.2).

Strengths of the theory of reconstructive memory	Limitations of the theory of reconstructive memory
<ul><li>The model can explain memory distortions well.</li><li>It is supported by many empirical studies and laboratory experiments (e.g Loftus and Palmer, 1974).</li></ul>	<ul><li>The model may focus too much on the inaccuracy of memory.</li><li>Schema processing is not fully understood.</li></ul>

Loftus and Palmer (1974) Reconstruction of automobile destruction (the first experiment)

Aim To investigate whether the use of leading questions would affect recall in a situation where participants were asked to estimate speed. This is a situation that could happen when people appear in court as eyewitness testimonies.

Procedure The student participants saw videos of traffic accidents and had to answer questions about the accident. In experiment 1, the participants were asked to estimate speed of the cars based on a critical question: "About how fast were the cars going when they smashed into each other?" "Smashed" was replaced by words such as hit, collided, bumped or contacted in other conditions (experiment 2 is not included here).

Results The mean estimates of speed were highest in the "smashed" condition (40.8 mph) and lowest in the "contacted" group (31.8 mph). The researchers calculated a statistical test and found that their results were significant at $p \leq 0.005$. The results indicate that memory is not reliable and that memory can be manipulated by using specific words. The critical word in the question consistently affected the participants' answer to the question. One explanation could be that the use of different words influenced participants' mental representation

of the accident, i.e. the verb "smashed" activates a cognitive schema of a severe accident and therefore speed estimates increase. It is not the actual details of the accident that are remembered but rather what is in line with a cognitive schema of a severe accident. This is in line with Bartlett's suggestion of reconstructive memory. It could also be that participants simply had difficulties estimating speed. This cannot be ruled out.

Evaluation The experiment was conducted in a laboratory. There may be a problem of ecological validity. Neisser has criticized laboratory experiments on memory for being too artificial. The fact that the experiment used students as participants has also been criticized because students are not representative of a general population. The films shown in the experiment were made for teaching purposes and therefore the participants' experience was not the the same as if it had been a real accident. The experiment was rigorously controlled so it was possible to establish a cause-effect relationship between the independent variable (the critical words) and the dependent variable (estimation of speed).

Loftus, E.F. and Palmer, J.C. (1974) "Reconstruction of automobile destruction: An example of the Interaction between language and memory", *Journal of Verbal Learning and Verbal Behavior* 13, 584–589.

Riniolo et al. (2003) on accuracy of eye witness testimony in a real life situation – the plunge of Titanic.

Aim To investigate the reliability of memory for a central detail of eye witnesses to the Titanic's final plunge (i.e. whether the Titanic sank intact or broke in two before it went down). It was believed at the time that the ship went down intact.

Procedure The researchers used archival data, i.e. transcripts from two hearings in 1912, one in the USA and one in the UK. The researchers identified 20 cases (N = 20) from the total amount of 91 survivors in the hearings who had explicitly addressed the state of the ship during its final plunge.

Results 75% of the eyewitnesses in this study, i.e. a total of 15, said that Titanic was breaking apart during sinking and 25% said Titanic was intact while it was going down. The majority of the 20 selected eyewitness testimonies in this study said that the ship broke in two before the plunge so *central traits* of the event were recalled accurately, although the memory was formed during traumatic conditions (high emotional arousal). After the hearings it was concluded that the Titanic sank intact and this "myth" has been repeated in the literature until the discovery of the wreck. Reasons for this could be that it was believed that the Titanic could not sink and the general belief that memory is impaired when witnessing a traumatic event.

Evaluation The case study only investigated memory for one central trait. The eyewitnesses used in this archival study were part of a subgroup and they are not representative of all the eyewitnesses. There might have been bias in the interrogations towards confirmation of a pre-existing belief of the intact ship. It is not possible to determine if post-event information could have influenced the testimony. The sample was small and it was not possible to interview the eyewitnesses for clarification because they were all dead at that time. It was not possible to measure the perceived trauma either. In spite of these methodological limitations, this case study contributes to our knowledge about the accuracy of eyewitness testimony from people who witnessed a traumatic event in real life.

Riniolo, T.C., Koledin, M., Drakulic, G.M., and Payne, R.A. (2003), *Journal of General Psychology*, 130 (1): 89–95.

Exam Tip You may also use Bartlett (1932) from unit 3.2. You need a minimum of two studies in an essay so you could choose an experimental study and one of the studies dealing with memory in real life.

3.7 Discuss the use of technology in investigating cognitive processes

- The use of advanced technology in research on cognitive processes provides insight into the complexity of the activity of the brain's neuronal network in cognitive processes that underpin behaviour.

- Cognition always involves neuronal activity in the brain. Modern technology, e.g. EEG (electroencephalography) and fMRI (functional magnetic resonance imaging), can be used to study cognitive processes while they are taking place (e.g. in traditional cognitive research on memory but also in research on neruroeconomics and neuromarketing).

- Neuroimaging, such as fMRI, can register changes in blood flow in the active brain (oxygen and glucose consumption in the brain). The researchers can then make a map of areas in the brain related to specific cognitive processes.

- Neuroimaging has revealed that cognitive processes are mediated by a network of distributed interacting brain regions and each area makes specific contributions.

EEG and MEG

EEG (Electroencephalography) refers to the recording of the brain's electrical signals, i.e. the firing of the many neurons in the cortex of the brain. Electrodes are placed on the scalp to register what parts of the brain are active and in what ways. EEG can be used to record electrical activity for research purposes (e.g. which areas are active when a child listens to its mother's voice).

MEG (magnetoencephalography) is a technique used to record magnetic fields produced by the natural electrical activity in the brain.

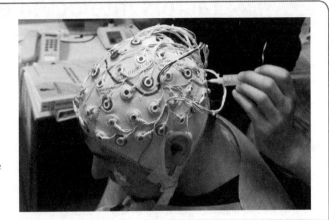

Palva et al. (2010) Working memory

Aim To investigate the interaction of neuronal networks in the cerebral cortex in relation to visual working memory.

Procedure Data from EEG and MEG was used to identify patterns of interaction between the neurons (neuronal synchrony) in the cerebral cortex during visual tasks.

Results The results showed synchronization of neuronal activity in different brain areas related to the maintenance and contents of working memory. Specific networks interacted (e.g. different areas of the brain's frontal and parietal lobes played a central role in coordinating attention and action in working memory). Handling and maintaining sensory information about visual stimuli showed activity in networks in the occipital lobe.

Evaluation The findings support Baddeley's model of working memory (e.g. the central executive could be linked to the activity in the frontal and parietal lobes). The activity in the networks in the occipital lobe could be linked to the visuo-spatial sketchpad (see more on the working memory model in unit 3.3). The neuroimaging technologies used were important to detect specific brain areas involved in cognitive processing. This could not be done otherwise.

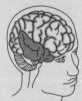  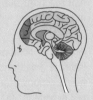

Phonological loop – temporal lobes of the left hemisphere

Visuo-spatial memory – right hemisphere

Central executive – dorsolateral prefrontal cortex

MRI

MRI (magnetic resonance imaging) produces three-dimensional images of brain structures. It is used to detect structural changes in the brain in cases of brain damage or illness.

- H.M. suffered from amnesia and was not able to form new explicit memories. This case study demonstrated that explicit memory processes are dependent on the hippocampus and adjacent cortical structures, but the exact damage to H.M.'s brain was not known before researchers could use brain imaging.

- **Corkin et al. (1997)** used MRI to study H.M.'s lesion in the first attempt to use modern technology to study his brain.

- The results of the MRI scan confirmed a relationship between damage to the medial temporal lobes (including the hippocampus) and H.M.'s amnesia. Although a tiny part of the hippocampus remained it was not enough to support normal memory function.

Strengths of using modern technology	Limitations of of using modern technology
- It provides the opportunity to see inside the working brain as it operates by mapping active brain areas. It is also possible to see synchronization between various brain areas involved in cognitive processes. - It is useful in diagnosing brain disease or damage that causes problems in cognitive functioning (for example memory problems in Alzheimer's).	- Scanning takes place in a highly artificial environment and some scanners are extremely noisy. This affects ecological validity. - Scanner studies can map brain areas involved in various cognitive processes but it is not yet possible to say anything definite about what these pictures actually mean.

To what extent do cognitive and biological factors interact in emotion?

- **Damasio (2000)** *Emotions* are physiological signals as a reaction to external stimuli, and *feelings* (conscious interpretation of the emotion) arise when the brain interprets the stimuli.

- The emotion "fear" is a useful survival mechanism as it allows animals (and humans) to react quickly to any possible sign of danger by starting the "fight or flight" reaction. In humans, cognitive factors such as *appraisal* may help to modulate physiological and psychological reactions to stimuli.

- Emotional arousal is a form of stress that activates the stress hormones adrenaline and cortisol. This is a useful survival mechanism. Memory of a fearful experience is stored in the cortex (explicit memory) and the emotional memory of the experience is stored via the amygdala (implicit memory). Normally humans can control irrational fear reactions but not always, and in some cases fear may be elicited without conscious control as in panic attacks.

- Anxiety, phobia, panic disorders, and PTSD in humans indicate a malfunction in the brain's ability to control fear reactions. Humans with damage to the amygdala do not experience fear in dangerous situations and this may endanger survival.

Brain, memory, and emotion

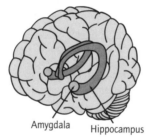

- Investigations into the role of emotion on explicit memory have focused primarily on the interaction of the **amygdala** (specialized for the processing of emotion) and the **hippocampus** (necessary for semantic and episodic memory).

Amygdala   Hippocampus

- **Phelps (2004)** suggests that in emotional situations the amygdala can modulate memory encoding and storage of explicit memories (hippocampal dependent memories) so that emotional events receive priority.

LeDoux's theory of the emotional brain (1999)

Humans' emotional reactions are flexible due to evolution. Learning to detect and respond to danger is important for survival (e.g. an instant response is needed in dangerous situations). Humans have also evolved "emotional feeling", i.e. a conscious experience of the emotion which helps to evaluate the level of danger before a response.

LeDoux's two pathways of emotions in the brain:

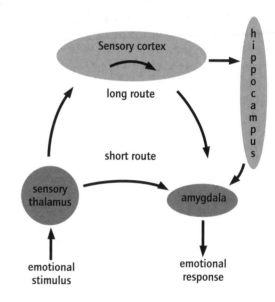

1 **The short route** The amygdala reacts immediately to sensory input and activates response systems (e.g. the physiological stress response "fight or flight"). This is very useful in the case of immediate danger where a quick reaction can make the difference between life and death.

2 **The long route** The sensory input goes via the sensory cortex to the hippocampus. This route involves evaluation of the stimulus and consideration of an appropriate response. This could link to the concept "cognitive appraisal" **(Lazarus, 1975)**.

Easterbrook (1959) Cue utilization theory (central traits and peripheral traits)

- The theory predicts that in situations with high levels of emotional arousal, people will tend to pay more attention to and encode details of the emotion arousing stimulus (central details) and not pay attention to details that are not central to the emotional arousal (peripheral details).

- See **Riniolo et al. (2003)** on memory for central traits in a traumatic event (The Titanic's final plunge) in unit 3.6.

Lazarus (1975) Appraisal theory

- According to appraisal theory, cognitive factors can modulate stress responses, i.e. the physiological and psychological reactions involved in the experience.

- Appraisal can be seen as an *evaluation* of a situation, including evaluation of one's psychological and material resources to cope with the stressful event.

Speisman et al. (1964) Experimental manipulation of emotions through cognitive appraisal

Aim To investigate the extent to which manipulation of cognitive appraisal could influence emotional experience.

Procedure

- In this laboratory experiment participants saw anxiety-evoking films, (e.g. a film of an aboriginal initiation ceremony where adolescent boys were subjected to unpleasant genital cutting).

- This film was shown with three different soundtracks intended to manipulate emotional reactions. The "trauma condition" had a soundtrack with emphasis on the mutilation and pain; the "intellectualization condition" had a soundtrack that gave an anthropological interpretation of the initiation ceremony; the "denial condition" showed the adolescents as being willing and happy in the ceremony.

- During each viewing of the film various objective physiological measures were taken, such as heart rate and galvanic skin response.

Results The participants in the "trauma condition" showed much higher physiological measures of stress than the participants in the two other conditions. The results support the appraisal theory in that the manipulation of the participants' cognitive appraisal did have a significant impact on the physiological stress reactions. The participants in the "trauma condition" reacted more emotionally.

Evaluation This was a laboratory experiment with rigorous control so it may lack ecological validity, but research on the role of appraisal in real-life emotional events tends to find the same relationship as laboratory research.

The study could be a demonstration of how biological and cognitive factors interact in emotion and it illustrates LeDoux's theory of the two pathways in emotional processing.

Summary of the interaction of emotion and cognition

Cognitive and biological factors do, to a large extent, interact in emotion, but in complex ways that are not yet well known. Emotions may influence cognitive processes such as memory, and cognitive processes such as appraisal may influence emotions, but little is known about the exact workings of the physiological correlates of emotion.

The influence is often bidirectional and this has been explored within health and abnormal psychology.

- Neuroimaging investigations of emotion have identified areas in the prefrontal lobes associated with active reappraisal of the emotional importance of events (**Ochsner and Gross, 2008**). This indicates that it is possible to regulate negative emotions via appraisal.

Evaluate one theory of how emotion may affect one cognitive process

Brown and Kulik (1977) The theory of flashbulb memory (FM)

- Flashbulb memories are a type of episodic memory (explicit memory). It is assumed that they are highly resistant to forgetting, i.e. the details of the memory will remain intact and accurate because of the emotional arousal at the moment of encoding. This is controversial.

- FM can be defined as a highly accurate and exceptionally vivid memory of the moment a person first hears about a shocking event.

- The "flashbulb" indicates that the event will be registered like a photograph, i.e. it will be accurate in detail.

- Brown and Kulik suggested that FM is often rehearsed because it is important or emotionally salient to the individual and this makes the memory more accessible and vividly remembered over time.

According to the theory, there are six important features about FM that people remember in detail:

- place (i.e. where they were when the incident happened)

- ongoing activity (i.e. what they were doing)

- informant (i.e. how they learned about the incident)

- own affect (i.e. how they felt – their emotional status or affect)

- other affect (i.e. how other people felt)

- aftermath (i.e. importance of the event – the consequences).

Brown and Kulik (1977) Research on FM

Aim To investigate whether shocking events are recalled more vividly and accurately than other events.

Procedure Questionnaires asked 80 participants to recall circumstances where they had learned of shocking events

Results

- The participants had vivid memories of where they were, what they did, and what they felt when they first heard about a shocking public event such as the assassination of John F. Kennedy.

- The participants also said they had flashbulb memories of shocking personal events such as the sudden death of a relative.

- The results indicated that FM is more likely for unexpected and personally relevant events. The researchers suggested 'the photographic model of flashbulb memory'.

- Brown and Kulik suggest that FM is caused by the physiological emotional arousal (e.g. activity in the amygdala).

Evaluation The reliance on retrospective data questions the reliability of this study. People tend to interpret an event from their current perspective. Research indicates that although an FM is emotionally vivid it is not necessarily accurate in regard to details. The photographic model of FM has been challenged.

Neisser (1982) is critical towards the idea of flashbulb memories, as certain memories are very vivid because they are rehearsed and discussed after the event.

Neisser and Harsch (1992) did a real life study on people's memory of the Challenger disaster. The first data were collected less than 24 hours after the event and the same participants were tested two and a half years later. Most participants did not remember anything correctly but were very confident that they did.

Neisser and Harsch (1992) Testing the FM theory

Aim To test the theory of flashbulb memory by investigating the extent to which memory for a shocking event (the Challenger disaster) would be accurate after a period of time.

Procedure

- 106 students in an introductory psychology class were given a questionnaire and asked to write a description of how they had heard the news. They also had to answer seven questions related to where they were, what they were doing, etc., and what emotional feelings they experienced at the time of the event.

- Participants answered the questionnaires less than 24 hours after the disaster.

- Two and a half years later, 44 of the original students answered the questionnaire again. This time they were also asked to rate how confident they were of the accuracy of their memory on a scale from 1 to 5. The participants were also asked if they had filled out a questionnaire of the subject before.

- Sometime after the last questionnaires, the researchers performed a semi-structured interview to test whether the participants could remember what they had written previously. Participants then saw their original reports from the first questionnaire.

Results

- Only 11 participants out of the 44 remembered that they had filled out the questionnaire before.

- There were major discrepancies between the original questionnaire and the follow-up two and a half years later. The mean score of correctness of recall of the seven questions was 2.95 out of 7. For 11 participants the score was 0, and 22 scored 2 or less. The average level of confidence in accuracy for the questions was 4.17.

- The results challenge the predictions of the FM theory and also question the reliability of memory in general. Participants were confident that they remembered the event correctly both times and they could not explain the discrepancies between the first and second accounts.

Evaluation

- The study was conducted in a natural environment and it has higher ecological validity than laboratory experiments on memory. The participants were psychology students who participated for course credits and they may not be representative.

- The degree of emotional arousal when witnessing a shocking public event may be different from experiencing a traumatic event in your own personal life, and the importance of the events may be very different. This could influence how well people remember a certain event.

Strengths of the FM theory	Limitations of the FM theory
- The theory can, to some extent, explain why very emotional memories are often more vividly remembered over time, but it cannot explain why these memories are often no more accurate than any other memory (except perhaps for some central details). - The theory has generated many research studies and the theory has been modified. The idea that emotional events are better remembered than non-emotional events is supported, but modified with the idea that the event should have specific personal relevance.	- "Flashbulb" refers to the flashbulb used in photography, but the name may not be well-chosen as the photograph taken with a flashbulb preserves everything in the scene as it was at the time the picture was taken. - An FM is a "reconstructed memory" where the emotional importance of the event may influence the way the memory is reconstructed – particularly if it is discussed with other people over time (confabulation) or if the memory does not have particular personal relevance.

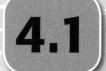

4.1 Outline principles that define the sociocultural level of analysis

Principle 1: Human beings are social animals with a basic need to belong.

This means that they are motivated to have important relationships with other people.

Principle 1 demonstrated in:

In the belongingness theory, **Baumeister and Leary (1995)** assert that humans are motivated to form and maintain interpersonal relationships and human culture is, to some extent, adapted to enable people to satisfy the psychological need to live together.

Howarth (2002) performed focus-group interviews with adolescent girls in Brixton to study how the girls described and evaluated themselves. She found that they had a positive view of "being from Brixton" which contrasted the view of people living outside Brixton. This can be seen as an example of creating a positive "social identity" based on group belonging.

Principle 2: Culture influences human behaviour.

This means that humans create and shape culture and they are influenced by their culture.

■ Cultural norms provide general prescriptions for behaviours that are expected in a given culture or society.

Principle 2 demonstrated in:

Berry (1967) investigated how conformity may be related to culture. He used a modification of the Asch experiment (see unit 4.8) with adults from two different cultures: the Temne culture of Sierra Leone, who rely on agriculture for survival, and adult Inuits from the Baffin Islands in Canada, who live on hunting and fishing. Temne people have to cooperate in order to grow a successful crop to feed the community, so they learn conformity and compliance from an early age. The Inuits must be able to ◀▶

track and hunt animals and fish on their own, so children in this culture learn independence. Berry found that Inuits were almost non-conforming whereas the Temne showed a high degree of conformity.

Principle 3: Humans have a social self which reflects their group memberships.

Group memberships give rise to social identities (ingroups) and comparison with other groups (outgroups). This might lead to bias in information processing (sterotyping) and discrimination.

Principle 3 demonstrated in:

Social identity theory (SIT) by **Tajfel and Turner (1979)** suggests that group-based social identities are based on categorization into **ingroups** (a group to which one belongs) and **outgroups** (a group to which one does not belong). Ingroups are generally seen as more positive than outgroups and ingroup favouritism is common. The outgroup is generally seen in a more negative light (outgroup negative bias).

Tajfel (1970) suggested the minimal group paradigm. He performed experiments with boys who were randomly divided into two groups. They were told that it was based on their estimation of dots or preference for paintings but in reality it was totally random. The boys just believed that they had been grouped according to their estimation and preference for paintings to award points to members of the groups; they consistently demonstrated ingroup favouritism by awarding more points to members of their own group. The experiments showed that a kind of social identity can be established even as a consequence of a minimal and unimportant task.

34

4.2 Describe the role of situational and dispositional factors in explaining behaviour

Attribution theory

Attribution theory (**Heider 1958**) is based on the assumption that people are **naive scientists** who try to explain observable behaviour. An essential feature of the original attribution theory is a fundamental distinction about *internal* and *external* causes of behaviour.

Attribution theory is based on the assumption that people:

- tend to look for causes and reasons for other people's behaviour because they feel that there are motives behind most of their own behaviour

- are "intuitive psychologists" who construct their own causal theories of human behaviour

- construct causal theories because they want to be able to understand, predict, and control the environment around them.

Why attributions?

- People seem to have a pervasive need for causal explanations because this makes the world more predictable.

- Most cultures have constructed causal explanations for the origin and meaning of life, (e.g. in myths and religions).

- The tendency to see motives and dispositions behind human actions may be so automatic that people sometimes find it difficult to override it even where motives and dispositions don't really apply (e.g. when people attribute motives to objects in computer games or believe in fate or witchcraft).

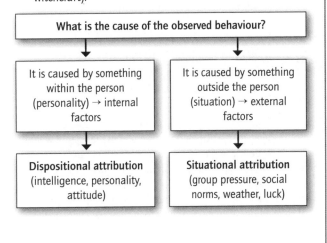

Empirical research

- **Simmel (1944)** performed an experiment where he showed moving geometric figures to participants and asked them to describe the movements of the figure. The participants all described them as if the geometric figures had intentions to act in the way they did.

- **Evans-Pritchard (1976)** described how the Azande people of central Africa believed that it was witchcraft that killed people when a granary doorway collapsed. The door had been eaten through by termites but the Azande believed that it was fate that made those people sit in the doorway just when it collapsed.

4.3 | Discuss two errors in attributions

Ross (1977) The fundamental attribution error (FAE)

FAE occurs when people overestimate personality traits (dispositional factors) and underestimate environmental factors when they explain other people's behaviour. According to social psychologist **Fiske (2004)**, people rely too much on personality in explaining behaviour and they underestimate – or never consider – the power of situations.

- In Western societies it could be because of the ideology that

people get what they deserve (**Gilbert 1995**).

- It makes life more predictable if people's behaviour is mainly caused by their personality. This gives the impression that people are understandable and easy to deal with.

- Explanations based solely on personality are incomplete. It would be wrong not to consider the power of situation.

Ross, Amabile, and Steinmetz (1977) FAE

Aim To investigate whether knowledge of allocated social roles in a quiz show would affect participants' judgements of people's expertise.

Procedure Eighteen pairs of students from an introductory class at Stanford University participated in a simulated quiz game where they were randomly assigned to the roles of either questioner or contestant. In the experimental condition the role of questioner or contestant was randomly allocated to one person in each pair. Twenty-four observers watched the quiz. The questioners were asked to compose 10 questions based on their own knowledge and the contestants were asked to answer these questions.

The questioner was instructed to ask each question and then wait around 30 seconds for a response. If the contestants did not answer correctly the questioner gave the correct answer. After the quiz, all participants and the observers were asked to rate "general knowledge" of contestants and questioners.

Results The contestants consistently rated the general knowledge of the questioners in the experimental condition as superior. The observers did the same.

This was a clear demonstration of the FAE. The contestants and the observers attributed the questioners' ability to answer the questions to dispositional factors and failed to take into consideration the situational factors that gave the questioners an advantage. The questioners themselves did not rate their own knowledge as being superior to that of the contestants.

Evaluation The experimental set-up was ingenious. It clearly gave the opportunity to demonstrate attributional biases because the questioners made up their own questions and this was known by all participants. The participants were university students so there may be sampling bias and it is difficult to generalize the results. The issue of ecological validity could also be raised.

Empirical research

Suedfeld (2003) investigated attributions made by Holocaust survivors. The researcher gave questionnaires to members of Holocaust survivor groups and age-matched Jewish participants who had not personally experienced the Nazi persecution (control). The two groups were asked for their views on possible factors in survival during the Holocaust. 91% of the survivors made situational attributions (e.g. luck and help from others) compared to 51% in the control group.

Only 34% of the survivors made dispositional attributions (e.g. psychological strength and determination) compared to 71% in the control group. This indicates that personal experiences during the Holocaust influenced survivors' attributions because they had witnessed that it was actually often luck or help from others that determined who survived and who didn't. The survivors had a clear picture of the power of the situation during the Holocaust.

Cultural bias in the FAE

Culture seems to be a determinant in attribution style.

- In collectivist cultures the emphasis is on the primary social relationships of an individual (family, social role, cultural activities).

- In individualistic cultures the emphasis on the individual as the primary cause of action leads to dispositional attributions. The individual is seen as the main cause of success and failure.

- **Norenzayan et al. (2002)** tested whether information given to Korean and American participants would influence their attributions. When participants only received information about individuals, both groups made dispositional attributions. When situational information was also provided, the Koreans tended to include this information in their explanations much more than the Americans did. This indicates that there may be universal features in the FAE and that available information influences attributions.

Strengths of the FAE	Limitations of the FAE
■ The theory has promoted understanding of common errors in explanation of what happens in the world. ■ The theory has proven very robust and has been supported by many research studies.	■ The theory is culturally biased with too much focus on individualism. ■ Much research on the theory has been conducted in laboratories and with a student sample (problems with generalization of findings).

The self-serving bias (SSB)

The SSB (i.e. a self-enhancing strategy) refers to people's tendency to evaluate themselves positively by taking credit for their success ("I am intelligent") and attribute their failures to situational factors ("The teacher is not competent").

A special version of the SSB is called "self-handicapping". For example, students who expect to fail an exam can openly make situational attributions before the exam by saying that they have hangovers or that they haven't slept the whole night.

Possible explanations

■ The SSB could be a way to uphold self-esteem (self-protection). People see themselves as responsible for success but not for their failures because they *want* to see themselves in this way.

■ Others have suggested that the SSB occurs when people don't have enough information and limit themselves to the available information. People typically *expect* to succeed and correlate success with their own effort and exaggerate the amount of control they have (**Miller and Ross, 1975**).

Empirical research

■ **Lau and Russel (1980)** found that American football coaches and players were more likely to attribute success to dispositional factors (e.g. talent or hard work) and failure to situational factors (e.g. injuries or bad weather).

■ **Posey and Smith (2003)** performed an SSB experiment with children. They were asked to do maths problems, sitting either with a friend or a non-friend. Although they sat in pairs the children had to do the maths problems alone, but the total score of the pair was noted. After the test the children were asked who did the better job. The results showed that children who worked with friends and failed were less likely to show the SSB and more likely to give their friends credit when they succeeded. Children who worked with a non-friend were more likely to demonstrate the SSB.

Cultural considerations in the SSB

Culture-specific attributional styles may be a natural part of enculturation and socialization. Some argue that the SSB is primarily linked to individualist cultures but others believe it is can be found in both individualistic and collectivist cultures.

■ **Kashima and Triandis (1986)** showed slides from unfamiliar countries to American and Japanese students and asked them to remember details. When the students were asked to explain their performance, the Americans explained their own success with internal factors, such as ability, and failure with external factors. The Japanese tended to explain their failure with lack of ability. This is called the modesty bias and is a cultural variation of the SSB.

■ **Bond, Leung, and Wan (1982)** argued that a possible explanation for the modesty bias in collectivist cultures could be a cultural norm in Chinese societies to maintain harmonious personal relationships. A person who makes self-effacing attributions could expect to be better liked.

Strengths of the SSB	Limitations of the SSB
The theory can explain why some people (mostly from individualist cultures) explain their failures as being caused by situational factors.	The theory is culturally biased. It cannot explain why some cultures emphasize a self-effacing attribution (modesty bias).

Social identity theory (SIT)

SIT is a theoretical framework developed by **Tajfel and Turner (1979)** for the analysis of intergroup relations. SIT is linked to the idea of self-categorization theory **(Turner 1991)**.

Social identity can be defined as the part of one's self-concept based on the knowledge of membership in social group(s) in combination with the *value* and *emotional significance* attached to that membership.

- Individuals strive to maintain a positive self-concept as well as a positive social identity. People make comparisons between ingroup and outgroup on valued dimensions to establish, maintain, and defend *positive ingroup distinctiveness* (social comparison).

- When a social comparison results in a positive outcome for the ingroup, the need for a positive social identity is satisfied but the opposite may also happen (e.g. for low-status minority groups).

- Intergroup discrimination can be one way to uphold a positive social identity for the ingroup (for example when women earn less than men for the same work or when whites think they are superior and discriminate against other ethnic groups).

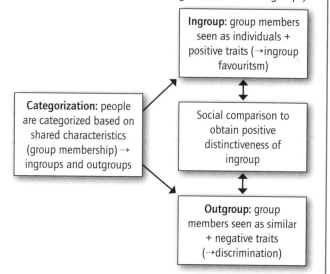

Tajfel (1970) Experiment in intergroup discrimination – the minimal group paradigm

Aim To investigate if boys placed in random groups based on an arbitrary task (minimal group) would display ingroup favouritism and intergroup discrimination.

Procedure The participants were 64 schoolboys (age 14–15) from a state school in the UK. They came to a psychology laboratory in groups of eight. They all knew each other well before the experiment. The boys were shown clusters of varying numbers of dots, flashed onto a screen and had to estimate the number of dots in each cluster. The experimenters assigned the boys to groups at random categorized as 'over-estimator', 'under-estimator' etc. Subsequently, the boys had to allocate small amounts of money to the other boys in the experiment. The only thing they knew of the boys was if they belonged to the same or a different category.

In a second experiment, boys were randomly allocated to groups based on their supposed artistic preferences for two painters. Then they had to award money to the other boys .

Results A large majority of the boys gave more money to members of their own category (ingroup) than to members of the other categories (outgroups).

In the second experiment the boys tried to maximize the difference between the two groups.

The results of both experiments indicate that the boys adopted a strategy of *ingroup favouritism*. This supports the predictions of social identity theory.

Evaluation The experiment contributed to the development of social identity theory, which states that the social groups and categories to which we belong are an important part of our self-concept. Tajfel demonstrated that a "minimal group" is all that is necessary for individuals to exhibit discrimination against outgroups. The experiment has been criticized for artificiality and demand characteristics. The boys may have interpreted the task as a sort of a competitive game and therefore reacted the way they did.

Howarth (2002) performed focus group interviews with adolescent girls in Brixton to study how the girls described and evaluated themselves. She found that the girls had a positive view of "being from Brixton" which contrasted with how people living outside Brixton perceived people from Brixton. This can be seen as an example of creating a positive "social identity" based on group belonging.

Strengths of SIT	Limitations of SIT
- SIT assumes that intergroup conflict is not required for discrimination to occur. This is supported by empirical research, e.g. **Tajfel (1970)**. - SIT can explain some of the mechanisms involved in establishing "positive distinctiveness" to the ingroup by maximizing differences to the outgroup. - SIT has been applied to understanding behaviours such as ethnocentrism, ingroup favouritism, conformity to ingroup norms, and stereotyping.	- Minimal group research has been criticized for artificiality. The experimental set-up is so far from natural behaviour that it can be questioned whether it reflects how people would react in real life. This could limit the predictive value of the theory. - SIT cannot fully explain how ingroup favouritism may result in violent behaviour towards outgroups. - SIT cannot explain why social constraints such as poverty could play a bigger role in behaviour than social identity.

4.5 Explain the formation of stereotypes and their effect on behaviour

How do stereotypes form? Sociocultural learning, categorization, and schema processing

- Stereotypes are a salient part of our social and cultural environment. We learn them through daily interactions, conversations and through the media.

- Stereotypes are, to some extent, based on individual experiences but cultural and social factors also play a role, i.e. stereotypes are contextualized and not simply the results of individual cognitive processing. Stereotypes can be shared by large sociocultural groups as **social representations**.

- The most common cognitive process involved in stereotyping is social categorization (**Tajfel, 1969**). Categorization (and stereotyping) seems to be fundamental to human nature and it helps to make the world more predictable. Once stereotypes are formed they act as cognitive schemas in information processing.

Empirical research: The Princeton Trilogy.

Study 1: Katz and Braley (1933) investigated whether traditional social stereotypes had a cultural basis by asking 100 male students from Princeton University to choose five traits that characterized different ethnic groups (for example Americans, Jews, Japanese, Negroes) from a list of 84 words. The results showed considerable agreement in stereotypes, especially of negative traits. Eighty-four per cent of the students said that Negroes were superstitious and 79% said that Jews were shrewd. They were very positive towards their own group (ingroup bias). Since most of the students did not have any personal contact with members of the ethnic groups they had to rate, it was suggested that stereotypes are learned (e.g. through the media or by gatekeepers, i.e. they are cultural products).

Study 2: Gilbert (1951) replicated the study of Princeton students. This time there was less uniformity of agreement, especially about unfavourable traits, than in the 1933 study. The stereotypes still demonstrated an ingroup bias. Stereotypes about Japanese were extremely negative and this was explained by the negative press about Japan after Pearl Harbour, so the original hypothesis about stereotypes as cultural products was confirmed. Many students expressed irritation at being asked to make generalizations at all and this could indicate a social change (e.g. that it was no longer as acceptable to express stereotypes openly).

Study 3: Karlins et al. (1969) replicated the study. Many students objected to the task but this time there was greater agreement on the stereotypes assigned to the different groups compared with the 1951 study. The researchers interpreted this as a re-emergence of social stereotyping but in the direction of a more favourable stereotypical image.

Devine (1989) argued that it is important to distinguish between knowledge of a stereotype and accepting it. According to her, the Princeton trilogy does not take this into account.

- Stereotypes are simplified mental images which act as templates to help interpret the social world (**Lipmann, 1922**).

- Stereotyping is, to a large extent, an automatic cognitive process (i.e. it occurs without intention, effort, or awareness and is not expected to interfere with other concurrent cognitive processes (**Posner and Snyder, 1975**).

Implicit personality theories (e.g. illusory correlations such as "blondes are stupid")

↕

Categorization: people are categorized based on shared characteristics (group membership) → stereotype (schema)

→

Generalization: attributes of the category (group) are) generalized to all members of the category

↕

Ingroup: group members seen as individuals + positive traits (→ingroup favouritsm)

↕

Outgroup: group members seen as similar + negative traits

↕

Schema processing: memory representations of stereotypes (schemas) influence perception and evaluation of stereotyped individuals. Stereotypes are often automatically activated.

↕

Confirmation bias: people tend to pay attention to information that confirms their beliefs→stereotypes resistant to change (stereotypes as defaults)

What is the effect of stereotypes on behaviour?

- Social groups are categorized into ingroups and outgroups. Once people are categorized as belonging to one group rather than another they tend to emphasize similarities to individuals in that group and exaggerate differences between groups. Stereotypes of outgroups are often central to group identity.

- People tend to pay attention to stereotype-consistent information and disregard stereotype-inconsistent information (confirmation bias).

- Negative stereotypes may be internalized by stereotyped groups (stereotype threat).

Empirical research

- **Darley and Gross (1983)** performed an experiment where the researchers showed videos of a girl to participants. In video 1 the girl was playing in a poor environment (poor stereotype); in video 2 the girl was playing in a rich environment (rich stereotype). Then they saw a video of the girl in what could be an intelligence test. When the participants were asked to judge the future of the girl they all said that the "rich" girl would do well and the "poor" girl would do less well. Based on a few salient details from the first video, participants formed an overall impression of the girl's potential future based on stereotypes.

- **Steele and Aronson (1995)** performed an experiment using African Americans and European Americans, who did a verbal performance test based on difficult multiple-choice questions. When told that it was a test on verbal ability, African Americans scored lower than European Americans. When told that it was a task used to test how certain problems are generally solved, African Americans scored higher and matched the scores of European Americans. The researchers concluded that the stereotype threat could affect behaviour in any stereotyped group if the members themselves believe in the stereotype.

4.6 Explain social learning theory, making reference to two relevant studies

- Bandura (1977) suggested social learning theory (SLT) as an extension of existing learning theories (classical and operant conditioning). SLT is based on the assumption that people learn behaviours, attitudes, emotional reactions and norms through direct experiences but also through observing other humans (models).

- We learn consequences of behaviour from watching what happens to other humans (vicarious reinforcement). Once such information is stored in memory it serves as a guide to future actions. People are more likely to imitate behaviour that has positive consequences.

- Social learning can be direct via instructions or indirect (e.g. role models and no direct instructions).

Four important factors in social learning (observational learning)

Attention
Paying attention to the model is a condition for learning

↓

Retention
Remembering what the model did is a condition for imitating the model's behaviour

↓

Reproduction
People must have the capacity (e.g. skills) for imitating the behaviour

↓

Motivation
People must be motivated to imitate behaviour (e.g. importance of model or reward)

Study 1: Bandura and Ross (1961) Experimental investigation on learning aggression from a model

Aim To see if children would imitate the aggression of an adult model and whether they would imitate same-sex models more than opposite sex models.

Procedure

- Participants were 36 boys and 36 girls from the Stanford University Nursery School (mean age 4.4) who were divided into three groups matched on levels of aggressiveness before the experiment.

- One group saw the adult model behave aggressively towards a bobo doll, one group saw the model assemble toys, and the last group served as control.

- The children were further divided into groups so that some saw same-sex models and some opposite-sex models.

- The laboratory was set up as a play room with toys and a bobo doll. The model either played with the toys or behaved aggressively towards the bobo doll. After seeing this, the children were brought into a room with toys and told not to play with them in order to frustrate them. Then they were taken into a room with toys and a bobo doll where they were observed for 20 minutes through a one-way mirror.

Results

- Children who had seen an aggressive model were significantly more aggressive (physically and verbally) towards the bobo doll. They imitated the aggressive behaviour of the model but also showed other forms of aggression.

- Children were also more likely to imitate same-sex models. Boys were more aggressive overall than girls.

Discussion of results

- This key study supports social learning theory. Aggressive behaviour can be learned through observational learning.

- It is not possible to conclude that children always become aggressive when they watch violent models (e.g. on television or at home). Generally, research supports that children tend to imitate same-sex models more and this is also the case for adults.

Evaluation The laboratory experiment is low in ecological validity. The aggression here is artificial and there may be demand characteristics. The children were very young and it has been criticized for ethical reasons.

Study 2: Charlton et al. (2002) Observation of the introduction of television in a remote community (St. Helena)

Aim To investigate whether children in St. Helena would exhibit more aggressive behaviour after the introduction of television to the island in 1995.

Procedure

- The study was a natural experiment. Children (aged three to eight years) were observed before and after the introduction of television through cameras set up in the playgrounds of two primary schools on the island. The level of aggression in television matched what children in the UK were exposed to.

- The researchers also conducted interviews with teachers, parents, and some of the older children.

Results There was no increase in aggressive or antisocial behaviour. This was also the case after five years.

Discussion of results

- The data showed that children did not change their behaviour after television had arrived although they saw the same amount of violent television as British children.

- The parents and teachers said that antisocial behaviour was not accepted on the island and that there was a high degree of social control in the community. It shows that people may learn aggressive behaviour but they may not exhibit it for several reasons.

- Social and cultural factors also play a role in what behaviours are acceptable, so even though the children had no doubt learned aggressive behaviour, they did not show it.

Evaluation The study investigated a real-life event and is high in ecological validity. It does not question SLT but rather the results of **Bandura and Ross (1961)**. The results also confirm the idea that people must be motivated to imitate behaviour.

The norm (or rule) of reciprocity

The social norm of reciprocity dictates that we treat other people the way they treat us (Cialdini, 1993). People are socialized into returning favours and this powerful rule underpins compliance. **Lynn and McCall (1988)** found that restaurants who offered a mint or a sweet with the bill received larger tips.

Tiger and Fox (1971) suggested that reciprocation (mutual indebtedness) could be a result of evolution. The feeling of future obligation has made an important difference in human social evolution, because it meant that one individual could offer something (e.g. food, or care) to another individual and be confident that he or she could expect something in return.

Regan (1971) A laboratory experiment to test reciprocity

Aim To test whether participants who had received a favour from another would be more likely to help this person than if they had not received a favour.

Procedure One participant and a confederate of the experimenter were asked to rate paintings. In the experimental condition the confederate left the experiment and returned after a few minutes with two bottles of coca cola. He had bought one for himself and one for the participant. In the control condition, the participant did not receive a coke.

When all the paintings had been rated the experimenter left the room again. The confederate told the naive participant that he was selling raffle tickets for a new car and that the one who sold the most tickets could win $50. He then asked the participant if he would buy some tickets and said that even a small amount would help.

Results The participants in the experimental condition bought twice as many raffle tickets than participants in the control condition who had not received a favour first.

As a follow-up to the experiment the researcher investigated how much "*liking*" the confederate influenced the participant. The participants were asked to fill out rating scales indicating how much they liked the confederate. The researcher then compared how many tickets the participants had purchased from the confederate in the control condition. Liking was associated with buying significantly more tickets from the confederate in this condition. In the experimental condition it made no difference whether the participants liked the person or not.

Participants who received a coca cola who did not like the confederate bought just as many tickets as those who liked him. This shows the powerful influence of the rule of reciprocity. Even if people don't like a person they will return a favour.

Evaluation This was a laboratory experiment with a high degree of control. It was possible to establish cause-effect relationships between "receiving a favour" and "returning a favour". This supports the principle of reciprocity. There may be issues of artificiality in the experiment as well as sample bias. This limits the possibility of generalization. The findings have been supported by observations in real life.

Foot-in-the-door technique (FITD)

With the FITD technique, the real (and large) request is preceded by a smaller one. The FITD technique has been used in fund raising and to promote environmental awareness.

Dickerson et al. (1992) did a field experiment where they asked university students to conserve water in the dormitory showers. The researchers first asked a group of students to sign a poster supporting shorter showers to save water. Then they asked students to do a survey asking them to think about their own water usage. Finally the students' shower time was monitored. Students who had signed the poster and had done the survey spent an average of 3.5 minutes less in the shower compared to the rest of the students in the dormitory.

Evaluation of FITD

- Compliance with a small request increases the likelihood of compliance with a second, much larger request. This can perhaps be interpreted in terms of commitment. Once people have said yes, they perceive themselves as committed and want to behave consistently with that commitment.

- Much research done in this area has used pro-social requests and it seems that such requests are generally more likely to be accepted with this technique. It is more likely to be successful if the second request is an extension of the first one instead of being something completely different. Such results could perhaps be linked to the principle of people's need for self-consistency.

- The foot-in-the-door technique is most powerful when the person's *self-image* is related to the request, i.e. a request needs to be kept close to issues which the person is likely to care about and support, such as helping other people or protecting the environment.

Cultural norms and reciprocity

Ting-Toomey (1986) compared reciprocity in three individualist cultures (Australia, the USA, and France) with reciprocity in two collectivist countries (Japan and China). She found that the principle of reciprocity is universal. This could support the evolutionary argument but reciprocity is displayed differently in the two types of culture. In individualist cultures: reciprocity is voluntary so people are free to choose if they want to return a favour. In collectivist cultures: obligatory reciprocity is the norm. It is seen as a moral failure if reciprocity is not honoured.

Exam Tip The learning outcome is "discuss the use of compliance techniques". This means that it is sufficient to discuss two compliance techniques. The command term "discuss" invites you to give a balanced review of factors that could be relevant in understanding how compliance techniques are used as well as the implications of their use.

4.8 Evaluate research on conformity to group norms

Sherif (1936) Experimental investigation of conformity to perceived group norm

Sherif used the autokinetic effect (an optical illusion where a fixed pinpoint of light in a completely dark room appears to move because of the eye movements). Half of the participants first watched the light alone and gave a verbal estimate of how much and in what direction the light moved. Sherif found that after a number of trials participants began to estimate based on their own frame of reference. Then the experiment continued in groups with three to four participants who took turns to estimate in random order. The participants now used each other's estimates as a frame of reference and these converged into more or less identical estimates. A group norm had developed, which participants conformed to once it had been established.

Then the other half of the participants performed the estimation task alone. Sherif found that participants continued to estimate based on the group norm when they did the task alone. The results showed that social norms emerge to guide behaviour when people find themselves in uncertain situations.

Strengths of Sherif's study

- Sherif's study is one of the most influential experiments in social psychology. It has generated a large amount of research.

- The study demonstrates how a group norm can be established and continue to influence a person's judgement even when the social influence is no longer present.

Limitations of Sherif's study

- The experiment was conducted in a laboratory. The task was artificial and ambiguous and this could influence the results.

- Ethics: participants were not informed about the purpose of the experiment (informed consent) but this was not the norm at the time of Sherif's experiment.

Asch (1951) Experimental investigation of conformity to the majority.

Aim To investigate whether perceived group pressure by a majority can influence a minority in an experimental set-up that is not ambiguous.

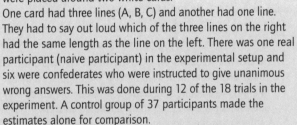

Procedure Seven male college students were placed around two white cards. One card had three lines (A, B, C) and another had one line. They had to say out loud which of the three lines on the right had the same length as the line on the left. There was one real participant (naive participant) in the experimental setup and six were confederates who were instructed to give unanimous wrong answers. This was done during 12 of the 18 trials in the experiment. A control group of 37 participants made the estimates alone for comparison.

Results In the control group 35 participants did not make a single error so in total 0.7% errors were made.

Strengths of Asch's study

- A high degree of control ensures that a cause-effect relationship can be established between variables.

- Asch's results have been replicated several times so the results are reliable.

- The results of the experiment in terms of conformity rates can, to some extent, explain why people conform to social and cultural norms in real life.

- Conformity may be universal to some degree but conformity rates vary cross-culturally.

Limitations of Asch's study

- Laboratory experiments are artificial and somewhat difficult to generalize to real life (issues of ecological validity).

- The experiment was conducted in the USA with male students as participants so this affects generalization.

- The results can only explain how a majority may influence a minority but not the other way round.

- The participants were deceived about the purpose of the experiment and they were exposed to embarrassing procedures. This raises ethical issues.

Can conformity research reveal anything about conformity in real life?

- Moghaddam et al. (1993) argue that the research may have a social and cultural bias. First, Sherif's study was conducted in the USA in a time when conformity was the norm and this may have changed since. **Nicholson et al. (1985)** suggest that participants now tend to conform less in Asch-like experiments. This could indicate that levels of conformity are context-dependent and may change over time. Second, conformity patterns may be different in other cultures.

- Moscovici (1976) argues that traditional conformity research cannot explain the minority influences on the majority, which have been observed in real life (e.g. various successful independence movements).

- Research shows that ingroup minorities have a greater chance of exerting influence than outgroup minorities.

4.9 Discuss factors influencing conformity

Informational conformity (informational influence)	Normative conformity (normative social influence)	Conformity (referent informational influence)
<ul><li>When an individual turns to members of a group to obtain information about what is right (e.g. when the available information is ambiguous).</li><li>Example of research study: Sherif (1935).</li></ul>	<ul><li>When an individual conforms in order to be accepted or liked by other members of the group.</li><li>People have a need for social approval and acceptance.</li><li>Example of research study: Asch (1951).</li></ul>	<ul><li>When an individual identifies with a particular social group (ingroup) and conforms to a prototypical group norm→increase in similarity between ingroup members as well as difference to outgroup.</li></ul>

Situational factors in conformity: group size and group unanimity

- **Group size:** Asch made variations of the original study by altering the amount of confederates. When there was only one confederate the participant answered correctly. With two confederates the minority participant's errors rose to 13.6%. With three confederates the errors jumped to 31.8%. Further increases in confederates did not increase errors so Asch concluded that the size of opposition is important only up to a point. Asch suggested that with larger groups, participants may become resistant to conform if they suspect that members of the majority are working together on purpose.

- **Group unanimity:** Asch introduced social support to the naive participant, either another naive participant or a confederate who had been instructed to go along with the naive participant. The presence of a supporter reduced errors from 35% to around 5.5%. This is particularly the case if the supporter responds before the majority. This effect was seen even if the supporter was more incorrect than the majority, so it seems that breaking group unanimity is the main factor in reducing conformity.

Cultural norms as a factor in conformity

- **Bond and Smith (1996)** performed a meta-analysis of 133 studies in 17 different countries on the Asch paradigm. They found higher conformity levels in collectivistic cultures than in individualistic cultures. The level of conformity (i.e. percentage of incorrect answers) ranged from 15% in an experiment with Belgian students (**Doms, 1983**) to 58% among Indian teachers in Fiji (**Chandra, 1973**). They also found that generally the conformity was higher when the majority group was large.

- **Berry (1967)** used a variation of Asch's conformity experiment to study whether conformity rates among the Temne in Sierra Leone in Africa and the Inuits of Baffin Island in Canada could be linked to social norms and socialization practices. He found that the Temne, who had an agricultural economy, had high conformity levels. The culture emphasized obedience in child-rearing practices because the culture is dependent on cooperation in farming. The Inuits are hunters and often hunt alone. They therefore need to be able to make decisions for themselves.

Child-rearing practices emphasize self-reliance because this is needed within this culture. This could perhaps explain why the Inuits tend to conform less.

- **Kagitcibasi (1984)** studied socialization patterns in nine different countries (Indonesia, South Korea, the Philippines, Sinagapore, Taiwan, Thailand, Turkey, the USA, and Germany). The study included 20,000 interviews with parents on the qualities they considered most desirable in children (e.g. if they wanted their children to be independent and self-reliant or if they wanted them to be obedient). Parents from Turkey and Indonesia found it important that children obeyed them and did not emphasize independence and self-reliance. The opposite pattern was found in the USA. Parents in Singapore, Taiwan, and Thailand also tended to emphasize self-reliance rather than obedience. The consequence of modernization is, to some extent, a breakup of the extended family system seen in collectivist cultures and placing more emphasis on individual effort and responsibilities.

4.10 Define the terms culture and cultural norms

Culture

It is difficult to give an exact definition of culture but here are three definitions from cultural researchers:

- **Lonner (1995):** Culture can be defined as the common rules that regulate interactions and behaviour in a group as well as a number of shared values and attitudes in the group.

- **Hofstede (1995):** Culture can be defined as a collective mental programming that is the "software of the mind" that guides a group of people in their daily interactions and distinguishes them from other groups of people.

- **Matsumoto (2004):** Culture can be defined as a dynamic system of rules, explicit and implicit, established by groups in order to ensure their survival, involving attitudes, values, beliefs, norms, and behaviours.

Cultural norms

- Cultural norms can be defined as the rules that a specific group uses for stating what is seen as appropriate and inappropriate behaviours, values, beliefs, and attitudes.

- Cultural norms give people a sense of order and control in their lives as well as a sense of safety and belonging. Cultural norms may encompass communication style, whom to marry and how, child-rearing practices, or interaction between generations.

- Cultural norms can be explicit (e.g. legal codes) or implicit (i.e. conventional practices and rituals).

4.11 Examine the role of two cultural dimensions on behaviour

A dimension of culture is an aspect of culture that can be measured relative to other cultures. The conceptual framework "cultural dimensions" was suggested by **Hofstede (1980)** in his survey of 88,000 IBM employees working in 66 countries across the world. Hofstede argues that differences in behaviour are a consequence of culture.

- Culture should be seen as a collective phenomenon that may distinguish one group from another on specific dimensions. Culture is seen as "mental programming" or "mental software".

- An individual's mental software will determine the way the person acts and thinks and the mental software is resistant to change. Unlearning what is once learned and internalized is very difficult.

- According to Hofstede, understanding the influence of cultural dimensions on human behaviour can facilitate international understanding and communication.

Two examples are:

1 **Collectivism and individualism:** This relates to the relationship between the individual and the group. In individualist countries (e.g. France, Germany, Denmark, and the USA) people tend to see themselves as individuals who must take care of themselves. Ties between individuals are loose and voluntary. Typical values are freedom, personal challenge, and personal time. In collectivist countries (e.g. Japan, Mexico, and Korea) the individual is tied to social groups such as families or clans throughout their lifetime. This extended social group provides safety in return for loyalty.

2 **Long-term orientation and short-term orientation (Hofstede and Bond 1988):** This relates to a cultural dimension found in Asian countries. China was not included in Hofstede's original study but **Hofstede and Bond (1988)** suggested this dimension based on the Confucian work dynamism. Values such as persistence, loyalty, trustworthiness, respect for tradition, and conservation of "face" are central to this dimension.

Cultural dimension: collectivism versus individualism

Wei et al. (2001) survey on collectivism vs. individualism on conflict resolution styles

Aim To investigate the extent to which the dimension of individualism vs. collectivism influenced conflict resolution communication styles.

Procedure A group of 600 managers working in companies in Singapore was randomly selected for this survey. The participants were divided into four groups: Japanese, Americans, Chinese Singaporeans working in multinational companies and Chinese Singaporeans working in local companies. Questionnaires and correlational analysis were used to find possible relationships between scores on cultural dimension and conflict resolution style.

Results Generally, the higher the score in the individualist dimension the more likely the manager was to adopt a dominating conflict resolution style. American managers (individualist dimension) were generally more likely to adopt a

dominating conflict resolution style and less likely to adopt an avoiding conflict resolution style than Asian managers. Asian managers did not always adopt an avoidant conflict resolution style as predicted by the collectivism-individualism dimension. In some cases, American managers who had been in Singapore for several years had adopted a more Asian conflict resolution style.

Discussion of results The collectivism vs. individualism dimension in relation to conflict resolution styles was only somewhat confirmed. The researchers conclude that conflict resolution styles are complex and cannot be reduced to cultural dimensions alone. For example, differences found *within* the groups of Asian managers were larger than between groups.

Evaluation: The survey used a large and representative cross-cultural sample of managers in Singapore so the results can be generalized. The study relies on self-reports so there may be issues of reliability of the data but overall the results are reliable.

Cultural dimension: long-term orientation versus short-term orientation

Basset (2004) qualitative research to compare perception of conflict resolution in Australian and Chinese students

Aim To investigate differences in Chinese and Australian students' perception of conflict resolution in relation to (1) the collectivist vs. individualist dimension and (2) long-term vs. short-term orientation.

Procedure The investigation was a qualitative cross-cultural study. The students were bachelor students of business and management. They were asked to analyse a potential conflict

situation between a Japanese supervisor and a Canadian visiting assistant teacher. The same question was answered by 30 students (15 Chinese and 15 Australian), each from their own cultural perspective: "Discuss how this conflict might be resolved in China (or Australia). "

Results Generally, the data confirmed Hofstede's individualist and collectivist dimensions but not all data could be explained by this. As for long-term orientation vs. short-term orientation, the Chinese data confirmed the importance of this dimension in understanding behaviour.

China	Australia
■ The Chinese are concerned about face-saving and interpersonal relationships. They want to solve problems and enhance relationships at a dinner table. ■ It is important to pay attention to a relationship; perhaps inviting the person to dinner or offering gifts could help the relationship.	■ Policies and procedures dictate the way employees and the organization operates rather than culture and tradition. ■ Issues such as saving face are not important since parties will push for arbitration and mediation if they feel that they are being treated unfairly.

Implications of research like this for negotiations with Chinese partners

■ Friendship is important. Banquets are seen as a relationship building exercise. Gifts act as expression of friendships and symbols of hope for good future business.

■ Guanxi is a network of relationships built by an individual through the exchange of gifts and favours to attain mutual benefits. This practice is based on the Confucian work ethics.

■ **Batonda and Perry (2002)** argue that the consequence of Guanxi for doing business in China is that the Chinese favour a process-oriented approach where Westerners tend to favour a more action-based approach.

4.12 Explain, using examples, emic and etic concepts

Pike (1967) suggested the emic and the etic concepts to address the issues of "culture specific" versus "universal", i.e. what is consistent across cultures.

Emic
■ Emic research studies one culture alone to understand culture-specific behaviour.

■ Researchers attempt to study behaviour through the eyes of the people who live in that culture. The way the phenomenon is linked to the culture (structure) and the meaning it has in this particular cultural (context) is emphasized. The focus is on the norms, values, motives, and customs of the members of the culture as they interpret and understand it themselves, explained with their own words.

Example 1: Bartlett (1932) mentioned the extraordinary ability of Swazi herdsmen to recall individual characteristics of their cattle. He explained that the Swazi culture revolves around the possession and care of cattle and it is important for people to recognize their animals because this is part of their fortune.

Example 2: Yap (1967) suggested the term "culture-bound syndrome" (CBS) as a culture-specific psychological disorder which can only be fully understood within a specific cultural context. Among the Yoruba people of West African it is believed that spirits may come into the possession of a person's soul and that the person can be treated by healing and spells spoken by a medicine man or a healer **(Ayode, 1979)**.

Etic
■ Etic research compares psychological phenomena across cultures to find out what could be universal in human behaviour.

■ The purpose of research is to compare and contrast cultural phenomena across cultures to investigate whether phenomena are culture-specific or universal.

Example 1: Kashima and Triandis (1986) found a difference in the way people explain their own success when they compared Japanese and American participants. The American participants tended to explain their own success by dispositional attributions whereas the Japanese participants made situational attributions. The American participants demonstrated the self-serving bias and the Japanese the self-effacing bias, which has also been observed in other Asian countries where people are socialized to see themselves as part of a social group.

Example 2: Berry (1967) used a variation of Asch's conformity experiment to study whether conformity rates among the Temne in Sierra Leone in Africa and the Inuits of Baffin Island in Canada could be linked to social norms and socialization practices. He found that the Temne, who had an agricultural economy, had high conformity rates. The culture emphasized obedience in child-rearing practices because the culture is dependent on cooperation in farming. The Inuits are hunters and often hunt alone. They therefore need to be able to make decisions for themselves. Child-rearing practices emphasize self-reliance because this is needed within this culture. This could explain why the Inuits score low on conformity.

Defining normality

Mental health model of normality (Jahoda, 1958)

The model suggests criteria for what might constitute normal psychological health (in contrast to abnormal psychological health). Deviation from these criteria would mean that the health of an individual is "abnormal":

- the absence of mental illness
- realistic self-perception and contact with reality
- a strong sense of identity and positive self-esteem
- autonomy and independence
- ability to maintain healthy interpersonal relationships (e. g. capacity to love)
- ability to cope with stressful situations
- capacity for personal growth and self-actualization.

Evaluation of the mental health model of normality

- The majority of people would be categorized as "abnormal" if the criteria were applied to them. It is relatively easy to establish criteria for what constitutes "physical health" but it is impossible to establish and agree on what constitutes "psychological health".
- According to **Szasz (1962)** psychological normality and abnormality are culturally defined concepts, which are not based on objective criteria.
- **Taylor and Brown (1988)** argue that the view that a psychologically healthy person is one that maintains close contact with reality is not in line with research findings. Generally people have "positive illusions" about themselves and they rate themselves more positively than others (**Lewinsohn et al. 1980**).
- The criteria in the model are culturally biased *value judgements*, i.e. they reflect an idealized rather than realistic perception of what it means to be human in a Western culture.

Defining abnormality

The mental illness criterion (the medical model)

- The mental illness criterion sees psychological disorders (abnormality) as *psychopathology*. Pathology means "illness" so it is literally "illness in the psyche".
- This criterion is linked to psychiatry, which is a branch of medicine. Patients with psychological problems are seen as "ill" in the same way as those who suffer from physiological illnesses.
- Diagnosis of mental illness is based on the clinician's observations, the patient's self-reports, a clinical interview and diagnostic manuals (classification systems) that classify symptoms of specific disorders to help doctors find a correct diagnosis.

Evaluation of the mental illness criterion

- Proponents of the mental illness criterion argue that it is an advantage to be diagnosed as "sick" because it shows that people are not responsible for their acts.
- Although the origin of some mental disorders (e.g. Alzheimer's disease) can be linked to physiological changes in the brain, most psychological disorders cannot.
- Critics of the mental health illness criterion argue that there is a *stigma* (i.e. a mark of infamy or disgrace) associated with mental illness.
- **Szasz (1962)** argues that it is not possible to identify the biological correlates of mental illness. Therefore, psychological disorders should rather be seen as "problems of living".

Abnormality as statistical deviation from the norm

- Deviance in this criterion is related to the statistical average. The definition implies that statistically common behaviour can be classified as "normal". Behaviour that is deviant from the norm is consequently "abnormal". In the normal distribution curve most behaviour falls in the middle.
- An intelligence quotient of 150 deviates from the norm of 100. It is statistically rare but it is considered desirable to have high intelligence. Mental retardation is also rare but this is considered undesirable.
- Obesity is becoming increasingly statistically "normal" but obesity is considered to be undesirable.

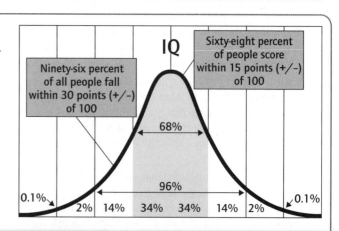

Evaluation of the statistical criterion

- The use of statistical frequency and deviation from the statistical norm is not a reliable criterion to define abnormal behaviour since what is "abnormal" in a statistical sense may both be desirable and undesirable.
- What may be considered abnormal behaviour can differ from one culture to another so it is impossible to establish universal standards for statistical abnormality. The model of statistical deviation from the norm always relates to a specific culture.

Abnormality as deviation from social norms

- Social norms constitute informal or formal rules of how individuals are expected to behave. Deviant behaviour is behaviour that is considered undesirable or anti-social by the majority of people in a given society. Individuals who break rules of conduct or do not behave like the majority are defined as "abnormal" according to this criterion.

- Social, cultural and historical factors may play a role in what is seen as 'normal' or 'abnormal' within a certain society. For example, homosexuality was seen as abnormal in Britain around 1900 where the famous writer Oscar Wilde was imprisoned for homosexuality. Homosexuality was classified as abnormal (sexual deviation) in the American Diagnostic and Statistical Manual DSM-II (1968). In later revisions of the manual homosexuality in itself was not seen as abnormal – only feeling distressed about it.

Evaluation of the deviation from social norms criterion

- This criterion is not objective or stable since it is related to socially based definitions that change across time and culture. Because the norm is based on morals and attitudes, it is vulnerable to abuse. For example, political dissidents could be considered "abnormal" and sent to hospitals for treatment as occurred in the former Soviet Union.

- Using this criterion could lead to discrimination against minorities including people who suffer from psychological disorders.

- Psychological disorders may be defined and diagnosed in different ways across cultures and what seems to be a psychological disorder in one culture may not be seen in the same way in another culture. The American classification system DSM includes disorders called "culture-bound syndromes". This indicates that it is impossible to set universal standards for classifying a behaviour as abnormal.

5.2 Discuss validity and reliability of diagnosis

Diagnosis

- Diagnosis within abnormal psychology means identifying and classifying abnormal behaviour on the basis of symptoms, the patients' self-reports, observations, clinical tests or other factors such as information from relatives.

- Clinicians use psychological assessment and diagnostic manuals to make diagnosis. The diagnostic manuals help to classify and standardize diagnosis.

- Diagnosis involves matching the results of the psychological assessment with classification systems such as DSM-IV-TR and ICD-10. The purpose of diagnosis is to find a treatment for the patient and to make a prognosis.

Diagnostic manuals

- DSM-IV, now in its fourth revised version, is developed by the American Psychiatric Association. The manual lists what it terms "mental disorders". For each of the 300 disorders there is a list of symptoms that the clinician could look for in order to diagnose correctly. A new fifth version is on its way. The diagnostic manual does not identify causes of psychological disorders (etiology) but merely describes symptoms.

- ICD-10 (The International Classification of Diseases) is published by WHO (World Health Organization). The manual uses the term "mental disorder". The diagnostic manual includes reference to causes of the disorders (etiology).

Reliability of diagnosis

- Reliability in diagnosis means that clinicians should be able to reach the same correct diagnosis consistently if they use the same diagnostic procedure (e.g. standardized clinical interview, observation of the patient's symptoms, neuropsychological examination with scanners and diagnostic manuals). This is called inter-judge reliability.

- Reliability can be improved if clinicians use standardized clinical interview schedules, which define and specify sets of symptoms to look for. The individual psychiatrist must still make a subjective interpretation of the severity of the patient's symptoms.

- The introduction of diagnostic manuals has increased reliability of diagnosis over the year even though the manuals are not without flaws.

- Reliability of diagnosis is a necessary prerequisite for validity. Rosenhahn (1973) performed a classic study that challenged reliability and validity of psychiatric diagnosis and showed the consequences of being labelled as "insane". In this study eight pseudo-patients were diagnosed as suffering from severe psychological disorders but they were in reality imposters.

Cooper et al. (1972) The US-UK Diagnostic Project

- The aim of the study was to investigate reliability of diagnosis of depression and schizophrenia.

- The researchers asked American and British psychiatrists to diagnose patients by watching a number of videotaped clinical interviews.

- The British psychiatrists diagnosed the patients in the interview to be clinically depressed twice as often. The American psychiatrists diagnosed the same patients to be suffering from schizophrenia twice as often.
- The results indicated that the same cases did not result in similar diagnosis in the two countries. This points towards problems of reliability as well as cultural differences in interpretation of symptoms and thus in diagnosis.

Fernando (1991) Diagnosis is a social process and it is not objective

- Clinical assessment, classification and diagnosis can never be totally objective according to Fernando since there are *value judgements* involved. The diagnostic process in psychiatry is not the same as making a medical diagnosis. There may also be problems in understanding symptoms from individuals in different cultures.

Validity of diagnosis

- Validity of diagnosis refers to receiving the correct diagnosis. This should result in the correct treatment and a prognosis (predictive validity). Validity presupposes reliability of diagnosis.
- It is much more difficult to provide a correct diagnosis and give a prognosis for a psychological disorder than for a physical disorder because it is not possible to observe objective signs of the disorder in the same way.
- The DSM-IV manual does not include etiology but only symptoms. Sometimes patients have symptoms that relate to different psychological disorders so it can be difficult to make a valid diagnosis.

Mitchel et al. (2009) Meta-analysis of validity of diagnosis of depression

- The study used data from 41 clinical trials (with 50,000 patients) that had used semi-structured interviews to assess depression.

- The general practitioners (GPs) had 80% reliability in identifying healthy individuals and 50% reliability in diagnosis of depression. Many GPs had problems making a correct diagnosis for depression.
- Generally GPs were more likely to identify false positive signs of depression after the first consultation. Mitchel et al. argued that GPs should see patients at least twice before making a diagnosis since accuracy of diagnosis was improved in studies that used several examinations over an extended period.
- **Evaluation of the study:** (1) The strengths of meta-analysis are that it can combine data from many studies and it is possible to generalize to a larger population; (2) Limitations of meta-analysis are that it may suffer from the problem of publication bias; since data from many different studies are used there may also be problems of interpretation of the data because it is not certain that each study uses exactly the same definitions.

Rosenhahn (1973) On being sane in insane places

Aim To test reliability and validity of diagnosis in a natural setting. Rosenhahn wanted to see if psychiatrists could distinguish between "abnormal" and "normal" behaviour.

Procedure This was a covert participant observation with eight participants consisting of five men and three women (including Rosenhahn himself). Their task was to follow the same instructions and present themselves in 12 psychiatric hospitals in the USA.

Results

- All participants were admitted to various psychiatric wards and all but one were diagnosed with schizophrenia. The last one was diagnosed with manic depression.
- All pseudo-patients behaved normally while they were hospitalized because they were told that they would only get out if the staff perceived them to be well enough.
- The pseudo-patients took notes when they were hospitalized but this was interpreted as a symptom of their illness by the staff. It took between 7 to 52 days before the participants were released. They came out with a diagnosis (schizophrenia in remission) so they were "labelled".

- A follow-up study was done later where the staff at a specific psychiatric hospital were told that impostors would present themselves at the hospital and that they should try to rate each patient whether he or she was an impostor. Of the 193 patients, 41 were clearly identified as impostors by at least one member of the staff, 23 were suspected to be impostors by one psychiatrist, and 19 were suspected by one psychiatrist and one staff member. There were no impostors.

Evaluation

- This controversial study was conducted nearly 40 years ago but it had an enormous impact in psychiatry. It sparked off a discussion and revision of diagnostic procedures as well as discussion of the consequences of diagnosis for patients. The development of diagnostic manuals has increased reliability and validity of diagnosis although the diagnostic tools are not without flaws.
- The method used raises ethical issues (the staff were not told about the research) but it was justified since the results provided evidence of problems in diagnosis which could benefit others. There were serious ethical issues in the follow-up study since the staff thought that impostors would present, but they were real patients and may not have had the treatment that they needed.

Exam Tip This study can be used as empirical research in unit 5.1 to examine concepts of normality and abnormality.

5.3 Discuss cultural and ethical considerations in diagnosis

Cultural considerations in diagnosis

Ballanger et al. (2001) suggest that variations in diagnosis across cultures do not necessarily reflect social or medical *reality*. There may be unknown factors influencing diagnosis, e.g. different methods of clinical assessment, differences in classification, lack of culturally appropriate instruments such as standardized clinical interviews, or problems in relation to translation of the clinical interviews. For these reasons, diagnosis is also linked to cultural variation in the prevalence of disorders.

Culture may influence psychiatric diagnosis in several ways.

1. Different cultural groups have different attitudes to psychological disorders that might influence the reporting of symptoms and diagnosis (e.g. due to stigmatization).

2. Cultural bias in diagnosis (i.e. the clinician does not observe certain symptoms because he or she is not familiar with the expression of distress in a particular culture).

3. Culture-bound syndromes (disorders that are specific to a particular culture) could be difficult to recognize for clinicians. This could prevent people from being treated.

Emic or etic in diagnosis?

- The **universalist approach** (etic) to diagnosis emphasizes the cross-cultural equivalence of diagnostic concepts and underlying processes. Symptoms and disorders are manifestations of universal underlying processes.

- The **relativist approach** (emic) to diagnosis emphasizes a fundamental role of culture in psychopathology. Culture shapes symptoms and how people experience distress as well as their beliefs about causes and consequences of such problems.

- Clinicians could use universal clinical interviews and a classification system like the DSM-IV (i.e. taking an **etic** approach); or they could use culturally specific instruments that are developed to be used in a specific culture (i.e. taking an **emic** approach). In reality, most clinicians use the universal classification systems.

- **Kirmayer (2001)** argues that even though DSM-IV includes suggestions for a cultural interpretation of disorders, it still represents Western concepts of illness and therefore it may not be easily applied to other cultures.

- **Bhui (1999)** argues that diagnostic systems are necessary for comparisons between different cultures, and therefore it is necessary to define concepts of depression in accord with psychiatric and indigenous belief systems.

Misdiagnosis due to cultural differences in expression of symptoms

- **Jacobs et al. (1998)** investigated a sample of Indian women in a general practice in London. The doctors were not likely to detect depression if the women did not disclose all their symptoms. The same has been found in research with cultural minorities in the USA and in Australia.

- People from traditional cultures may not distinguish between emotions and physical symptoms. For example, Chinese people have lower rates of depression and tend to deny depression or express it somatically (**Zhang et al. 1998**). In the 1980s, four fifths of psychiatric patients in China were diagnosed with "neurasthenia", a disorder that includes somatic, cognitive and emotional symptoms in addition to any depressive symptoms. This concept fits well with the traditional Chinese explanation of disease as a disharmony of vital organs and imbalance of **"Qi"** (the Chinese term for "life force" or "energy flow").

- **Bhugra et al. (1997)** carried out a focus group interview with Punjabi women in London. The women knew the term "depression" but the older ones used terms like "weight on my heart" or "pressure on the mind". They also talked about symptoms of "gas" and "heat". These terms are in accordance with traditional Indian medicine models of hot and cold.

Case: culture and depression in China

- One of the most discussed cross-cultural differences in psychopathology was that depression was apparently very rare in China. **Zhang et al. (1998)** reported a survey in 12 regions in China in 1993 where only 16 out of 19,223 people said they had suffered from a mood disorder at some point in their life. This suggests a prevalence rate substantially lower than in the USA.

- According to **Tseng and Hsu (1970)** the Chinese are very concerned with the body and tend to manifest neurasthenic symptoms such as exhaustion, sleep problems, concentration difficulties, and other symptoms similar to the physical aspects of depression and anxiety.

Neurasthenia – the Chinese version of depression?

- 'Neurasthenia' is a diagnosis that is not present in the DSM system. It is a Chinese diagnostic category signifying 'a weakness of nerves'.

- The diagnosis could be seen as a Chinese variation of depression characterized by bodily symptoms, fatigue and depressed feelings. This disorder is much more common in China than depression. One reason could be that this diagnosis is less stigmatizing in the Chinese culture.

- Another reason could be that the concept of neurasthenia fits better with the traditional way of explaining causes of disease in terms of disharmony of vital organs and imbalance of Qi. Diagnosis in traditional Chinese medicine means finding how Qi is blocked or imbalances of Qi.

Kleinman (1982) Neurasthenia at a psychiatric hospital in China

- The aim of the study was to investigate if neurasthenia in China could be similar to depression in DSM-III.

- Kleinman interviewed 100 patients diagnosed with neurasthenia using structured interviews based on DSM-III diagnostic criteria.

- He found that 87% of the patients could be classified as suffering from depression; 90% complained of headaches, 78% of insomnia (sleep problems), 73% of dizziness, and 48% of various pains. Depressed mood was only given as the main complaint in 9% of the cases.

- Neurasthenia could be a specific Chinese way of expressing depression in somatic ways since the majority of the patients in the study only presented physical symptoms.

- It would be difficult to compare these data to Western data because patients do not make the same complaints during diagnosis. This shows one of the concerns in cross-cultural diagnosis. Somatization is perhaps the cultural mode of distress in China but in the West the most common mode of distress is *psychologization* (e.g. reference to mood).

- The implication of such findings are that Western clinicians should pay attention to somatization when they work with Chinese patients but they should at the same time be careful not to overdiagnose depression just because the patient complains of pain.

Ethical considerations in diagnosis

- **Correct diagnosis and treatment**: Ethical consideration in diagnosis could refer to *reliability and validity of a diagnosis.* A reliable and valid diagnosis is the prerequisite for a *correct treatment* but unfortunately the diagnostic process is not without problems. Many disorders are not easy to identify correctly because they often occur together with symptoms of other disorders (the problem of comorbidity). For example, many patients with bulimia also suffer from depression.

- **Biases in diagnosis**: There may be various biases in the diagnostic process (e.g. gender bias, ethnicity bias or age bias) preventing a correct diagnosis. Clinicians may also be influenced by confirmation bias, i.e. having made a diagnosis they may not perceive information that contradicts it.

- **Considerations of normality and abnormality**: Ethical issues in diagnosis could also refer to *considerations of normality and abnormality* (see unit 5.1). It would be ethically wrong to diagnose a patient with a psychiatric disorder if the patient is not ill and in need of treatment. It would also be ethically wrong not to make a correct diagnosis if a patient needs treatment.

- **Stigmatization: Rosenhahn (1975)** claimed that a psychiatric diagnosis carries a personal, legal, and social *stigma*. He demonstrated that a diagnosis of a serious mental illness (schizophrenia) could be based on limited information. He also argued that a psychiatric diagnosis is often associated with significant consequences in terms of being considered "deviant" (social stigma).

Jenkins-Hall and Sacco (1991) Ethnicity bias in diagnosis?

- The researchers presented videotapes of a person in therapy to a number of European American male and female therapists. The videos presented different situations (e.g. the patient was male or female, black or white, with depressed symptoms or non-depressed symptoms).

- The results showed that white therapists were more likely to make a false-positive diagnosis if the patient was black.

For example, a black patient would be diagnosed as depressed even in the absence of depressed symptoms.

Broverman et al. (1970) Gender bias in diagnosis?

- **Rosser (1992)** argued that many psychiatrists are males whose perspective is situated within normative gender roles and a patriarchal culture. For example , if a woman is unhappy about her role as housewife and mother because she is stressed and bored, a male psychiatrist could diagnose her with depression. This would be an example of overdiagnosis.

5.4 Describe symptoms and prevalence of two disorders (anxiety, affective, or eating disorders)

Prevalence is a statistical concept in medicine (or psychiatry). It refers to the percentage of individuals within a population who are affected by a specific disorder either currently or during their lifetime. Prevalence rates change cross-culturally and between genders.

Affective disorder: major depression

Symptoms
Typical symptoms of major depression (depressive episodes without mania) according to the DSM-IV-TR include

- **Physiological:** Fatigue or loss of energy, significant weight loss or gain, loss of appetite, headaches, and pain.

- **Cognitive:** Feelings of worthlessness or excessive guilt; difficulties concentrating; negative attitudes towards the self, the world and the future. (Feelings of guilt and worthlessness seem to be symptoms that are primarily experienced in Western cultures).

- **Emotional:** Distress and sadness, loss of interest in the world.

- **Behavioural:** Disturbed sleep patterns, self-destructive behaviour (suicidal thoughts), and avoidance of social company.

Prevalence
- The National Comorbidity Study (1994) found that prevalence for lifetime major depression in the USA was 17.1%. The National Institute of Mental Health (NIMH) in the USA found that lifetime prevalence of depression was 16.6% with 13.2 % for males and 20.2 for females (**Kessler et al. 2005**).

- **Andrade and Caraveo (2003)** found that lifetime prevalence of depression varies across cultures (e.g. 3% in Japan and 17% in the USA).

- **Poongothai et al. (2009)** found an overall prevalence rate of depression in the city of Chennai in South India of 15.9. The study was based on 25,455 participants. Depression was assessed through a self-report instrument (The Patient Health Questionnaire). Depressed mood was the most common symptom (30.8%) followed by fatigue (30.0%). Suicidal thoughts were less common (12.4%). Generally, depression rates were higher in the low income group (19.3 %) compared to the higher income group (5.9). Prevalence of depression was also higher among divorced (26.5%) and widowed (20%) compared to currently married respondents (15.4%).

- **Kessler et al. (1993)** found a lifetime prevalence for major depression of 21.3% in women compared to 12.7% in men.

Eating disorder: bulima nervosa

Symptoms
Typical symptoms of bulimia according to the DSM-IV-TR include:
- **Physiological:** Nutritional deficiencies and hormonal changes could lead to disturbances in the menstrual cycle, fatigue, digestive problems, muscle cramping.

- **Cognitive:** Distorted body image, low self-esteem, sense of lack of control during binge-eating episodes.

- **Emotional:** Fear of becoming fat (fat phobia), body dissatisfaction, and depressed mood.

- **Behavioural:** Self-starvation in combination with recurrent binge eating episodes and compensatory behaviour such as vomiting and misuse of laxatives to avoid weight gain.

Prevalence
- **Fairburn and Beglin (1990)** found that bulimia nervosa affected between 1 and 2 % of young women in the USA and the UK. APA (200) estimated 1–3% of young adult females to have Bulimia. The disorder occurs much less frequently in men.

- **Drewnowski et al. (1988)** conducted a telephone survey with a representative sample of 1,007 male and female students in the USA. They found that 1% of the women and 0.2% of the men were classified as bulimic. Bulimia nervosa was most prevalent among undergraduate women living on campus (2.2%).

- **Keel and Klump (2003)** performed a meta-analysis of research on bulimia nervosa and found an increase in people diagnosed with bulimia from 1970 to 1993. There are no incidence data for bulimia prior to 1970. The diagnostic criteria for bulimia have become more stringent over the years and this has resulted in the increase of incidences. According to the researchers, self-report surveys tend to produce higher estimates of bulimia nervosa prevalence than structured clinical interviews.

5.5 Analyse etiologies (in terms of biological, cognitive and/or sociocultural factors) of one disorder from two of the following groups: anxiety disorders, affective disorders, eating disorders

Etiology means the scientific study of causes or origins of diseases or abnormal behaviour. The reason psychiatrists are interested in etiology is the assumption that treatment should be related to the cause of the disorder, e.g. if the disorder is biological in origin, the treatment should also be biological (the biomedical model). This unit will analyse etiologies of one affective disorder (major depression) and one eating disorder (bulimia nervosa).

Affective disorder: major depression

Biological factors

Neurotransmitters: The serotonin hypothesis
- The serotonin hypothesis suggests that depression is caused by low levels of serotonin **(Coppen, 1967)**. Serotonin is a neurotransmitter produced in specific neurons in the brain and they are called "serotonergic neurons" because they produce serotonin.

- Anti-depressants in the form of selective serotonin reuptake inhibitor (SSRI) block the reuptake process for serotonin. This results in an increased amount of the serotonin in the synaptic gap. The theory is that this increases serotonergic nerve activity leading to improvement in mood.

- SSRI drugs such as Prozac, Zoloft, and Paxil are now among the most commonly sold anti-depressants and this has been taken as indirect support of the serotonin hypothesis. According to **Lacasse and Leo (2005)** this is an example of backward reasoning. Assumptions about the causes of depression are based on how people respond to a treatment and this is logically problematic.

Henninger et al. (1996) performed experiments where they reduced serotonin levels in healthy individuals to see if they would develop depressive symptoms. The results did not support that levels of serotonin could influence depression and they argued that it is necessary to revise the serotonin hypothesis.

Kirsch et al. (2002) found that there was publication bias in research on effectiveness of SSRI in depression. In fact, if the results of all studies (including the ones that had not been published) were pooled it would seem that the placebo effect accounted for 80% of the anti-depressant response. Of the studies funded by pharmaceutical companies, 57% failed to show a statistically significant difference between anti-depressant and a neutral placebo. This and similar studies cast doubt on the serotonin hypothesis.

Evaluation of the serotonin hypothesis of depression:
- There is some evidence that serotonin may be involved in depression and that this may be linked to stress and stress hormones such as cortisol.

- Scientific research has failed to show a clear link between serotonin levels and depression. The fact that anti-depressant drugs like the SSRIs can regulate serotonin levels and produce an effect does not mean that low serotonin levels cause depression.

Genetic predisposition
This theory of genetic predisposition is based on the assumption that disorders have a genetic origin. In order to study this, researchers study twins and families. In the twin method both monozygotic twins (MZ) and dizygotic twins (DZ) are compared. MZ twins share 100% of their genes but DZ twins share only around 50%. The assumption is that *if* a predisposition for a psychiatric disorder is inherited, then concordance rates should be higher in MZ twins than in DZ twins. If one twin is diagnosed with a disorder and the other twin is also diagnosed with the same disorder, the twins are said to be concordant.

Nurnberger and Gershon (1982) reviewed seven twin studies on major depression. The results indicated that genes could be a factor in depression. The concordance rates for major depression were consistently higher for MZ twins (65% on average across the studies) than for DZ twins (14%). This supports the theory that genetic factors could predispose people to depression. Since the concordance rate is far below 100% nothing definite can be said about genetic inheritance except that environmental and individual psychological factors could also play an important role in etiology. There is also the problem with co-morbidity: people suffering from depression often suffer from other psychological disorders as well (e.g. anxiety, and eating disorders).

Sullivan et al. (2000) conducted a meta-analysis of twin studies including 21,000 twins to investigate the genetic influence on major depression. They found that MZ twins were more than twice as likely to develop major depression if their co-twin had the disorder compared to DZ twins. On average the study showed that genetic influence in developing major depression was between 31% and 42%. The study also showed that non-shared environmental factors were important. The researchers concluded that major depression is a familial disorder with a strong genetic component and that it is a complex disorder resulting from the interaction of genetic and environmental influences.

Evaluation of the genetic theory of depression
There seems to be a genetic vulnerability to depression (as seen in the twin studies) but depression is a complex disorder and environmental factors such as continuous stress seem to play an important role in the development of the disorder as well.

Cognitive factors
This approach to etiology deals with the role of "thinking" and "negative cognitive schemas" called "depressogenic schemas".

Beck (1976) Cognitive theory of depression (negative cognitive triad)
- According to this theory depression is caused by inaccurate cognitive responses to events in the form of negative thinking about oneself and the world. People's conscious thoughts are influenced by negative cognitive schemas about the self and the world (depressogenic schemas). This results in negative automatic thoughts and dysfunctional beliefs. This explanation is contrary to traditional theories about depression where negative thinking is seen as a *symptom* of depression and not the cause.
- Beck's theory can be seen within the *diathesis-stress model* of depression. Depressive thinking and beliefs (depressogenic schemas) are assumed to develop during childhood and adolescence as a function of negative experiences with parents or other important people. The depressogenic schemas constitute a vulnerability (diathesis) that influences an individual's reaction when faced with stressors (e.g. negative life events or rejection), Such events tend to produce negative automatic thoughts (cognitive biases) based on three themes: negative thoughts about the self, the world, and the future (negative cognitive triad).

Negative views about the world
"Everybody hates me because I am worthless"

Negative views about oneself
"I am worthless"

Negative views about the future
"I'll never be good at anything because everyone hates me"

- Boury et al. (2001) investigated Beck's theory and found a significant correlation between amount of negative automatic thoughts and the severity of depression. The study also showed that the duration of depression was influenced by the frequency of negative cognitions. The researchers argued that it is difficult to determine whether cognitive distortions caused depression or if depression resulted in cognitive distortions.

Evaluation of Beck's cognitive theory of depression
- The theory has resulted in a valuable instrument to measure depression (The Beck Depression Inventory: BDI) and an effective psychological treatment (cognitive behavioural therapy). The theory has also generated a large amount of research.
- The theory is effective in *describing* many characteristics of depression. For example, depressed individuals are considerably more negative in their thinking than non-depressed individuals. People who suffer from depression generally think more negatively about themselves and the world, even when they are not depressed.
- The limitation of Beck's theory is perhaps that it is difficult to confirm that it is the negative thinking patterns that cause depression but there has been some empirical support of the causal aspects of the theory. Lewinshohn et al. (2001) found that negative thinking, dissatisfaction with oneself and high levels of life stressors preceded episodes of depression. The study was a longitudinal prospective study with 1,500 adolescents. The participants who started out with high levels of dysfunctional beliefs were more likely to develop major depression after a stressful life event. This confirms that dysfunctional beliefs (cognitive vulnerability) may play a role in triggering depression after major stress since participants who scored low or medium in dysfunctional beliefs did not develop depression after a stressful life event.

Sociocultural factors

- Social factors such as poverty or living in a violent relationship have been linked to depression. Women are more likely to be diagnosed with depression than men and one reason could be linked to the stress of being responsible for many young children and lack of social support.

Brown and Harris (1978) Social factors in depression

Aim: To investigate how depression could be linked to social factors and stressful life events in a sample of women from London (vulnerability-stress model of depression).

Procedure In London, 458 women were surveyed on their life and depressive episodes. The researchers used interviews where they addressed particular life events and how the women had coped.

Results In the previous year, 37 women (8% of all the women) had been depressed. Of these, 33 (90%) had experienced an adverse life event or a serious difficulty. Working-class women with children were four times more likely to develop depression than middle-class women with children. The researchers found that vulnerability factors such as lack of social support, more than three children under 14 years at home, unemployment and early maternal loss, in combination with acute or ongoing serious social stressors, were likely to provoke depressive episodes.

Evaluation The study was exceptional in that it showed that social factors (and not only personality factors) were involved in development of depression. The results were extremely important at establishing a new approach in understanding depression. Etiology of depression now often includes consideration of social factors. The sample in the study was gender biased (only female respondents) so it is not possible to generalize the findings to men. The semi-structured interview was useful to gather in-depth information of how the women perceived their own situation.

Evaluation of the sociocultural theory of depression

The theory has received support not only from the key study by Brown and Harris (1978). It is generally accepted that social stressors (e.g. war, urbanization, or restricted gender roles) play a role in mental health. In the case of women, there are cultural expectations of women taking care of the children and the household. Women are also more likely to be exposed to violence, which could explain the higher prevalence of depression in women.

Eating disorder: Bulimia nervosa

Bulimia nervosa is a serious psychological disorder characterized by binge eating episodes followed by compensatory behaviours such as dieting, vomiting, excessive exercise and misuse of laxatives (see unit 5.4 for symptoms).

Biological factors

Kendler et al. (1991) Twin research to study genetic vulnerability in bulimia nervosa

Aim To investigate risk factors and genetic inheritance in bulimia nervosa.

Procedure A sample of 2,163 female twins participated in the study. One of the twins in each pair had developed bulimia. The study was longitudinal and the researchers conducted interviews with the twins to see if the other twin would develop bulimia and if concordance rates were higher in monozygotic twins (MZ) than in dizygotic twins (DZ).

Results Overall the concordance rate for bulimia was 23 % in MZ twins compared to 9% in DZ twins.

Evaluation The results indicate a heritability of 55%, but this leaves 45% for other factors. Genetic vulnerability may predispose an individual but other factors trigger the disorder and it is important to investigate environmental factors that might interact with the genetic predisposition. The study was a "natural experiment" so the researchers did not manipulate variables and there was no control, so it is not possible to establish a cause-effect relationship. The participants were all women so the findings cannot be generalized to men. It is also questionable whether twins are representative of the population. The study does not take environmental factors into account. It could be that twins grow up in the same dysfunctional environment. It is very difficult to find out the relative importance of genetic inheritance and environmental factors.

Cognitive factors

Body-image distortion hypothesis

- **Bruch (1962)** claimed that many patients with eating disorders suffer from the cognitive delusion that they are fat. It may be that when patients evaluate their own body size, they are influenced by emotional appraisal rather than their perceptual experience.

- **Fallon and Rozin (1985)** showed nine pictures of different body shapes, from very thin to very heavy, to 475 US undergraduates of both sexes and asked them to indicate the body shape (1) most similar to their own shape, (2) most like their ideal body shape, and (3) the body shape of the opposite sex to which they would be most attracted. Women consistently indicated that their current body shape was heavier than the most attractive body shape. Their ideal body shape was also much thinner than the one they had chosen as similar to their own body shape. Men chose very similar figures for all three body shapes. The researchers concluded that men's perceptions helped them stay satisfied with their body shape whereas women's perceptions put pressure on them to lose weight. These sex differences could probably be linked to a higher prevalence of dieting, anorexia, and bulimia among American women than among American men.

Weight-related schemata model

- **Fairburn (1997)** suggested that people with eating disorders had distorted weight-related schema and low self-esteem. The distorted beliefs and attitudes towards body shape and weight develop partly because of the high status given to looking thin and attractive. Individuals strive to control body weight to stay thin and they base their self-worth on being thin, i.e. they have a weight-related self-schema that distorts the way they perceive and interpret their experiences. For some people, their concerns and prioritization of weight control may reflect a wider lack of self-esteem and a vulnerability to cultural messages about body weight. They think they will feel better if they lose weight but this obsession with weight control may lead to depression and intensified feelings of low self-esteem because weight control is the major way of maintaining self-worth.

Sociocultural factors

- Perceptions of the perfect body are influenced by cultural ideals. In the West, images of the ideal body shape for women have changed over the years from an hourglass shape to a slimmer shape.
- According to **Wardle and Marsland (1990)** body shape can be a major criterion in self-evaluation and evaluation of others. Many people have prejudices against overweight people.

Levine et al. (1994) investigated the relationship between sociocultural factors and eating attitudes and behaviours.

- In the USA, 385 middle school girls (aged 10–14 years) answered questions about eating behaviour, body satisfaction, concern with being slender, parents' and peers' attitudes, and magazines with regard to weight management techniques and the importance of being thin.

- The majority of the respondents said they received clear messages from fashion magazines, peers and family members that it is important to be slim. They also said that the same sources encouraged dieting or other methods to keep a slender figure.

- The study found two important factors in the drive for thinness and disturbed patterns of eating: (1) reading magazines containing information about ideal body shapes and weight management and (2) weight-related or shape-related teasing or criticism by family.

- The results indicate that body dissatisfaction and weight concerns reflect sociocultural ideals of a female role and raises the possibility that some adolescent girls live in a subculture of intense weight and body-image concern that places them at risk for disordered eating behaviour such as bulimia nervosa.

Jaeger et al. (2002) conducted a cross-cultural investigation of the relationship between body dissatisfaction and the development of bulimia nervosa.

- A cross-cultural sample of 1,751 female medical and nursing students from 12 nations participated.

- The participants saw a series of 10 body silhouettes, designed to be as culture-neutral as possible in order to measure body dissatisfaction. The participants' BMI was taken, and they answered questions on body dissatisfaction, self-esteem, and dieting behaviour.

- The most extreme body dissatisfaction was found in northern Mediterranean countries, followed by northern European countries. Countries in the process of westernization showed an intermediate amount of body dissatisfaction. Non-western countries showed the lowest levels. Body dissatisfaction was the most important factor in dieting behaviour in most countries and it was found to be independent of self-esteem and BMI.

- The results indicated that the body shapes represented in the media could encourage dissatisfaction with body shape and dieting behaviour.

- The study used culture as a variable but it is impossible from these results to say that culture causes bulimia because "culture" is not a controlled variable. The study only focused on sociocultural factors and other factors (e.g. biological) were not considered. The results cannot be generalized to men.

Prevalence is a statistical concept in medicine (or psychiatry). It refers to the percentage of individuals within a population who are affected by a specific disorder at a given time. Two disorders (major depression and bulimia nervosa) will be addressed in this section.

Cultural variation in prevalence of depression

- **Weisman et al. (1996)** found cross-cultural variation in data from 10 countries. The study found that the lifetime prevalence of depression ranged from 19.0 % (Beirut in Lebanon) to 1.5 % (Taiwan). Korea had rates of depression twice as high as those in Taiwan (2.9%) although they are both Asian countries. Paris had a rate (16.4%) close to that of Beirut although Beirut had experienced war for 15 years. Women had a higher rate than men in all countries. The researchers argue that different risk factors, social stigma, cultural reluctance to endorse mental symptoms as well as methodological limitations of the study may account for some of the differences.

- **Marsella et al. (2002)** argue that depression has long been a major topic of concern in Western medical history but it seems that depression is now becoming the world's foremost psychiatric problem because of global challenges such as war, natural disasters, racism, poverty, cultural collapse, ageing populations, urbanizations, and rapid social and technological changes. There is growing evidence that rates of depression are increasing, particularly in individuals born after the Second World War.

Possible explanations of cultural variation in the prevalence of depression

Differences in social and cultural background

- **Dutton (2009)** finds that cultural variation in prevalence of major depression could be due to cultural differences in stress, standards of living, and reporting bias. People in some countries have much harder lives. They may be exposed to war, civil war, rapid political and economic changes, crime, and discrimination. Unemployment and standards of living also differ across cultural groups.

- **Sartorius et al. (1983)** found that there are substantial cultural differences in the *stigma* associated with mental health problems. It could be that individuals in cultures where psychological disorders are associated with stigma (e.g. the Middle East or China) are more likely to report physical pain instead of psychological problems.

Variation in symptoms could indicate that symptoms of depression can be culturally influenced. See **Kleinman (1982)** on neurasthenia as an alternative diagnosis for depression which could explain a cultural variation in the prevalence of depression (unit 5.3).

Urbanization

- **Marsella (1995)** proposed that urban settings are associated with increased stress due to problems of housing, work, marriage, child rearing, security, and other urban difficulties. Urban crowding, poor working conditions or underemployment, chronic hunger, gender discrimination, limited education and human rights violations are all thought to weaken both individuals and the social support that could serve as buffers against mental health problems.

Gender variation in prevalence of depression

- According to **Nolen-Hoeksema (2001)** women are about twice as likely as men to develop depression. She argues that in spite of three decades of research on gender difference in depression, it has not been possible to find a variable that single-handedly can account for the gender difference in depression.

- Women's lifetime prevalence for major depressive disorder in the USA was found to be 21.3% compared to 12.7% for men **(Kessler et al. 1993)**. Females are more likely to report physical and psychological symptom and to seek medical help.

- According to **Piccinelli and Wilkinson (2000)** the gender differences in depression are genuine and not just a result of differences in diagnostic procedures.

Possible explanations for gender variation in prevalence of depression

Biological factors: hormones

- Biological explanations for women's higher vulnerability to depression have focused on the effect of sex hormones (oestrogen and progesterone) on mood. According to **Nolen-Hoeksema (2001)** there is little scientific support to the theory that women are more depressed than men only because of differences in sex hormones.

- Adverse experiences in childhood (e.g. childhood sexual abuse) have been linked to increased risk of developing depression partly because of long-term dysregulation of the stress response system (HPA axis). Weiss et al. (1999) suggested that women are more likely than men to have a dysregulated response to stress because they are more likely to have been exposed to regular episodes of traumas early in life.

- **Nolen-Hoeksema (2001)** suggests that women and men experience the same stressors but women seem to be more vulnerable to develop depression because of gender differences in biological responses to stressors, self-concepts or coping styles. Experiences of continuous stress could increase physiological and psychological reactivity to stress and lead to hyperactitviy of the stress system. This could increase vulnerability to depression (diathesis-stress model).

Sociocultural factors

- **Women's low power and status**: Nolen-Hoeksema (2001) Women have less power and status than men in most societies. They are more likely to experience sexual abuse, constrained choices, poverty, and lack of respect. These factors can contribute directly to depression because they make women feel that they are not in control of their lives. Women's social roles carry a number of chronic strains, which could contribute directly or indirectly to depression. Higher rates of depression in women could be due to the fact that women face a number of chronic burdens in everyday life as a result of their social status and roles. This is supported in **Brown and Harris (1978)** in unit 5.5.

- **The role strain hypothesis** suggests that social roles and cultural influences contribute to the higher ratio of female depression. In many cultures married women have no paid employment and they have to rely on the role of housewife for identity and self-esteem. This may be rather frustrating at times and it is not highly valued in modern society. **Bebbington (1998)** found that marriage could have negative effects on women. The researcher speculated that many women have limited choices after marriage. Staying at home and looking after small children is generally associated with higher levels of depression.

Cultural variation in prevalence of bulimia

- Cultural beliefs and attitudes have been identified as factors leading to the development of eating disorders (etiology). Prevalence of eating disorders varies among different ethnic and cultural groups and across time within such groups. Bulimia nervosa was first identified and classified as a specific disorder in 1979.

- **Makino et al. (2004)** compared prevalence of eating disorders in Western and non-Western countries based on a review of published medical articles. They found that prevalence rates in Western countries for bulimia nervosa ranged from 0.3% to 7.3% in females and from 0% to 2.1% in males. Prevalence rates for bulimia in non-Western countries ranged from 0.46% to 3.2% in females. The study concluded that prevalence of eating disorders appears to be increasing in non-Western countries but it is still lower than in Western countries.

Explanations of cultural variation in prevalence of bulimia

The Westernization hypothesis

- According to **Rubinstein and Caballero (2000)** eating disorders seem to have become more common among younger females after the Second World War, where female beauty ideals have gradually become thinner. This is reflected in the increase of articles on dieting in women's magazines in the same period as well as in thinner icons of female beauty (e.g. Miss America).

- One explanation for the development of eating disorders such as bulimia in non-Western countries is a perceived social pressure to conform to the standards of female beauty imposed by modern industrial society or Western culture.

Nasser (1994) used questionnaires to investigate eating attitudes in a sample of 351 girls in secondary school in Egypt. He found that 1.2% of the girls fulfilled the criteria for a diagnosis of bulimia nervosa and 3.4% qualified for a partial diagnosis. The results indicate that eating disorders are emerging in cultures that did not know such disorders in the past where a round female body was still considered attractive and desirable, and was associated with prosperity, fertility, success, and economic security. The researcher concluded that no society is truly immune to the development of eating disorders because of the globalization of culture through the media.

Becker et al. (2002) Impact of introduction of Western television on disordered eating patterns among Fijian adolescent girls

- The field study investigated changes in eating patterns in 1995 after television had been introduced to a remote province in Fiji, and again in 1998 when television had been available for three years). The traditional Fiji body ideal at the time was robust and the pressure to be thin found in many Western countries was absent.

- The study used quantitative (survey) and qualitative methods (semi-structured interviews) on issues such as television viewing, dieting, body satisfaction, and purging. Adolescent girls from two secondary schools participated.

- The results showed an increase in dieting and self-induced vomiting to control weight from 0% in 1995 to 11.3% in 1998.

- The researchers suggested that increasing globalization and exposure to Western media could explain the increase in symptoms related to eating disorders in non-Western countries. The specific combination of binge eating and purging to control weight, which is the core symptom of bulimia nervosa, only appeared after introduction of television. This could support that bulimia is a culture-bound syndrome.

- The study did not use clinical diagnoses, which is a limitation. There may be a tendency to report symptoms (e.g. purging) in anonymous self-reports but a clear diagnosis cannot be made. The questionnaires revealed clinical signs (vomiting and body dissatisfaction) associated with eating disorders and in particular bulimia. The study only included girls so nothing can be concluded on changes in eating behaviour among males (sample bias).

Gender variation in prevalence of bulimia

Makino et al. (2004) reviewed studies on eating disorders in 11 Western countries. They found that more female participants suffered from eating disorders and had abnormal eating attitudes than male participants.

Males

- Men are generally less likely to develop eating disorders, perhaps due to less pressure on men to conform to an ideal body weight or shape **(Rolss et al. 1991)**. Men who develop eating disorders tend to resemble females in terms of dissatisfaction with their body **(Olivardia et al. 1995)**.

- Certain sub-populations of men with jobs that require weight restrictions (e.g. wrestlers and jockeys) seem to be at increased risk of developing eating disorders. There may be a possible link between male homosexuality and eating disorders because of a higher emphasis on attractiveness and slimness in gay subcultures **(Silberstein et al. 1989)**.

Females

- There has been a steady increase in diagnosis of bulimia nervosa in the UK from 1988 to 2000 **(Currin et al. 2005)** but since 1996 there has been a decline. This meta-analysis used data from general practitioners (GPs) in the UK. The study found that incidence of bulimia nervosa per 100 was 94 cases for females and five cases for males. Overall females are more likely to be diagnosed with bulimia than males.

- **Currin et al. (2005)** found that the highest risk for bulimia nervosa is in young women between 10 and 19. Certain sub-populations such as ballerinas and models have been associated with increased risk for developing eating disorders because of high pressure to be thin.

5.7 Examine biomedical, individual and group approaches to treatment

Biomedical treatment of depression

- The biomedical approach to treatment is based on the assumption that if a mental problem is caused by biological malfunctioning, the cure is to restore the biological system with drugs. For example, the serotonin hypothesis of depression suggests that *depression* is linked to low levels of the neurotransmitter serotonin (see unit 5.5). Anti-depressant treatment should therefore aim to regulate serotonin levels.

- Anti-depressants are often used in the treatment of *bulimia nervosa* because some patients also suffer other disorders such as depression (comorbidity).

- Anti-depressants are also used to treat minor depressive symptoms but the American Food and Drug Administration (**FDA, 2004**) warned that use of anti-depressants for children and adolescents could perhaps lead to an increased risk of suicide.

Selective serotonin re-uptake inhibitors (SSRI)

- Drugs that interfere with serotonin re-uptake (SSRI) are used in the treatment of depression. They interfere with serotonin levels and affect mood and emotional responses positively in most people. Anti-depressants normally take seven to 14 days to relieve depressive symptoms.

- Currently the most widely used drugs are SSRI. They all increase the level of available serotonin by blocking the reuptake process for serotonin. This results in an increased amount of serotonin in the synaptic gap. The theory is that this increases serotonergic nerve activity leading to improvement in mood in depressive patients.

- SSRI are popular because they have fewer side effects than previous drugs such as the tricyclic antidepressants but not everyone can use SSRI. The most common side effects are headache, nausea, sleeplessness, agitation, and sexual problems.

Neale et al. (2011) conducted a meta-analysis of published studies on the outcome of anti-depressants versus placebo. The study focused on: (1) patients who started with anti-depressants and then changed to placebo, (2) patients who only received a placebo, and (3) patients who only took anti-depressants.

The study found that patients who do not take anti-depressants have a 25% risk of relapse, compared to 42% or higher for those who have been on medication and then stopped it.

According to the researchers, anti-depressants may interfere with the brain's natural self-regulation. They argue that drugs affecting serotonin or other neurotransmitters may increase the risk of relapse. The drugs reduce symptoms in the short term but, when people stop taking the drug, depression may return because the brain's natural self-regulation is disturbed.

Individual treatment

In individual therapy, the therapist works one-on-one with a client. One of the most widely used individual therapies is cognitive behavioural therapy (CBT).

CBT

- The therapy is linked to Beck's explanation of depression (see unit 5.5) where automatic negative thinking is assumed to cause depression. CBT aims to change negative thinking patterns (cognitive restructuring).

- CBT includes around 12 to 20 weekly sessions combined with daily practice exercises, with a focus on helping people with major depression to identify automatic negative thinking patterns and change them.

How CBT works

Step 1: Identify and correct faulty cognitions and unhealthy behaviour (cognitive triad)

The therapist encourages the client to identify thinking patterns associated with depressive feelings. These false beliefs are challenged (reality testing) to give the client the possibility to correct them (cognitive restructuring).

Step 2: Increase activity and learn alternative problem solving strategies

The therapist encourages the client to gradually increase activities that could be rewarding such as sport, going to concerts, or meeting other people (behavioural activation).

- **Paykel et al. (1999)** conducted a controlled trial of 158 patients who had experienced one episode of major depression. The patients received antidepressant medication but some of them also received cognitive therapy. The CBT group had a relapse rate of 29% compared to those who only had medication. Paykel argues that cognitive therapy appears to be effective to prevent relapse, particularly in combination with medication.

How CBT works in treating bulimia (Fairburn, 1997)
CBT is considered the best psychological treatment for bulimia. The treatment involves:
- replacing binge eating with a pattern of regular eating (three planned meals and two planned snacks) and trying to avoid vomiting or other compensatory behaviours
- therapy sessions with the client and later with important friends and relatives who will support behavioural change
- therapy sessions that address both behaviour (e.g. food that provokes anxiety or desire to binge and purse) and cognitive distortions (e.g. concerns about weight and body shape)
- maintenance of the programme and considerations of strategies to prevent relapse.

Hay et al. (2004) studied the effectiveness of CBT in the treatment of bulimia and binge eating. The aim of this meta-analysis was to evaluate the effectiveness of CBT, and a specific form of CBT developed for the treatment of bulimia (CBT-BN).

The study showed that CBT was an effective treatment for eating disorders. CBT was effective in group settings. CBT-BN was particularly effective in the treatment of bulimia but also other eating disorders that involve bingeing.

Wilson (1996) reported that 55% of participants in CBT programmes no longer purged at the end of therapy, and those who continued to purge did so much less (86% reduction in purging).

Fairburn et al. (1995) found that after nearly six years, 63% of the participants in their study had not relapsed.

Interpersonal psychotherapy (IPT)
Klerman et al. (1984) developed IPT as a short-term, structured psychotherapy for depression, but it has been adapted for bulimia nervosa by **Fairburn et al. (1993)**. The aim of the therapy is to help clients identify and modify current interpersonal problems as these problems are assumed to maintain the eating disorder. The therapy does not focus directly on eating disorder symptoms.

Elkin et al. (1989) found that IPT was effective in relieving major depression and to prevent relapse when treatment was continued after recovery.

Fairburn et al. (1993) compared IPT with CBT and found that IPT was less effective than CBT at post-treatment, but follow-up studies after one and six years found that the two treatments were equally effective.

Group treatment
In group therapy, the therapist meets with a group of people (e.g. a family or a group of individuals suffering form the same disorder). Group therapy is generally less expensive than individual therapy. Group therapy based on mindfulness is becoming increasingly popular and studies indicate that it may be a useful approach.

Mindfulness-based cognitive therapy (MBCT) to treat depression
MBCT is based on Kabat-Zinn's mindfulness-based stress reduction programme (see unit 7.3). The MBCT is developed by **Segal, Williams and Teasdale (2001)**. The aim of this psychosocial group-based therapy is to prevent people becoming depressed again (relapsing) after successful treatment for major depression.

How MBCT works
- MBCT is based on Buddhist meditation and relaxation techniques. These help people to direct their focus and concentrate so they are able to observe intrusive thoughts and gradually become more able to prevent the escalation of negative thoughts.
- The goal of MBCT is to teach people to recognize the signs of depression and adopt a "decentred" perspective, where people see their thoughts as "mental events" rather than something central to their self-concept or as accurate reflections of reality.

Mindfulness-based treatment of bulimia
Proulx (2008) used an eight-week mindfulness-based intervention to treat six college-age women suffering from bulimia. Participants were interviewed individually before and after treatment. They all reported that they could control emotional and behavioural extremes better after the treatment and had reached a greater self-acceptance. Generally, they felt less emotional stress and were more able to manage stress and the symptoms of bulimia.

Kuyken et al. (2008) Randomized controlled trial of MBCT and anti-depressive medication
- The study investigated the effectiveness of MBCT in a randomized controlled study with 123 participants with a history of three or more episodes of depression. All participants received anti-depressive medication.
- Participants were randomly allocated to two groups. Over the 15-month study, the control group continued their medication and the experimental group participated in an MBCT course and gradually diminished their medication.
- People in the control group who received anti-depressive medication had a relapse rate of 60% compared to the experimental group of 47%. Participants in the MBCT group overall reported a higher quality of life, in terms of enjoyment of daily living and physical well-being. Anti-depressive medication was significantly reduced in the MBCT group and 75% of the patients stopped taking the medication.

Evaluation of a biomedical treatment of depression

- Drugs are nearly always part of the treatment for severe depression. The biomedical approach to the treatment of depression is under debate. The most common treatment for depression includes drugs. Anti-depressants may reduce depressive symptoms but they have side effects and do not cure patients. Studies indicate that the placebo effect could account for the effectiveness of medication.

- Some researchers and psychiatrists now criticize the heavy use of medication on the grounds that it is not well known how it affects the brain long term (see **Neale et al. 2001**). There is also increasing criticism of the role of pharmaceutical companies and their marketing of anti-depressants, which has led to an increase in the prescription of SSRI.

Leuchter et al. (2002) Changes in brain function during treatment with placebo

- The study examined brain function in 51 patients with depression who received either a placebo or an active medication. An EEG was used to compare brain function in the two groups. The design was double-blind and ran over nine weeks. The study used two different SSRI, which were randomly allocated to the participants.

- Results showed a significant increase in activity in the prefrontal cortex nearly from the beginning in the trial in the placebo group. This pattern was different from the patients who were treated with the SSRI but patients in both groups got better. This indicates that medication is effective but placebo seems just as effective.

- The findings from the study are intriguing. The difference in activity in the brain indicates that the brain is perhaps able to heal itself since there was a positive effect in both groups. Believing they are being treated could be enough for some patients.

Kirsch et al. (2008) Meta-analysis of clinical trials

- This meta-analysis used clinical trials of the six most used anti-depressants (including Prozac) approved between 1987 and 1999.

- The study analysed all clinical trials of anti-depressants submitted to the FDA (US Food and Drug Administration).

- The results showed that the overall effect of new-generation anti-depressant medication (SSRI) was below the recommended criteria for clinical significance. This indicates that placebo may be just as effective.

- The highest effect of the medication was in the most severe cases of depression but the researchers speculate whether this is a real effect or due to a decrease in responsiveness to placebo rather than an increase in responsiveness to medication.

- According to the researchers, the placebo effect may account for any observed effect and they are very sceptical about the increasing use of anti-depressants on the basis of the results of the clinical trials.

Evaluation of an individual approach to the treatment of depression

- Individual treatments are normally effective. Cognitive theories have been criticized for focusing too much on symptoms (distorted thinking patterns) rather than causes of depression.

- The combination of behavioural techniques with cognitive restructuring in CBT seems to be effective, even in the absence of medication **(Luty et al. 2007)**. Studies that combine medication with CBT have good results, see unit 5.7 **(Paykel et al. 1999)**.

Luty et al. (2007) Randomized controlled trial of IPT and CBT

- The study investigated the relative effectiveness of the two treatments for major depression.

- A 16-week therapy with 8 to 19 individual sessions was attended by 177 patients diagnosed with major depression. Patients were randomly allocated to either CBT or IPT. They did not receive medication and those who eventually decided to use it were not included in the study.

- Generally the results showed no difference in effect of the two forms of psychotherapy but CBT was more effective in severe depression. Only 20% of patients with severe depression responded to IPT, whereas 57% of patients responded to CBT.

- The results indicate that psychotherapy alone could relieve symptoms of depression even when no drugs are given.

Elkin et al. (1989) Controlled outcome study of treatment for depression.

- The study is one of the best controlled outcome studies in depression. It involved 280 patients diagnosed with major depression who were randomly assigned to either (1) an anti-depressant drug plus the normal clinical management, (2) a placebo plus the normal clinical management, (3) CBT or (4) IPT. The treatment ran for 16 weeks and the patients were assessed at the start, after six weeks, and after 18 months.

■ The results showed a reduction of depressive symptoms of over 50% in the therapy groups and in the drug group. Only 29% recovered in the placebo group. There was no difference in the effectiveness of CBT, IPT or anti-depressant treatment. This indicates that psychotherapy might be an alternative in some cases.

■ The recovery rate for therapy (psychological and drug) was only 50% in this study so neither of the treatments can guarantee recovery for all patients.

Evaluation of a group approach to treatment of depression

■ Group therapy has been used to treat depression but it may not be appropriate as the only therapy and it should only be used when clients are positive about treatment in a group.

■ Modern forms of group therapy include ideas from Buddhism and ideas from cognitive therapy. It seems to be a promising way to treat depression but it may be suitable only for clients who are not severely depressed.

McDermut et al. (2001) Meta-analysis on effectiveness of group therapy for depression

■ The study was a meta-analysis based on 48 studies published between 1970 and 1998. The patients' mean age was 44 years and 78% of patients were women. All but one study included a cognitive and/or behavioural treatment group.

■ Results showed that 45 of the 48 studies reported that group psychotherapy was effective for reducing depressive symptoms. The overall results showed that group psychotherapy was more effective than no treatment around 19 weeks after the end of treatment. Nine studies showed that individual and group psychotherapy were equally effective.

■ The conclusion was that there is sound empirical support that group therapy is effective for relieving depressive symptoms. **Truax (2001)** commented on the results saying that group therapy should only be used when clients are positive about treatment in a group. The meta-analysis did not include severely depressed and suicidal patients in the study so it is not possible to conclude anything in relation to this group.

Exam Tip Kuyken et al. (2008) on MBCT in unit 5.7 can also be used to answer a question on the effectiveness of group therapy.

Discuss the use of eclectic approaches to treatment

Eclectic approaches to the treatment of depression

- The most common approach to the treatment of depression is antidepressive medication. This often relieves the depressive symptoms although it may take weeks before there is an effect and dropout rates are quite high because of the adverse effects of anti-depressants.

- Although nearly 50% to 60% of depressed outpatients experience an improvement in mood to the first trial of antidepressants, only 1 in 3 patients will experience a full and complete recovery with no symptoms **(Keller et al. 2004)**. The risk of relapse is also high and there is risk of repeated depressive episodes (chronic depression). The combination of psychotherapy and drugs seems to be particularly valuable in the prevention of relapse.

Klerman et al. (1974) Treatment of depression by drugs and/or psychotherapy

- The aim of this controlled study was to test the efficacy of treatment with anti-depressants and psychotherapy, alone or in combination.

- Participants were 150 females diagnosed with depression. Patients were divided into three groups: (1) anti-depressants alone, (2) anti-depressants and psychotherapy, and (3) no medication but more psychotherapy or (4) placebo and no psychotherapy.

- The results showed that relapse rates were highest for patients in the placebo group alone (36%). The group with anti-depressants alone had a relapse rate of 12%; the

psychotherapy (IPT) alone had a relapse rate of 16.7%; combination of drug and IPT had a relapse rate of 12.5%.

- There was no significant difference between drug therapy alone or drug therapy in combination with psychotherapy.

This study could also be used in unit 5.7 to address the effectiveness of biological treatment and individual treatment of depression.

Pampallona et al. (2004) Meta-analysis of efficacy of drug treatment alone versus drug treatment and psychotherapy in depression

- The aim of the study was to analyse whether combining anti-depressants and psychotherapy was more effective in the treatment of depression.

- 16 randomized controlled studies were conducted including 932 patients taking antidepressants only and 910 receiving combined treatment. The patients had all been randomly allocated to the treatments.

- The results showed that patients in combined treatment improved significantly more compared to those receiving drug treatment alone. This was particularly true in studies that ran over more than 12 weeks and there was also a significant reduction in dropouts.

Why eclectic approaches could be more efficient than medication alone

- There is always a risk that patients stop taking their medicine (e.g. anti-depressants). This could be because the patient feels somewhat better after a while and then stops, or it could be because he or she experiences too many negative side effects.

- According to Pampallona et al. (2004) this could be a very good reason for the clinician to combine anti-depressants with psychotherapy. Their review of randomized controlled trials shows that the combination of drugs and psychotherapy generally leads to greater improvement. The study also showed that psychotherapy helps to keep patients in treatment.

5.10 Discuss the relationship between etiology and therapeutic approach in relation to one disorder

- **Etiology** means explaining the *cause* of a disorder. This is often very difficult within abnormal psychology. There are no simple explanations of complex psychological disorders. Logic suggests that the cause of a disorder should dictate the treatment. This is done in medicine but it is not possible in the case of psychiatric disorders such as major depression because the causes of disorders are not well known and cures have yet to be found.

- Scientific research has failed to show a clear link between serotonin levels and depression. The fact that anti-depressant drugs like SSRI can regulate serotonin levels and produce an effect does not mean that low serotonin levels cause depression.

Etiology and therapeutic approach in major depression

- Treatment of major depression often involves anti-depressant medication that interferes with neurotransmission (e.g. serotonin and dopamine) in the brain. This can be seen as an attempt to regulate what is believed to be an imbalance in the serotonin system.

- Some psychiatrists question the usefulness of anti-depressants that interfere with serotonin balances in the brain on the grounds that:

  - the serotonin system in the brain is very complex and not much is known about the drugs' long-term effect

  - the drugs do not cure depression and have side effects

  - studies show that placebo might be just as effective

  - psychotherapy (particularly CBT) is just as effective and in some cases more effective.

- **Henninger et al. (1996)** performed experiments where they reduced serotonin levels in healthy individuals to see if they would develop depressive symptoms. The results did not support that levels of serotonin could influence depression and they argued that it is necessary to revise the serotonin hypothesis.

Etiology: the serotonin hypothesis

- The serotonin hypothesis suggests that depression is caused by low levels of serotonin in the brain (**Coppen, 1967**).

- Anti-depressants in the form of SSRI block the re-uptake process for serotonin. This results in an increased amount of serotonin in the synaptic gap. The theory is that this improves mood.

- SSRI such as Prozac, Zoloft and Paxil are now among the most sold anti-depressants, and the drug companies spent millions of dollars on advertising campaigns all over the world. This has been taken as indirect support of the serotonin hypothesis. According to **Lacasse and Leo (2005)** this is an example of backward reasoning. Assumptions about the causes of depression are based on how people respond to a treatment and this is logically problematic. For example, it is clear that aspirin can cure headaches but this does not prove that low levels of aspirin in the brain cause headaches.

Elkin et al. (1989) Controlled outcome study of treatment for depression

- The study is one of the best controlled outcome studies of depression. A sample of 280 patients diagnosed with major depression were randomly assigned to either an anti-depressant drug plus the normal clinical management, a placebo plus the normal clinical management, CBT (cognitive-behavioural therapy) or IPT (interpersonal therapy). The treatment ran for 16 weeks and the patients were assessed at the start, after 6 weeks, and after 18 months.

- The results showed a reduction of depressive symptoms of over 50% in the therapy groups and in the drug group. Only 29% recovered in the placebo group. There was no difference in the effectiveness of CBT, IPT or anti-depressant treatment. For the most severely depressed patients, medication and clinical management was most effective in reducing symptoms but this does not prove that serotonin causes depression.

Brain development and neuroplasticity

Developmental cognitive neuroscience is an area of research that studies the relationship between brain development and cognitive competence. Research in this field explores the developing brain in order to understand healthy development but also how various factors may interfere with normal brain development and lead to problems in cognitive functioning.

- The basic functional elements of the brain are neurons that connect to each other (synaptic growth) to form a network of neurons (information processing networks). Neuronal networks change as a result of learning, experience, and age. Each human brain has a unique neural architecture due to differences in individual experience.

- The neural connections (dendritic branching) in the brain grow in size and complexity after birth and myelination (covering the neuron with myelin – white matter) is accelerated. Synaptic growth is most significant in childhood and adolescence.

- Interaction with loving and responsive caregivers contributes to healthy brain development. Various factors such as early social deprivation, inadequate nutrition, or living in a polluted environment may interfere with normal brain development. This can have adverse effects on cognitive, emotional, and social development.

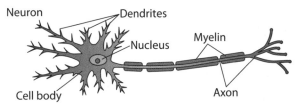

Brain development and cognitive functioning

- The brain doubles in size from birth to young adulthood and the brain's surface folds become more complex, especially in the areas that process cognitive and emotional information. The growth in complexity of the neuronal network permits the neurons to process increasingly complex information.

- Developmental neuroscientists use brain imaging (e.g. PET and MRI) to study the relationships between brain development and cognitive processes in infants and young children.

Chugani (1999) used PET scans to investigate glucose metabolism in the brains of newborn human babies. He found:

- There was little activity in the cerebral cortex (executive function)

- There was activity in the brain stem and the thalamus (inborn reflexes such as grasping)

- There was activity in the limbic system (amygdala, hippocampus, and the cingulate cortex). These areas are associated with emotional processing, memory, and bonding. They are used in observing and reading the emotional content of faces and in communicating via facial expressions and eye contact. Lack of stimulation in these areas in early life can lead to abnormal behaviour and attachment difficulties.

The research found that the lower levels of the brain are developed first (measured as activity) and over time glucose consumption can be registered in higher levels of the brain. For example, from age six to nine months there is increasing activity in the frontal lobes, prefrontal areas of the cortex and evidence of improved cognitive competence.

Giedd (2004) performed MRI scans in a longitudinal study of healthy children. He found that 95% of the brain structure is formed when the child is around five or six years old, but areas in the prefrontal cortex (PFC) start growing again in adolescence. The PFC is the last part of the brain to mature. It is responsible for cognitive processes such as planning, impulse control, direction of attention, and decision making.

Waber (2007) peformed the **MRI Study of Normal Brain Development**, a longitudinal representative study of 450 healthy children aged 6–18 that began in 1999. The research includes MRI scans of the brain and a battery of tests to measure the children's cognitive function (e.g. mental processing speed, memory, reading, and calculation) as well as IQ and psychosocial function. The first analysis of data showed that age predicts performance on every measure of cognitive function. There was a steep increase in cognitive function from age six but this levelled off in the majority of cases between 10 and 12 years of age. This indicates that as children mature the speed of mental processing generally increases.

Strathearn et al (2001) found that child neglect is associated with significantly delayed cognitive development and head growth in young children.

Chugani et al. (2001) found that Romanian children who had spent time in institutions before being adopted showed deficits in cognitive tasks dependent on prefrontal function such as attention and social cognition.

Strengths of neurobiological theories	Limitations of neurobiological theories
■ Neuroscientific evidence provides a valuable insight into how the brain develops from the simple to the more complex and this can, to some extent, be linked to increasing cognitive competence. ■ Animal research shows that an enriched environment results in synaptic growth (for example **Rosenzweig and Bennet, 1972**, on brain plasticity, see unit 2.5 for more on this). This is also the case in humans. ■ Developmental cognitive neuroscience has provided evidence of the devastating effects of neglect on the developing brain, which is useful for treating children with cognitive, emotional, and behavioural problems due to long- term stress (see more in units 6.4 and 6.6).	■ It is not possible at this point to establish a direct cause-effect relationship between brain development and cognitive growth. Much of the empirical research within cognitive developmental neuroscience is correlational. ■ Little is known about the exact neural basis of cognition in normally developing children but longitudinal brain imaging studies like the MRI Study of Normal Brain Development will perhaps provide more knowledge on this.

Piaget's method

Piaget based his theory on observations and open-ended interviews. This clinical method enabled Piaget to gain insight into the children's judgement and explanations of events. He presented children with a number of tasks designed to discover the level of logical reasoning underpinning their thinking. He was interested in the way they arrived at their conclusions. His method has been criticized for:

■ using a small and non-representative sample

■ lack of scientific rigour and cross-sectional design which makes it difficult to make conclusions about changes over time (a longitudinal design would be better to do this)

■ asking questions that are too complex for children.

Piaget's theory of cognitive development

According to Piaget, there are qualitative differences between the way adults and children think. Action and self-directed problem solving are at the heart of learning and cognitive development in children. Formal logic is seen as the highest and last stage in intellectual development.

■ **The child is seen as an active "scientist":** He or she actively constructs knowledge about the social and physical world as he or she interacts with it (constructionist approach). Each child builds his or her own mental representation of the world (**schemas**) used to interpret and interact with objects, people, and events. Piaget used the term "operation" to describe physical or symbolic manipulations (thinking) of things.

■ **Stage theory:** Children's cognitive development progresses through stages over time. According to Piaget, the content and sequence of stages in cognitive development is the same for all humans (universal theory). Children cannot learn or be taught how to function at higher levels of cognition before they have passed through the lower levels.

Key concept: schema
■ Knowledge is seen as cognitive structures or mental representations (schemas) that change over time. The baby uses an innate genetically based repertoire of schemas (sucking, grasping) to explore the world.

■ Knowledge comes from the baby's actions upon objects in the environment. At later stages, action is replaced by "thinking", which Piaget sees as a kind of action.

■ Schemas are integrated and modified as a result of experience (adaptation) and new schemas emerge when existing schemas are inadequate.

Adaptation (learning) can take two forms →

Assimilation: New information is integrated into existing cognitive schemas (for example "dog" is categorized as "animal". Knowledge is consolidated.

Accomodation: Existing schemas are modified to fit new information or new schemas are created. New knowledge is created.

Piaget's stages of cognitive development

Stage	Some characteristics
Sensorimotor (0–2 years)	Baby goes from reflexive instinctual action (sucking, grasping) to constructing knowledge via coordination of sensory experiences with physical actions.
Preoperational (2–7 years)	Thinking is intuitive and dominated by the appearance of things and focusing on one dimension at a time. Shows **egocentrism** (difficulty seeing things from the perspective of others) and lack of **conservation** (cannot see that things remain constant in spite of change in visible appearance). Not able to use formal logic.
Concrete operational (7–11 years)	Can carry out mental operations but needs to see the objects being concretely manipulated (e.g. understanding what happens in the conservation test and why objects remain the same in spite of changing form).
Formal operational (11–15 years)	Ability to use abstract reasoning and logic. Can deal with hypothetical problems and mentally manipulate ideas, numbers, and concepts. Can use deductive reasoning.

Egocentrism in the preoperational stage

Egocentrism is the idea that a child can only see the world from his or her own viewpoint and is not able to understand that others might see things differently. **Piaget and Inhelder (1956)** showed preschool children a scene with three mountains, each with a distinctive landmark. A doll was placed opposite to the child. The researchers asked the child to choose a picture that represented what the doll would see from the other side. The child then changed position and was asked the same question. Children between four and five years old picked the picture of the mountains showing the mountains from their own perspective. Children who were around six years tended to do the same but showed awareness that there could be other viewpoints.

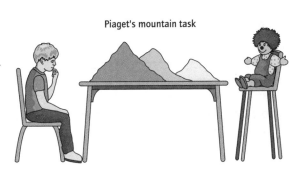
Piaget's mountain task

Hughes (1975) made a variation of the study. The children were asked to hide a doll from two policemen dolls. He found that, in this version, younger children were able to take the perspective of the dolls most of the time. The explanation was that the task was made more relevant to the children. The results indicate that it is possible for children to take the perspective of others if they understand the task.

Conservation in the preoperational stage

Piaget did a number of tests like this one: A child is presented with two glasses of water. The researcher asks if there is the same amount of liquid in the two. The child will say yes. The same question is asked after the water from one of the glasses is poured into a tall glass. The child will now typically say that there is more water in the tall glass because it is taller. Piaget argued that this is because the child is not able to mentally reverse the operation and in this way understand that it must be the same amount of water. He or she focuses on only one dimension of the situation (the size of the glasses) and cannot *conserve* the quantity of water. Piaget's findings have been replicated many times, also in cross-cultural studies. The researcher asks the same question twice – in the first situation and in the second – and this has been criticized for creating demand characteristics.

McGarrigle and Donaldson (1974) argued that demand characteristics could flaw the conservation task. They used an experimental set-up with two rows of counters in parallel lines. First children were asked whether the two rows contained the same or a different number. Children said they were the same.

Then a glove puppet called "naughty teddy" appeared and messed up the two rows so that one appeared longer. The same question as before was asked. Most children between four and six years old said that there was the same amount of counters. This indicates that if a less artificial task is used, children can conserve earlier than predicted by Piaget.

Strengths of Piaget's theory	Limitations of Piaget's theory
■ Piaget has contributed substantially to the study of cognitive development. His work laid the foundation for much of the early work on cognitive development. ■ Piaget's work has had a major influence on education (e.g. "discovery learning" and the teacher as "facilitator" rather than transmitter of knowledge). Piaget's theory has generated a lot of research over time. ■ Piaget showed that the way children think is qualitatively different from the way adults think.	■ Piaget focused primarily on cognitive development as a process located within the individual child and placed less importance on how contextual (e.g. social and cultural) factors contributed to cognitive growth. ■ Researchers have questioned the timing of Piaget's stages. Vygotsky criticized Piaget for underestimating the role of instruction in cognitive development. ■ Piaget's methods have been criticized for lack of scientific rigour and sampling bias. He also used tasks that were too difficult for children to understand and this could explain some of the results.

Vygotsky's sociocultural approach to cognitive development

Vygotsky was a Russian psychologist. Like Piaget he thought that children's thinking is different from adults'.

■ Children grow up in a specific historical, social, and cultural context and their knowledge and intelligence develop within the framework of that culture's characteristics (e.g. history, artefacts, language, science).

■ The historical and cultural characteristics of each society influence the way people come to act upon and think about the world. Vygotsky talks about "cultural tools" that individuals must learn to handle in order to function in that culture. For example, today an important cultural tool in the West could be the computer.

■ Vygotsky emphasizes *language* and *instruction* as the most important factors in intellectual and personal development. Instruction through cooperation and interaction is the main vehicle for the cultural transmission of knowledge. This is a contrast to Piaget's view of children,, who must discover everything by themselves through concrete or mental "operations".

■ If children receive instructions from other, more skilled individuals they can understand and accomplish things that they would not be able to achieve alone. The **"zone of proximal development"** refers to the gap that exists for an individual child between what he or she is able to do alone (zone of competence) and what he or she can achieve with help from someone who has more knowledge. The concept of **"scaffolding"** refers to the assistance that a more skilled individual can provide to increase a child's performance on a particular task.

Evaluation of Vygotsky's theory
■ According to **Wood (1998)** Vygotsky's perspective on cognitive development can hardly be called a full-fledged theory, but his ideas have been integrated into the development of other theories (e.g. **Bruner, 1966**) and visions about education (e.g. collaborative learning).

■ Vygotsky has inspired sociocultural approaches to learning based on the assumption that cognitive development and learning must be seen in relation to an individual's historical, social, and cultural context (see **Cole and Scribner, 1974**, in unit 3.5).

Biological theories	Piaget (cognitive)	Vygotsky (sociocultural)
■ The brain develops according to a genetically determined programme but environmental factors influence the end result. ■ Healthy brain development is a prerequisite for optimal cognitive functioning. ■ Negative environmental and social factors can interfere with normal brain development.	■ Children pass through stages as they construct their ability to reason through individual action. ■ Instruction (teaching) is only possible if the child is cognitively ready (i.e. the necessary cognitive structures have developed). ■ Constructivist theory (and focus on development of independent thinking based on individual experience).	■ Children can learn more at each stage than predicted by Piaget through instruction from adults because of the potential of the "zone of proximal development". ■ Observation, social interaction, cooperation, and cultural practices are important in cognitive development. ■ Social constructivist theory (and related to Marxist thinking).

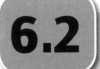

6.2 Discuss how social and environmental variables may affect cognitive development

- Cognitive development is affected by a number of social and environmental variables that interact with the child's genetic inheritance in complex ways that are not yet fully understood. Stimulation, adequate nutrition, and parental nurturance are important factors in brain development and therefore also in developing cognitive competence.

- A relevant social variable could be socioeconomic status (SES), i.e. family income and educational level). Adequate parenting and healthy nutrition facilitates cognitive development.

- Relevant environmental variables influencing cognitive development are, for example, access to stimulating toys and good schools. Living in a polluted environment may affect brain development negatively.

Social variables

SES is a total measure of a person's social and economic position based on income, education, and occupation. SES has been found to correlate with parenting (social variable) and environmental enrichment (environmental variable). **Farah et al. (2005)** found that low SES children performed worse on all tests of cognitive performance compared to middle SES children.

- Findings from neuroscientists show that children growing up in very poor families experience high levels of stress and this could impair brain development and general cognitive functioning.
- **Krugman (2008)** argued that children born to poor parents (low SES) have a 50% chance of remaining in lifelong poverty because the brains of poor children do not develop optimally and they therefore miss social and economic opportunities.

- One effect of poverty is chronic malnourishment, which is linked to less activity and interest in learning. Malnutrition is associated with impaired or delayed brain development. A number of cognitive deficits have been reported in malnourished children.
- **Bhoomika et al. (2008)** studied the effect of malnutrition on cognitive performance in a sample of 20 Indian children in two age groups, one aged from five to seven and another aged between eight and ten. The data was compared to those in a control group. Malnourished children in both age groups scored lover in tests of attention, working memory, and visuospatial tasks. Older children showed less cognitive impairment, which suggests that the effects of malnutrition on cognitive competence may result in delayed cognitive development during childhood but it is not a permanent generalized cognitive impairment.

Environmental variables

Animal research suggests that there is a specific relationship between early experience and brain development. Research showed that manipulating environmental variables, such as toys and other animals to play with, influenced the number of neurons as well as the animal's behaviour (see **Rosenzweig Bennet, and Diamond (1972)** on dendritic branching in unit 2.5). Animal research has also demonstrated that stress (e.g. due to maternal separation) interferes with normal brain development. This kind of research cannot take place using humans for ethical reasons.

Liu et al. (2000) performed an experiment with rats and found that prolonged maternal separation and brief handling affect later life stress regulation ability and memory ability as a result of their impact on hippocampal development. Brief separations seemed to be positive because they resulted in intensified nurturing behaviour after the separation. The more the mother rat licks her pup following a brief stressor, the better regulated the pup's response to stressors and the better its learning ability.

It is perhaps not possible to generalize directly to humans from animal research but it is possible to measure some of the same naturally occurring variables in human experiences (e.g. neglect and institutionalization) known to be related to cognitive function.

Farah et al. (2008)

Aim To investigate the relationship between *environmental stimulation* and *parental nurturance* on cognitive development.

Procedure

- This was a longitudinal design with 110 African-American middle-school children (mean age 11.8 years). Children were recruited at birth and evaluated at age four and eight years in the home.

- Interviews and observational checklists were used to measure environmental stimulation (e.g. variety of experience, encouragement to learn colours, music, and art) and parental nurturance (e.g. warmth and affection, emotional and verbal responsivity, and paternal involvement).

- The researchers also performed cognitive tests on language and memory in the laboratory.

Results There was a positive correlation between environmental stimulation and language development. Age was also a factor. There was also a positive correlation between parental nurturance and long-term memory performance.

Evaluation

- The data shows the importance of environmental and social factors in cognitive development although it is not possible to establish a cause-effect relationship since the study did not manipulate variables.

- The children in this sample were from a low economic status and the sample is not representative, although 17% of American children live below the poverty line according to the 2004 census.

- Low SES is associated with a number of adverse factors that can affect cognitive development, (e.g. physical and mental health problems, social and psychological stress, and poverty.

- The correlation between parental nurturance and memory has also been found in animal research. Prolonged stress due to maternal separation affects the hippocampus, which is vital in memory processing.

Exam Tip The discussion refers to how and why cognitive development may be influenced by social and environmental factors. It could be relevant to include knowledge from unit 6.3 on how cognitive development is dependent on brain development (e.g. with reference to how neglect could affect cognitive development).

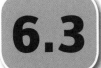

Examine attachment in childhood and its role in the subsequent formation of relationships

Attachment in childhood

Attachment theory was suggested by **Bowlby (1951)** and it has become one of the most influential theories in understanding children's emotional and social development as well as adult love relationships.

- Attachment can be defined as the emotional bond between an individual and an attachment figure (caregiver who is responsive and sensitive to the child's needs).

- Parental sensitivity is important in the development of attachment. Attachment can be observed from around the age of seven months. From this age, the baby shows separation distress when the primary attachment figure (often the mother) leaves the child. "The strange situation" (**Ainsworth et al., 1978**) can test if attachment has formed.

Ainsworth: Attachment classification and the Strange Situation paradigm

Ainsworth (1969) carried out the Ganda Project which was an observational study of 28 mothers interacting with their child performed in Uganda over nine months (longitudinal). The observations were naturalistic (in the family living room). Ainsworth interviewed the mothers and measured maternal sensitivity to the infant's signals and needs as these were considered to be important factors in the development of attachment. The study was replicated in the USA in 1971 with 26 families.

Ainsworth et al (1978) suggested a classification system with three attachment patterns based on "The Strange Situation paradigm", a procedure with several sequences performed in a laboratory to test a child's attachment pattern to the mother. Key features of the procedure are:

1 the child's reaction to the mother's departure
2 how the child reacts to her when she returns
3 how the child reacts to a stranger.

Different patterns of responses to the Strange Situation are assumed to show three particular attachment patterns:

- **Secure attachment (type B):** This pattern is displayed by 70% of American infants. The infant shows distress when the mother leaves the room and quickly seeks contact with her when she returns. The infant is easily soothed by the mother.

- **Ambivalent attachment (type C):** This pattern is displayed by 10% of American infants. The infant shows distress when the mother leaves the room. The baby seeks contact on her return but at the same time rejects it.

- **Avoidant attachment (type A):** This pattern is displayed by 20% of American infants. The infant does not show distress when the mother leaves the room and avoids contact when she returns. The baby is not afraid of a stranger. Mothers to avoidant children tend to be unresponsive and uninterested in the child's signals.

Campos et al (1983) performed a review of American studies on infant attachment patterns and found the following distribution: secure (62%), ambivalent (15%), and avoidant (15%).

Attachment and internal working model

Bowlby (1973) claims that there is a *continuity* between childhood and adult relationships, i.e. early attachment patterns formed with parents continue in later relationships because they create an **internal working model**. The internal working model is a mental representation of the self, about the attachment figure, and how others will react (social life).

- **Internal working model:** The child's experiences with attachment figures during infancy, childhood, and adolescence result in expectations (mental representations or schemas) that persist relatively unchanged throughout the rest of life. If the child is confident that the attachment figure is available when needed, the child will feel loved, secure and worthy of love and attention. According to Bowlby, the internal working model tends to be reproduced in later relationships (parenting, romantic love).

- **Attachment history:** The internal working model reflects the various experiences concerning accessibility and responsiveness of the attachment figures that an individual has experienced. Differences in experience with attachment figures may explain different attachment patterns as well as attachment disorders. The Strange Situation Paradigm was developed by **Ainsworth et al. (1978)** to test if attachment has formed.

Social and cultural factors in attachment

Attachment research has primarily been conducted in the West but cross-cultural research tends to find similar attachment categories but different distributions. **Van Ijzendorn and Kroonenberg (1988)** reviewed 32 studies from eight countries including 2,000 infants. In Japan, ambivalent attachment (type C) was more common than in the West, but there was no avoidant (type A). Secure attachment (type B) was the most common in the West. Differences in attachment patterns are associated with differences in child-rearing practices.

Continuity in attachment patterns in romantic love

- **Hazan and Shaver (1987)** suggested that romantic love is an attachment process which is experienced differently by different people because of variations in their attachment histories.

- People have formed "inner working models" of themselves and social interaction with partners based on their attachment history. These inner working models are an important source of continuity between early and later feelings and behaviour.

Hazan and Shaver (1978)
The research consisted of two different studies.

Aim To investigate:

1 whether the same distribution of childhood attachment patterns was manifested in a study on adult love relationships

2 whether the difference in attachment patterns could be linked to different attachment histories

3 whether respondents' descriptions of their love relationships could be classified as secure, avoidant, or ambivalent.

Procedure

- The first was a "love quiz" (survey with forced choices) in a local newspaper. The researchers used 620 participants (205 males, 415 females, mean age 36, 91% were heterosexual).

- The questionnaire included statements characterizing the *most important love relationship* and *childhood relationship with parents* (attachment history).

- **Ainsworth et al.'s (1978)** attachment categories were translated into terms appropriate to adult love. It was assumed that *beliefs* about romantic love could be measured as an "inner working model".

Results

- Around 56% of the respondents classified themselves as secure, 25% as avoidant, and 19% as ambivalent.

- **Secure lovers** described their most important love relationships as trusting, happy, and friendly. **Avoidant lovers** were characterized by fear of intimacy, emotional highs and lows, and well as jealousy. **Ambivalent lovers** believed that romantic love is characterized by obsession, emotional highs and lows, extreme sexual attraction, and jealousy.

- The best predictors of adult attachment type were respondents' perception of the quality of their relationship with each parent as well as parental relationships. The results showed that loving and affectionate parenting correlated positively with secure attachment. Participants classified as avoidant reported cold and rejecting mothers.

Evaluation

- The results supported that three different attachment styles could be found in adult love. The study confirmed Bowlby's theory about continuity of attachment (inner working model).

- The study had a biased self-selected sample so results could not be generalized. More females than males responded (gender bias). This could affect the estimates of prevalence of each attachment type. Use of questionnaires with forced choices may may limit the validity of the findings.

- **Hazan and Shaver (1988)** was a seminal study, which conceptualized adult romantic relationships as an attachment process. The study provided a bridge between infant attachment theory and theories of romantic love. The findings have been replicated and researchers have linked adult attachment to existing theories of love.

Conclusion

- There are different attachment styles which seem to be related to an individual's attachment history. People's inner working models include different beliefs about romantic love, whether they are worthy of love, and what to expect from a partner.

- **Feeney, Noller and Callan (1994)** found that attachment patterns in stable couples tend to be secure. Attachment patterns seem to be flexible and may change when events in the social environment disconfirm existing expectations. Becoming involved in a stable, satisfying relationship can lead to change in internal working models of self and others. Likewise, a secure person who is involved in a negative relationship may become insecure.

Healthy development is influenced by factors such as access to loving caregivers, adequate nutrition, sensory and cognitive stimulation, and linguistic input.

A child reared in a severely deprived setting will not experience such factors and this can affect the child's development negatively. However, even children who are exposed to deprivation may eventually develop normally (see units 6.5 and 6.6).

- **Deprivation** in childhood can be seen as living in a state of various forms of neglect to provide basic needs – physical, emotional, or social. Deprivation is often related to

institutionalization, growing up in poverty, and parental problems (e.g. alcoholism or mental illness.

- **Trauma** in childhood can be seen as experiencing a powerful shock (e.g. divorce, death of a parent, physical or sexual abuse, natural disasters, or war. Such experiences may have long-lasting effects on development.

- It is not possible to make a clear-cut distinction between effects of deprivation or trauma: they are much the same. Experiences of deprivation can also be traumatizing for the child.

Potential effect of trauma: PTSD

Children who have experienced severe and repeated trauma may develop post-traumatic stress disorder (PTSD), which could interfere with normal development. If left untreated children may exhibit impulsivity, agitation, hyper-vigilance, avoidance behaviour, and emotional numbness.

Carion et al. (2009) performed fMRI scans and found that children suffering from PTSD after experiencing extreme stressors such as abuse or witnessing violence performed worse on a simple verbal memory test and showed less hippocampal activity compared to a control group. The participants who performed worst on the test were those who also showed

specific PTSD symptoms such as withdrawal from those who wanted to help them. They also had difficulties remembering the trauma, felt cut off from others, and showed lack of emotion.

Yehuda et al. (2001) studied the mental health of 51 children of Holocaust survivors who were raised by traumatized parents and made comparisons to a control group. The mean age of the sample was 40.9 years. The results showed that children of Holocaust survivors were more likely to develop PTSD (33.3 % compared to 12.2% in the control group). Childhood trauma was associated with parental PTSD and the results indicate that PTSD can be transmitted from parent to child.

Potential effects of deprivation: cognitive impairment and attachment disorder

The English and Romanian adoptees study

This is a longitudinal study of 324 Romanian adoptees that entered the UK between February 1990 and September 1992. The aim was to investigate potential long-term effects of severe deprivation in childhood. All the children had been reared from infancy in very deprived institutions in Romania and adopted into UK families at various ages up to 42 months.

Rutter et al. (2004) investigated a sample of 144 children who were, at that time, six years of age. The parents were interviewed at home and answered questionnaires on the family and the child's behaviour. Three months later the child was assessed using observations and standard cognitive and developmental measures including tests on general cognitive functioning and attachment behaviour. The focus was on **cognitive impairment** and **attachment disturbance** in children who had spent more than six months in the institutions. The study found no major deficits in children who had spent less than six months there.

Cognitive impairment

- Cognitive impairment was found in 15.4% of the adoptees from Romania but in only 2.3% of the adoptees from the UK.
- There was a persistent cognitive deficit at age six in the children who remained longest in the deprived Romanian

institutions before being adopted. This was particularly the case for those children who had also suffered from severe malnutrition.

- These children also had a much smaller head circumference at the time they entered the UK and this could also be observed at age six. This could suggest neural damage.

- This is supported by **Perry and Pollard (1997)** who used CT scans and found that the brain size of a severely deprived three-year-old was significantly smaller than average (see also unit 6.1).

- Cognitive functioning at age six was not associated with the educational level of the adoptive parents. This supports that cognitive impairment could be related to neural damage.

Cognitive impairment related to time of institutionalization	
Time spent in depriving institution	% of the children with cognitive impairment
From 6–24 months	12%
From 24–42 months	36%

Attachment disorder

- Data was collected in semi-structured interviews with parents to assess the child's behaviour toward the parent and other adults in both novel and familiar situations.

- There was a relationship between length of institutional deprivation and attachment disorders. No significant deficits were found in the children who entered the UK below the age of six months.

- A number of children showed an insecure attachment pattern called **disinhibited attachment disorder** characterized by:

  - lack of preference for contact with caregivers versus relative strangers (i.e. lack of differentiation among adults)

  - definite lack of checking back with the parent in anxiety-provoking situations.

Disinhibited attachment behaviour related to time of institutionalization

Time spent in depriving institution	% of the children with disinhibited attachment behaviour
From 6–24 months	16%
From 24–42 months	33%

Conclusion

- According to **Rutter et al. (2004)** a lack of personalized caregiving may well be the key factor that puts children's social development at risk. This is in line with **Bowlby (1969)** who argued that emotionally available caregiving is a crucial factor in determining a child's development and future mental health (see more on this in unit 6.3).

- Generally the data revealed a major degree of recovery in children suffering from profound institutional deprivation: the effects were not fixed and irreversible. Most of them did *not* show cognitive impairment and disinhibited attachment (see more on resilience in units 6.5 and 6.6).

6.5 Define resilience

- **Rutter (1990):** Resilience can be seen as maintaining adaptive functioning in spite of serious risk factors.
- **Wyman et al. (2000):** Resilience can be defined as a child's achievement of positive developmental outcomes and avoidance of maladaptive outcomes under adverse conditions.

Approaches to resilience research

Approaches to resilience research

- Focus is on *risk factors* in development as well as *protective factors*. A risk (or protective) factor in psychosocial development could be the early relationships with caregivers as these relationships provide the foundations for developing secure attachments, feelings of self-worth, and regulations of emotions.

- The child is seen as part of multiple systems where risk factors and protective factors are included in the overall understanding of development.

- Focus on how to promote resilience by preventative interventions to help children at risk (e.g. parenting programmes, academic programmes, family support).

Wright and Masten (2006) claimed that resilience should not be seen as an **individual trait**. Individual resilience must be studied in the context of adversity and risk in relation to multiple **contextual factors** that interact (e.g. family, school,

neighbourhood, community, and culture) with individual factors (e.g. the child's temperament, intelligence, and health).

Schoon and Bartley (2008) highlighted the importance of examining the factors and processes that enable individuals to beat the odds instead of focusing on "adaptive functioning of the individual" as this could lead to the misunderstanding that resilience is a matter of personality traits and that everyone can make it if they try hard enough. Such a dispositional approach can lead to blaming the victim of adverse circumstances. Instead, there should be a focus on how to promote resilience by removing obstacles and creating opportunities.

Werner (2005)
Werner performed a large-scale longitudinal study (Kauai study) with a multi-racial cohort of children born in 1955 on the Hawaiian island of Kauai. Children who had experienced four or more risk factors by the age of two were likely to have developed behavioural problems by the age of 10 as well as mental or delinquency problems. One third of the children had developed into normal healthy individuals at the age of 40. This indicates that multiple risk factors may be a major threat to children but also that adversity can be overcome by building resilience.

Exam Tip The points made here on resilience and the research can be included in a discussion on how to promote resilience.

- Adversity in childhood can be seen as a situation where a child's basic emotional, social, physiological, or cognitive needs are not met.
- Early **risk factors** include poor attachment to caregivers, poor parenting skills, and multiple family (e.g. poverty, and violent neighbourhoods). Such risk factors may directly affect the child's development and lead to psychological and social problems (e.g. depression, low education, early pregnancy, delinquency).
- Resilience programmes typically target the promotion of **protective factors** such as parenting skills, academic tutoring (e.g. reading skills), training of social skills, and self-regulation. It has been found that early interventions have better long-term results than programmes introduced later in life.

The Triple P – Positive Parenting Programme

The Triple P is based on social learning principles. Its goal is to target behavioural, emotional, and developmental problems in children aged 0–16 years, through enhancing the knowledge, skills, and confidence of parents. It includes a short, video-based programme and group-based interventions.

- **Sanders et al. (2002)** found that this programme was effective in reducing children's disruptive behaviour. A number of randomized controlled trials show success in promoting effective parenting and children's prosocial behaviour through The Triple P.
- These findings are supported by **Love et al. (2005)** who found that parents who had participated in a parental skills training programme were more supportive, better at stimulating language development, and used less corporal punishment.

The High/Scope Perry Preschool Project to prevent juvenile delinquency

The project is an ongoing longitudinal study (field experiment) that began in 1962. The project is based on an active learning model with focus on children's intellectual and social development.

Aim To study how juvenile delinquency can be prevented in a high-risk population.

Procedure Participants were 123 high-risk African-American children of low SES, with low IQ scores and at risk of failing schools. At between three and four years of age they were split into two groups: 58 children in the programme group and 65 acting as control. ▶▶

The programme consisted of preschool for two and a half hours every day for two years. The teachers made home visits once a week and the parents participated in monthly meetings with staff. This was to increase parents' involvement in the children's education.

Results There were a number of positive outcomes in the treatment group compared to the control, such as significantly lower rates of crime and delinquency, lower rates of teenage pregnancy, and dependence on welfare. The rates of prosocial behaviour, academic achievement, employment, income, and family stability were also higher in the treatment group.

Evaluation The intervention programme is a field experiment and not all variables can be controlled. The results so far show positive correlations between the intervention on a number of variables but it is difficult to determine cause-effect relationships. The control group did not show the same positive development, so it may be unethical not to include that group in the programme.

The Big Brothers Big Sisters (BBBS) mentoring programme

This is a resilience-based mentoring programme for high-risk children and adolescents in the USA. The programme is based on the idea that social support from a caring adult to a high-risk child or adolescent can promote a healthy development in spite of environmental risk factors.

Tierney et al. (1985) studied the impact of **mentoring** on the behaviour of 959 high-risk children and adolescents, aged 10–16, from low-income families. Many had experienced family violence or substance abuse. Half of them were assigned a mentor and half of them acted as control. The researchers were interested in the outcome of mentoring on factors such as antisocial behaviour, academic performance, relationships with family members and friends, and self-concept.

The results showed a positive outcome if the adult provided a caring relationship and had positive expectations. The programme did not target any specific problem behaviour but was merely investigating whether social support from an adult could promote resilience.

Exam Tip A discussion of two strategies to build resilience is enough. In an essay on strategies to promote resilience, it would be a good idea to outline what is meant by resilience and how adversity in childhood may endanger healthy development. Then refer to two different strategies and discuss them (or follow what the command term invites you to do).

6.7 Discuss the formation and development of gender roles

Sex	Gender	Role	Gender role
Biological sex determined by chromosomes (XY for boys and XX for girls)	The social and psychological characteristics associated with being male or female.	A set of social and behavioural norms linked to a specific sociocultural setting.	Gender role characterizes activities as masculine or feminine.

Gender role theories

Evolutionary theory

- Biological and psychological differences in men and women are natural and result in different gender roles. Men are naturally more competitive and aggressive because this increases chances of attracting a partner and providing resources for offspring. Women are nurturing because this is needed to attract a partner and take care of offspring.

- **Evaluation** The theory is controversial. There are cross-cultural differences as well as similarities in gender roles so it is more logical to assume that gender roles should be seen as an interaction of biological and sociocultural factors.

Theory of psychosexual differentiation

- Gender role identity is related to genetic sex determined by chromosomes (XX for girls and XY for boys). During prenatal development, sex hormones are released. These prenatal hormones cause the external genitals of the foetus and the internal reproductive organs to become masculine or feminine. It's the *presence* or *absence* of male hormones (androgens) that makes a difference in psychosexual differentiation.

- Androgens (e.g. testosterone) in the male foetus stimulate the development of male sex characteristics and have a masculinizing effect on the brain of the developing boy.

- In this theory humans are born with innate predispositions to act and feel female or male due to the presence or absence of prenatal androgens. Socialization plays a subsidiary role.

The biosocial theory of gender role development

- **Money and Ehrhardt (1972)** claim that children are gender neutral at birth. Development of gender identity and adherence to gender role is primarily a consequence of socialization.

- The theory is based on case studies of individuals born with ambiguous genitals called **intersex** in medical literature. Money found children who had been born as females genetically but were raised as boys and thought of themselves as boys. Money theorized that humans are not born with a gender identity and therefore it is possible to reassign sex within the first two years of life.

- The theory is supported by animal research. Female rat foetuses injected with testosterone tend to behave like male rats as adults. They do not exhibit normal female sexual behaviour in adulthood even if they are injected with the female hormone oestrogen at that time.

- David Reimer was a twin boy who accidentally lost his penis under a routine circumcision, when he was 8 months. Dr. John Money suggested that the parents change the sex of the boy through surgery, hormone replacement and raise him as a girl. David Reimer was changed into a girl, Brenda.

- Money used the identical twin as a matched control and believed that this case would support the biosocial theory. In Money's scientific articles the sex change seemed to be a success but he failed to publish evidence that went against his theory. Brenda (David) was not happy and felt different from the other girls.

- At the age of 15 her parents revealed the truth. Brenda decided to become a male again and had reconstructive surgery to create a penis.

- **Evaluatio5** This case study seriously questions the biosocial theory that socialization can override biological make-up. In fact, it rather lends support to the theory of hormonal psychosexual differentiation.

Social learning theory

Bandura's (1977) theory assumes that gender roles are *learned* through the observation of same-sex models, direct tuition, and modelling.

1. **Direct tuition:** Acceptable gender behaviour is rewarded (social approval) by significant others (parents, peers) and gender inappropriate behaviour is discouraged (social disapproval).

2. **Modelling** of gender role behaviour by same-sex models: the child observes how others behave and then imitates (models) that behaviour.

Smith and Lloyd (1978): the **Baby X experiment** asked adults to interact with infants dressed in unisex snowsuits of either blue or pink. The snowsuits were randomly distributed and not always in line with the infants' true sex. The adults played with the infants according to what they believed was the gender of the child (colour of snowsuit). This indicates that a baby's perceived gender is part of the baby's social environment because people treat the child according to perceptions of gender. This could influence the child's own perception of gender and become a determining factor in the development of the child's gender role identity.

Sroufe et al. (1993) observed children around the ages of 10 and 11 and found that those who did not behave in a gender-stereotyped ways were the least popular. These studies indicate that children establish a kind of social control in relation to gender roles very early and it may well be that peer socialization is an important factor in gender role development.

Strengths of social learning theory	Limitations of social learning theory
■ It predicts that children acquire internal standards for behaviour through rewards and punishment, either by personal or vicarious experience. ■ A number of empirical studies support the notion of modelling.	■ It cannot explain why there seems to be considerable variation in the degree to which individual boys and girls conform to gender role stereotypes. ■ It suggests that gender is more or less passively acquired but research shows children are *active* participants in the socialization process.

Gender schema theory

- Gender schema theory is based on the assumption that cognitive processes play a key role in the development of gender identity and gender roles.

Gender schemas are generalized ideas about what is appropriate behaviour for males and females. People are categorized as either male or female and given specific gender attributes (gender stereotypes). Gender schemas thus organize knowledge and information processing.

- The most important factor in the development of gender role identity is children's ability to *label* themselves as boys or girls, i.e. the establishment of gender identity. Gender schemas guide subsequent information processing.
- Children are motivated to be like others in their group (conformity) and they tend to observe same-sex role models more carefully. Cultural beliefs about female and male gender roles are included in gender schemas and influence the way children think about themselves and their possibilities.

- **Martin and Halvorson (1978)** found that children actively construct gender identity based on their own experiences. The tendency to categorize on the basis of gender leads them to perceive boys and girls as different.
- According to Martin and Halvorson, children have a gender schema for their own sex (the ingroup) and for the opposite sex (the outgroup).
- Gender schemas determine what children pay attention to, whom they interact with, and what they remember. Gender schemas thus serve as an internal, self-regulating standard. This could be the reason that gender schemas may become a self-fulfilling prophecy or a stereotype threat.

Martin and Halvorson (1983) performed an experiment with boys and girls aged between five and six years. They saw pictures of males and females in activities that were either in line with gender role schemas (e.g. a girl playing with a doll) or inconsistent with gender role schemas (e.g. a girl playing with a gun). A week later, the children were asked to remember what they had seen on the pictures. The children had distorted memories of pictures that were not consistent with gender role schemas. They remembered the picture of a girl playing with a gun as a boy playing with a gun. This shows how information may be distorted to fit with existing schemas.

Fagot (1985) observed "gender policing" in children aged between 21 and 25 months. She found that boys made fun of other boys who played with dolls or who played with a girl. The girls did not like it when a girl played with a boy. This indicates that gender schemas had been established and that peers can reinforce gender schemas (gender stereotypes), which could then act as an internal self-regulating standard.

Strengths of gender schema theory	Limitations of gender schema theory
■ It can explain why children's gender roles do not change after middle childhood. The established gender schemas tend to be maintained because children pay attention to and remember information that is consistent with their gender schemas (confirmation bias). ■ The theory depicts the child as actively trying to make sense of the world using its present knowledge and gender schemas serve as an internal, self-regulating standard.	■ There is too much focus on individual cognitive processes in the development of gender roles. Social and cultural factors are not taken into account. ■ It is not really possible to explain how and why gender schemas develop and take the form they do.

Matsumoto (1994) defines culture as a set of attitudes, values, beliefs, and behaviours shared by a group of people and communicated from one generation to the next though cultural practices and language.

- If gender roles were based on *biology* alone it would be natural to assume that gender roles are universal and based on evolution. For example, women have traditionally done most of the household work and spent more time on childcare than men, but does this indicate that housework and child caring is based on women's biology?

- If gender roles were based on *culture* it would be natural to assume that gender roles vary across cultures according to a specific culture's beliefs and expectations with regard to men and women's roles (gender role ideology). In most cultures, women have had the major responsibility for taking care of the children and house work.

- **Eagly's (1987)** social role theory suggests that gender stereotypes arise from the different roles occupied by males and females. Women and men are seen as best suited for the roles they occupy respectively and this gives rise to beliefs about how women and men behave and feel respectively. Some of these stereotypes may become cognitive schemas, which are resistant to change (see more on stereotypes in unit 4.7).

- In modern societies, physical strength is no longer the only way to assure "bread winning". Women and men are more likely to have the same jobs and share the responsibility for the family.

Goffman (1977) predicted that gender roles will shift as societies shift from a belief that gender roles are based on biological differences to a belief in general social equality.

Support for this could be research on new male gender roles in Western cultures:

- **Reinicke (2006)** found that young fathers in Denmark find childcare important. Being a father is an important part of their identity and they want to be close to their children.

- **Engle and Breaux (1994)** found that, if fathers participated in programmes on parenting and child development, they became more involved with their children.

Sociocultural factors and gender roles
Societies that accept social inequality seem to accept not only class differences but also social differences between men and women. In societies where males control resources and dominate the political system, women are more likely to conform to the stereotypical gender role.

Gender equality may be the road to change in traditional stereotyped gender roles. The women's movement for social equality started in individualistic societies and ideas of social equality of men and women have been adopted in most individualist societies.

Mead (1935) compared gender roles in three New Guinean tribes.

She argued that masculine and feminine roles are not related to biology but gender role ideology. Cultural differences in gender roles are more likely to reflect cultural expectations than biology.

Arapesh tribe	Mundugumor tribe	Tchambuli tribe
■ Both men and women were cooperative, gentle, and loving (a traditional stereotype of female traits). ■ Men and women cooperated in tasks relating to crops and children.	■ Both men and women were arrogant, competitive, and emotionally unresponsive (a traditional stereotype of male traits). They were constantly quarrelling. ■ Neither men nor women were interested in children. The children quickly became independent and this trait was highly valued in the tribe.	■ Men were interested in body adornments and spent their time gossiping with other men (a traditional female stereotype). ■ Women were responsible for food production, tool making, and producing clothes.

6.9 Describe adolescence

- Adolescence is historically a new concept and it may be culturally specific to some extent. In the Western world, adolescence is defined as the period of development between puberty (the time where individuals become capable of sexual reproduction) and adulthood.

- The concept of adolescence is controversial because:
  1. not everyone agrees that it is a unique life period across all cultures
  2. there are enormous individual and cultural differences in the adolescent experience
  3. most research on adolescence has been conducted in the West.

- **Schlegel and Berry (1991)** argue that even if there is no specific word for adolescence, almost all cultures have a notion of what it is. In some non-industrialized cultures, the beginning of adolescence is marked by **initiation ceremonies** or rites of passage, which are major public events.

- Themes of initiation ceremonies may be related to adult responsibilities (e.g. productivity or fertility) in the various societies. In industrialized societies, there are no formal transition ceremonies and this leaves adolescence with no clear beginning or end.

- **Hall (1904)** described adolescence as a period of "storm and stress". While it is true that some adolescents in the West may experience some problems during adolescence, it is not the norm.

6.10 Discuss the relationship between physical change and development of identity during adolescence

Physical changes in adolescence

Physical maturation and adult reproductive functioning are controlled by the endocrine system that operates through the hypothalamus-pituitary-gonadal system. During the prenatal period, hormones called androgens organize the reproductive system but these hormones are suppressed after birth. They are reactivated in early childhood (around the age of eight for girls and six for boys) and this starts the puberty process with gradual maturation of the body and the reproductive system. All individuals experience the same bodily changes during puberty but the sequence of changes may vary.

- Until puberty, boys and girls produce roughly the same amount of "male hormones" (e.g. testosterone) and "female hormones" (e.g. estrogens). At the start of puberty, the pituitary gland causes an upsurge of sex hormones so that girls now produce more estrogen and boys more testosterone.

- The physical "growth spurt" is characterized by an increase in the distribution of body fat and muscle tissue. The body grows taller and heavier and gradually becomes more adult-like. The adolescent has to become familiar with this new body and integrate a revised body image.

- Girls experience physical changes two to three years before boys (between the ages of 10 and 13). The most important changes are the development of breasts and a widening of the hips. The gain in body fat and rapid weight gain may be seen as a problem for some girls because it clashes with the Western ideal of a slim female figure.

- Boys experience the growth spurt as a broadening of the shoulders and an increase in muscle strength. Having a masculine body is welcomed because it brings boys closer to their body ideal. Boys whose bodies do not appear masculine may experience identity problems.

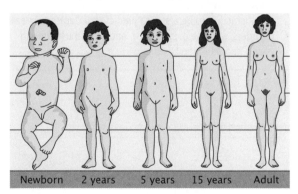

| Newborn | 2 years | 5 years | 15 years | Adult |

Relationship between physical change and development of identity

Sexual identity

- The physical changes of the adolescent body are related to changes in identity including an emerging sexuality. This includes learning to handle sexual desires and sexual attitudes and values, and integrating all this with feelings and experiences into a new self-image.

- Social and cultural norms determine the extent to which adolescents can explore their sexuality. In some cultures, adolescent sexual activity is seen as inappropriate whereas in others it is seen as normal and healthy.

- The entry into sexual maturity may increase girls' concerns about sexual attractiveness as well as awareness that they may become the targets of sexual violence.

Body image and identity

- **The cultural ideal hypothesis** by **Simmons and Blyth (1987)** suggests that puberty brings boys closer to their ideal body while girls move further away from theirs. A cultural ideal is that a male body should be big and strong. The ideal female body in Western culture is a slim body.

- The cultural ideal hypothesis predicts that, since the cultural ideal for the female body is being slim, adolescent girls should be more likely to express body dissatisfaction and resort to dieting than boys. This is supported by research.

- **Caufmann and Steinberg (1996)** found that girls in Western cultures are more concerned about their appearance and express more worry about how other people will respond to them than in other cultures. Teenage girls want to be seen as attractive. If their body is far from the dominant cultural ideal of slimness, they may develop a negative body image and low self-esteem.

- **The objectification theory** suggested by **Fredrickson and Roberts (1997)** holds that Western girls are socialized to constantly think of whether their bodies and physical appearances are pleasing to others. A chronic state of anxiety may be generated by their concerns about maintaining a satisfactory appearance.

- **Stice and Withenton (2002)** found body image dissatisfaction to be a strong predictor of depression, eating disorders, exercise dependence, and steroid use among young people in the USA.

Ferron (1997)

Aim To investigate possible cultural differences in the way adolescents relate to bodily changes in puberty.

Procedure This was a small-scale survey using semi-structured interviews to collect data in a cross-cultural sample consisting of 60 American and 60 French adolescents. Boys and girls were equally represented. One of the themes in the interview was how the bodily changes during puberty affected body image and how they coped with it.

Results

- Seventy-five per cent of the American adolescents did not accept any biological predisposition in terms of body shape. They believed it was possible to obtain a perfect body if one tried hard enough and adhered to specific rules. Eighty per cent of the Americans believed in the effectiveness of specific diets or exercise programmes.

- The Americans were also more likely to suffer from self-blame and guilt and adopt unhealthy weight regulating strategies such as unbalanced diets or continuous physical exercise.

- Seventy-five per cent of the American girls believed that their personal worth depended on looks and would do nearly anything to get close to an ideal body image.

- Less than half of the French adolescents believed they could obtain a perfect body. They had perceptions of ideal body image but 75% of them believed that physical appearance is genetically determined and could not possibly be extensively modified through willpower or particular behaviour. The only thing they considered blameworthy was physical carelessness.

Evaluation The study was conducted in the West but it shows interesting differences between two Western countries. The results may not be generalized to non-Western countries. It was a small-scale survey using self-reported data, which can be somewhat unreliable.

6.11

The theory of psychosocial development (Erikson, 1968)

The theory is partly based on psychoanalysis but it departs from Freud's heavy emphasis on sexuality. According to the psychosocial theory of development the individual develops through a series of stages from birth to death.

- The fifth stage concerns adolescence: **identity versus role confusion.** This stage of **identity crisis** is marked by the rapid physical growth and hormonal changes which take place between the ages of 12 and 18.

- The bodily changes may be confusing and the adolescent has to search for a *new* sense of continuity and sameness. Questions of sexuality, future occupation, and identity are explored. This is called a **moratorium**, i.e. a time to experience different possibilities.

- If the identity crisis is solved successfully, the adolescent will feel confident about his or her own identity and future. The danger of this stage is *role confusion*, i.e. uncertainty about one's identity and future role.

- If the identity crisis is not solved successfully, the adolescent may join a subgroup and develop a negative or socially unacceptable identity. According to Erikson, a negative identity may be preferable to no identity at all.

- Adolescents must establish an adult personality and develop commitment to work and role (for example as partner and parent) in life to prepare for the next stage, **intimacy versus isolation**, where the goal is to commit oneself to another person.

Key concepts in the psychosocial theory are ide versus role confusion, identity crisis, and psycho moratorium.

Support for the theory's concept of deve crisis in adolescence

Espin et al. (1990) conducted a longitudinal tested Erikson's ideas. The researchers perform analysis of 71 letters from a Latin-American gi over a period of nine years, between the ages was a very traumatic period in her life because parents were arrested for political reasons. The analysed the letters and found changes of ther in relation to age. Themes of identity appeared letters, and increased from the ages of 13 to 18 declined. This confirms that issues of identity w this period, as predicted by Erikson. Themes of 'intimacy' which

appear in early adult life, according to Erikson's theory, increased steadily through the next period but became predominant after the age of 19. It was a single case study so the results cannot be generalized.

Challenge to the theory's concept of identity crisis in adolescence: Rutter et al. (1976)

Aim To investigate the concept of developmental crisis in a representative sample of adolescents.

Procedure All adolescents on the Isle of Wight aged between 14 and 15 (cohort) participated in the study (N=2,303). Data were collected with questionnaires and interviews from parents, teachers, and the adolescents.

Results Only a minority of the adolescents showed signs of crisis or conflict with parents and this was mostly related to psychiatric problems. This is not in line with predictions of the theory of psychosocial development. Only one fifth of the adolescents reported feeling miserable or depressed.

Evaluation The fact that it was a cohort study, i.e. all adolescents born on the island in the same years, increases the validity of the results. The combination of interview and questionnaires with adolescents as well as parents and teachers gave credibility to the results because the data could be corroborated. There may be problems with the reliability of the self-reported data.

Evaluation of the theory of psychosocial development

- Identity formation is perhaps not a project undertaken during adolescence alone. **O'Connel (1976)** performed retrospective interviews with a sample of married women with children in school. The women reported changes in identity after ... g parent, etc. This ... be a life-long project t life.

... ultures young people ... ood. **Condon (1987)** ... the Inuit of the ... th century. At ... arried and had ... re treated as adults ... ge animals on their ... families. The ... ung people had to ... ible. The Inuits did ... y.

... on the assumption ... l, and characterized ... stage. Today stage ... lopment are questioned.

[handwritten notes:] →Discuss the relationship between physical change and development of identity. (Thrs)

→ 2 x Psychological theories of adolescence (Ytctr) (22)

Describe stressors

- Stress can be defined as a negative emotional experience accompanied by various physiological, cognitive, and behavioural reactions. Stress is thought to be one of the principal causes of psychological distress and physical illness.

- Stressors are described as **acute** (i.e. sudden) or **chronic** (i.e. persisting over a longer period of time). Stressors may or may not cause stress in an individual depending on the person's capacity to cope with the stressors.

- A stressor is any adverse experience (physiological, psychological or social) that causes a stress response. The stressor must be perceived as stressful by an individual to activate the stress response. There are individual variations as to what is perceived as stressful and research shows that humans can *imagine* stressors and experience the same physiological arousal as from external environmental stressors **(Sapolsky, 1998)**.

Acute stressors
Examples are:
- being diagnosed as seriously ill, being involved in an accident or being injured
- life events such as the death of a loved one, divorce, being fired, or not getting admitted to a university.

Chronic stressors
Examples are:
- social stressors such as poverty, illness, or being responsible for many young children
- unemployment, being bullied at work, or work place stressors
- violent relationships.

Life events as stressors
Holmes and Rahe (1967) observed that major life changes often preceded illness. These events could be both positive and negative but they were perceived as stressful because the change required that the person should adapt to a new situation. The list of life events presented by Holmes and Rahe may not apply to all or in that order. If an individual perceives one of these life events (or another which is not on the list) as serious and threatening to their well-being, it is a stressor.

SOCIAL READJUSMENT RATING SCALE

LIFE EVENT	LIFE-CHANGE UNIT
Death of one's spouse	100
Divorce	73
Marital separation	65
Jail term	63
Death of close family member	63
Personal injury or illness	53
Marriage	50
Being fired	47
Retirement	45
Pregnancy	40
Change in one's financial state	38
More arguments with one's spouse	35
Change in responsibilities at work	29
Son or daughter leaving home	29
Trouble with in-laws	29
Beginning or ending school	26
Change in living conditions	25
Trouble with one's boss	23
Change in work hours or conditions	20
Change in eating habits	15
Vacation	13
Christmas	12

Workplace stressors (UK National Work Stress Network)
Examples are:
- monotonous, unpleasant or meaningless tasks
- working under time pressure or working long hours
- lack of clear job description
- no recognition or reward for good job performance
- heavy responsibility but lack of control or influence over the demands of the job
- harassment or bullying
- new management techniques or new technology
- poor leadership and poor communication.

Social stressors
- Social stressors (e.g. chronic poverty, discrimination, trying to manage both family and job commitments, unemployment, living in a violent environment or relationship) could lead to a number of physical and mental health problems.
- Exposure to stressful conditions has been associated with smoking, alcohol, or other substance abuse and dependence. There is also increasing evidence that stress could be linked to overeating and obesity.

Physiological aspects of stress

Cannon (1914) The fight or flight theory

- The fight or flight response is a physiological stress response evolved to help organisms (i.e. animals and humans) to survive immediate danger. **(Cannon, 1914).**

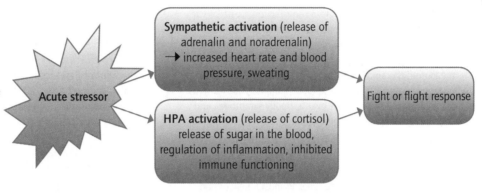

- The theory proposes that when an organism faces an imminent danger (acute stressor), the body is rapidly aroused and motivated to act via two systems: the sympathetic nervous system and the endocrine system. These two physiological systems interact to mobilize the organism to fight against or flee the danger.

- The fight or flight theory is only addressing the physiological aspects of stress. This could be because Cannon only studied animals. The exclusive focus on physiological aspects of stress is a limitation in relation to humans. It is now known that cognitive factors can mediate the stress response **(Lazarus and Folkman, 1988)**.

- On the one hand, the fight or flight response is adaptive because it enables the organism to respond quickly to an acute stressor. On the other hand, the response may be harmful if stress persists (chronic stress) because long-term stress may result in physiological as well as psychological health problems.

Selye (1956) GAS (General Adaptation Syndrome).

- The theory is based on animal research (rats) and it extends Cannon's theory. Selye did experiments where he exposed rats to various stressors (e.g. cold, surgical injury, excessive exercise).

- The animals all showed the same *general* physiological responses such as enlarged adrenal glands, diminished thymus (important organ in the immune system) and ulcers when they were exposed to stressors. Some of them died.

- Selye concluded that rats (and humans) would respond with the same physiological pattern of physiological changes no matter the stressor. With prolonged exposure to stress (chronic stress), the physiological system will be damaged and the organism may eventually die. It may be problematic to generalize such results to humans but research in health psychology has confirmed a link between stress and low immune functioning (e.g. **Kiecolt-Glaser et al. 1984**).

The three stages of stress

- **Alarm:** Physiological mobilization to respond to the danger. It is the same as the fight or flight response.
- **Resistance**: Attempts to cope with the stress response.
- **Exhaustion**: Occurs when the organism fails to overcome the danger and is incapable of further coping.

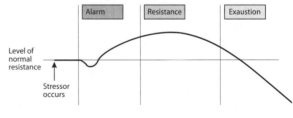

The general adaptation syndrome

Strengths of the GAS model	Limitations of the GAS model
<ul><li>The GAS model has generated a lot of research and it remains an important theory in the field.</li><li>It provides an explanation of the *interaction* of environmental stressors and physiological responses.</li><li>Research confirms Selye's suggestions of a link between exhaustion and physical illness (e.g. that chronic stress can affect immune functioning and cause shrinking of the hippocampus).</li></ul>	<ul><li>There is no reference to individual differences, social or cognitive factors in the model.</li><li>**Taylor et al. (2000)** argue that in addition to fight or flight, humans (especially females) respond to stress with social affiliation and nurturant behaviour.</li><li>The model cannot explain that humans can experience stress by merely *thinking* of stressful events (**Sapolsky, 1998**).</li></ul>

Kiecolt-Glaser et al. (1984) Stress and immune functioning
- The aim of this natural experiment was to investigate if the stress of an important exam had an effect on the body's immune functioning.
- A sample of 75 volunteer medical students participated. Blood tests were taken twice: one month before and on the first day of the final exam. Immune functioning was assessed by measuring the amount of the natural killer cells in the immune system (T cells) in the blood samples. The students also completed scales of life events, bodily symptoms, and satisfaction with interpersonal contacts.
- The results showed a significant decrease in the amount of T-cells in the second blood test. The high stress in relation to the exam had diminished the effectiveness of the immune system. Students who reported feeling most lonely or had experienced other stressful life experiences had the lowest T-cell counts.
- It is not possible to establish a cause-effect relationship in a natural experiment. The study was longitudinal and conducted in a natural environment so it has high ecological validity.

Taylor et al. (2000) Gender differences in stress responses: Tend and befriend theory
- The theory suggests that evolution has presented women with different adaptive challenges than men who were responsible for hunting and protection. The theory proposes that women are biologically prepared to react with affiliation and nurturant behaviour toward offspring in times of stress.
- The fight or flight response to stress depends on underlying biological mechanisms. The tend and befriend response to stress could also involve underlying biological mechanisms such as oxytocin. Research shows that high levels of oxytocin are associated with calmer and more relaxed behaviour in animals and humans, which could contribute to nurturant and social behaviour according to Taylor.
- The theory is supported by evidence that women are consistently more likely than men to respond to stress by turning to others (**Tamres et al. 2002**). The theory includes social aspects of the stress process and focuses on humans as affiliative creatures.

Psychological aspects of stress
- Humans respond to stressors in different ways and cognitive appraisal seems to be an important determinant of whether an event is *perceived* as stressful or not. If an event is not perceived as stressful, it is not likely that there is a physiological stress response.

Lazarus and Folkman (1984) The transactional model of stress and coping cognitive appraisal model
The model is based on the assumption that stress involves a *transaction* (i.e. a two-way process) between an individual and the external world. In the face of potential stressors, the individual engages in a process of primary and secondary appraisal.
- **Primary appraisal**: the event is perceived to be either neutral, positive, or negative in its consequences.
- **Secondary appraisal:** this is assessment of one's coping abilities and resources. Various coping strategies are considered before choosing a way to deal effectively with the stressor.

The *interaction* between psychological and physiological factors is illustrated in stress processes. The cognitive appraisal of a stressor influences the extent of the physiological response.

- **Lazarus (1975)** claimed that **cognitive appraisal** is an important part of stress reactions and that stress experiences are not only physiological as claimed by traditional theories. People are psychological beings who are not simply passively responding to the world but actively interpret and evaluate what is happening to them.

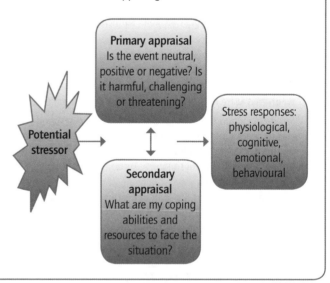

Speisman al (1964) Experiment on the role of appraisal in stress experience

- The aim of the experiment was to investigate if it was possible to manipulate the participants' emotional reaction to an unpleasant film on genital mutilation (stressor).
- The participants (college students) all watched a film about a tribal initiation ceremony that involved genital mutilation. The researchers manipulated the participants' cognitive appraisal by showing the film with different sound tracks:
  - *the trauma condition* (sound track emphasized the pain and the mutilation)
  - *the denial condition* (sound track emphasized the participants as willing and happy)
  - *the intellectualization condition* (sound track gave an anthropological interpretation of the ceremony).
- The researchers took various measures of arousal or stress (e.g. heart rate, galvanic skin response) during the viewing of the film. The participants also answered questions on their responses (self-reports).
- The results showed that participants in the denial and intellectualization conditions experienced considerably less stress than participants in the trauma condition. The manipulation of cognitions had a significant impact on the physiological stress responses.
- The results suggest that stress was not intrinsic to the unpleasant film but rather dependent on the participants' appraisal of it. This seems to support Lazarus' theory. It is not the events themselves that elicit emotional stress, but rather the individual's interpretation or appraisal of those events.
- The experiment was conducted in a laboratory with high control of variables. This can establish a cause-effect relationship between appraisal and stress reaction but there may be issues of artificiality. The study was to some extent unethical because it used deception and put participants in unpleasant situations.

Social aspects of stress

- Social factors such as lack of education, a low standard of housing, noise and crowding, homelessness, lack of social support, domestic violence, and economic hardship put individuals under greater stress, contributing to poor health and family problems.

Evans and Kim (2007) Effects of long-term exposure to poverty in childhood

- The aim of the study was to investigate the long-term relationship between poverty or low socioeconomic status, cumulative risk factors and physiological stress.
- Participants were 200 seven-year-olds. The researchers measured blood pressure and cortisol levels. Stress regulation was assessed by measurement of the heart's reactivity to a standard acute stressor, and recovery after exposure to the stressor. Exposure to risk factors such as substandard housing, and family violence were included to have a measure of cumulative stress factors.
- The results showed that there was a positive correlation between long-term exposure to a social risk factors on physiological measures of stress. A greater number of years spent living in poverty correlated with more elevated cortisol levels and more problems for the heart to recover after exposure to the stressor.
- The conclusion was that there is a negative effect on the stress regulation system in children from poor backgrounds and that this effect can be explained by the cumulative risk factors associated with chronic poverty in childhood. Socioeconomically deprived children are exposed to a number of social stressors that disadvantage their development and health. For example, they experience more family violence, separation from their families, and chaotic households.
- The accumulation of risk factors and the lack of protective factors associated with poverty seem to have long-term effects on both physical and mental health.

Folkman and Lazarus (1988) Two ways of coping

Problem-focused coping

- This is an attempt to remove or correct a problematic situation (e.g. as quitting an abusive relationship, drafting a revision plan, or taking extra courses to qualify for a new job).

- A special form of problem-focused coping is called pro-active coping that is used to avoid a future problem (such as studying hard for an exam to avoid the stress of failing).

Emotion-focused coping

- This is an attempt to manage the emotional aspects of stress (e.g. example, changing the way one thinks about a problem or learning to accept it, using relaxation techniques, seeking social support, or using drugs to alleviate tension).

- A special form of emotion-focused coping is *avoidance coping* (for example, denying the problem or drinking alcohol to forget the problem. Avoidance coping could be effective in the short-term. Some coping strategies may be problematic, for example, if people become dependent on alcohol.

Problem-focused coping may be the most adaptive in situations perceived as controllable. Emotion-focused coping may be the most adaptive in situations that are perceived as uncontrollable.

People's appraisal of their situation and own resources to cope with the challenge are important
Conway and Terry, (1992)

Gender differences in coping strategies: Taylor (2002) Tend and befriend theory of coping

- The physiological stress reactions (fight or flight and GAS) are the body's instinctual coping mechanisms to deal with imminent threat. These reactions are adequate in dangerous situations but there may be gender differences in managing stress.

- The tend and befriend theory suggests that evolution has provided males and females with different challenges.

- Males tend to exhibit the fight or flight response, which is triggered by adrenaline.

- Females tend to exhibit the tend and befriend response, which is triggered by the hormone oxytocin. "Tend" refers to nurturing activities and "befriend" refers to seeking social support.

- The theory was formulated on the basis of a meta-analysis on research on stress and coping. The study found that women tend to use social support more than men as coping strategy. Women also provide more social support to others, and draw on socially supportive networks more consistently in times of stress.

Thoits (1995) found that women were more involved than men in both giving and receiving social support. It seems that across the lifespan women are generally more likely to mobilize social support – especially from other women – in times of stress.

Social support as coping strategy

- Seeking social support is a coping strategy related to emotion-focused coping. Social support can act as a buffer against the physiological and psychological effects of stress but it can also protect against potential stress on a daily basis without apparent stressors. Social support can be defined as the experience of being part of a social network with access to mutual assistance and obligations.

- Social support can come from a partner, relatives, friends, or various social support groups. Social support from others indicates that you "belong" and this is an important factor in the face of stress. Social support from pets also seems to have a beneficial effect against stress. The perception or belief that emotional support is available appears to be a much stronger influence on mental health than the actual receipts of social support (**Wethering and Kessler, 1986**).

Social support may manifest as:

- **Emotional support**: verbal or non-verbal communication of caring and concern. It could include listening, empathizing, and comforting.

- **Informational support**: information to guide and advice to help a person to understand and cope better with a stressful situation.

- **Practical support**: tangible assistance such as transportation, assistance with household chores or financial assistance.

Neuling and Winefield (1988) Longitudinal study of the role of social support in a group of female cancer patients

- The researchers performed a longitudinal study with 58 women recovering from surgery for breast cancer. Each woman was interviewed three times within three months. Participants also rated the frequency of social support (emotional, informational, practical) from family, friends, and doctors.

- The results showed that the patients needed a large amount of emotional support from family and that this was also the most frequent kind of support they received. The patients also expressed a wish for more informational support from doctors.
- Participants reported that social support helped them. This perception could be beneficial in adjustment to cancer. Since the data were descriptive it is not possible to conclude that social support was a more effective strategy than other strategies. This can only be concluded with randomized controlled studies.

Allen et al. (1999) Pets as social support

- The researchers investigated whether owning a pet could reduce stress in a sample of 48 participants (New York City stockbrokers) who suffered from mental stress. They were living alone and had all been treated with drugs against high blood pressure (hypertension) – a consequence of stress. There was an equal distribution of men and women and they all had to be willing to acquire a pet as part of the experiment.
- Half of the participants were randomly allocated to a condition, where a cat or dog was added to their treatment. Blood pressure and heart rate were measured before the drug therapy began and six months later.

- Results showed that in tests where participants were stressed, the pet owners remained significantly more stable than the participants who did not own a pet. According to the researchers, a loving pet can have a calming influence on stress symptoms such as blood pressure and heart rate. This is particularly the case for individuals who have a limited social network.

Evaluation of social support as a coping strategy

- Social support comes primarily from other human beings (disclosure and actively seeking help) but it seems that pets could have a beneficial effect.
- Seeking social support may be particularly common among women in times of stress.
- In some cultures, it may not be the norm to seek and use advice and emotional support (explicit social support). **Taylor et al. (2007)** found that Asians and Asian Americans were less willing to seek explicit social support for dealing with stressful events and benefited less from social support. It seems that Asians and Asian Americans are more concerned about the negative relational implications of seeking social support than European Americans are.

Mindfulness-based stress reduction (MBSR) as coping strategy

- MBSR is a group-based stress reduction programme based on Buddhist principles of meditation developed by **Kabat-Zinn (1979)**. The focus in MBSR is on awareness of the present moment, relaxation of the body, meditation and daily practice to learn the technique.
- MBSR has been used to address adjustment to the stress of chronic illness, pain, anxiety and depression.

- MBSR can be seen as an *emotion-focused coping strategy* in that it deals with the physical and emotional aspects of stress. It can also be seen as a *problem-focused coping strategy* in that an individual learns new skills to prevent the harmful effects of stress in the future.
- MBSR teaches awareness of the moment to avoid automatic negative thinking. The use of gradual relaxation is an attempt to deal with the physiological and psychological aspects of stress.

Shapiro et al. (1998) MBSR and coping with exam stress

- The aim of the study was to investigate effectiveness of MBSR as a coping strategy to control exam stress.
- The study used a controlled experimental design. Some premedical students at the University of Arizona were offered an introductory course of MBSR for course credits.
- The participants were randomly assigned to the MBSR course (37) or to a waiting list (36). An equal number of men and women were in the sample. Participants in the MBSR group and the waiting list group filled out a questionnaire assessing stress at the start of the term (before the course) and during the exams at the end of the term (after the course). They also completed a questionnaire on empathy.
- The results showed no difference in stress between the two groups at the beginning of the term. There was a difference

at the time of the exams. Students on the waiting list expressed more perceived stress compared to those who had participated in the MBSR class. The MBSR students were in fact less anxious than at the start.

- The results suggest that the course had taught them to cope effectively with the stress of the exams.
- MBSR seems to be an effective means of coping with stress but people must be willing to learn MBSR and it may not suit everybody.
- The participants were students and participated for course credits. This means that the findings cannot be generalized. The results have been replicated in another controlled study with 130 medical students. This indicates that MBSR is effective in stress reduction.

Grossman et al. (2003) Meta-analysis of MBSR and health benefits.

The study is a review of 20 controlled studies and observations of clinical individuals and stressed non-clinical individuals. All the studies included standardized measures of physical and mental well-being.

The results suggest that MBSR could be helpful to a broad range of individuals to cope with their clinical and non-clinical problems. The sample in this meta-analysis was small but overall there was a positive effect in all the studies.

Evaluation of MBSR as a coping strategy
Group-based psychosocial interventions such as MBSR that facilitates adaptation and adjustment to stress are both cost-effective and time-efficient. The method is gaining increasing popularity and a number of clinical trials have been conducted at this point.

Clinical trials in relation to cancer patients indicate that MBSR is a promising approach but more research is needed.

7.4 Explain factors related to the development of substance abuse or addictive behaviour

- **Substance abuse** refers to the continued use of the substance despite knowing problems associated with the substance such as persistent desire to use it and/or unsuccessful efforts to control substance use. Smoking could be an example of substance abuse when smokers want to quit but find they are unable to.

- **Substance dependence** This is demonstrated in *craving* (i.e. a strong desire to get the substance or engage in a behaviour) and in *withdrawal symptoms* (i.e. the unpleasant physiological and psychological symptoms when people don't get the substance on which they are dependent).

- **Addiction** (or addictive behaviour) occurs when people become physically or biologically dependent on a substance because of repeated use over time.

Smoking

Biological factors

- The psychoactive drug in tobacco is **nicotine**. Nicotine alters levels of neurotransmitters (e.g. acetylcholine, dopamine, adrenaline, vasopressin). Secretion of adrenaline results in temporarily increased heart rate and blood pressure. Secretion of dopamine is involved in the alteration of mood. Secretion of acetylcholine appears to enhance memory. Nicotine is also associated with relaxation and changes in mood.

- Nicotine is a highly **addictive substance**. A habitual smoker will experience withdrawal symptoms if the level of nicotine is not constant in the body. This could explain why up to 80% of smokers in the USA who would like to quit are not able to do it (**Benowitz, 2009**).

- **Marks et al. (2005)** report that although teenagers' initial reaction to tobacco smoke is generally negative, they quickly develop a taste for it. Young smokers report that smoking has a *calming effect* and that they experience *craving* if they cannot smoke. This is confirmed in measurement of nicotine levels in the saliva. Within a couple of years, teenagers report that they find it difficult to stop.

- **Heath and Madden (1995)** reviewed the evidence from national twin studies in Scandinavia and Australia. They found that genetic factors increased both the likelihood of becoming a regular smoker ("initiation") and of these smokers becoming longterm smokers ("persistence").

DiFranza et al. (2006) Research on adolescents' smoking history and addiction

- The aim of the study was to investigate the relationship between attitudes to smoking and smoking habits.
- The design was longitudinal and used questionnaires and interviews for data collection. In Massachusetts 217 adolescents (mean age 12) answered questionnaires on their smoking history, social environment (e.g. family and peers) as well as beliefs and attitudes towards smoking. All participants reported having smoked a cigarette at least once.
- Eleven of the participants were interviewed. Tobacco dependence was assessed based on reported cravings, and inability to quit.

- The results showed that of those adolescents who recalled a relaxation effect after their first inhale, 67% became dependent compared to 29% of those who did not experience such an effect.
- Feelings of relaxation after inhalation were the main risk factor for addiction. Of the participants who the experienced relaxation effect, 91% reported that it was not possible for them to quit smoking even though they wanted to and 60% said they felt they had lost control.
- The conclusion was that for some people addiction to smoking seems to start almost after the first puff but it is unknown why some are more vulnerable to nicotine addiction than others. It could be genetic but smoking is a complex behaviour where both genes and environmental factors interact.

Sociocultural factors

According to social learning theory (SLT) smoking is learned through modelling (see unit 4.6 for more on SLT). This could apply to the role of parents and peers in the initiation of smoking.

Parents play a significant role (modelling and attitudes to smoking).

- **Bauman et al. (1990)** found that 80% of a sample of American adolescents aged 12–14 whose parents did not smoke had never tried to smoke themselves. If the parents smoked, half of the children had tried smoking. **Murray et al. (1984)** found that in families where the parents were strongly against smoking, the children were up to seven times less likely to smoke.
- **Powel and Chaloupka (2003)** investigated the impact of parental influences on the probability of youth smoking both in terms of modelling and the parents' attitudes to smoking. The results showed that parental influences play a significant role in youth smoking decisions, especially for adolescent girls.

Peer pressure

- According to the UN Department of Health and Human Services (2001) peer smoking appear to be the most important factor in smoking initiation. More than 70% of all cigarettes smoked by adolescents are smoked in the presence of a peer according to **Biglan et al. (1984)**.

Unger et al. (2001) Cross-cultural survey on adolescent smoking

- The aim of the study was to investigate smoking habits in relation to peers and cultural background.
- The sample consisted of adolescents from California (N=5,143, mean age 13).
- The results showed that white students with close friends who smoked were much more likely to smoke than non-white students (e.g. Asian American and Hispanic students).
- The researchers explained that in individualistic cultures, adolescents typically create their own youth culture characterized by rebellion in order to set themselves apart from their parents. In collectivistic cultures, the bond between the teen and the parents is considered important. Rebellion is not tolerated so adolescents are more likely to conform to the roles and norms that parents prescribe for them.

Role of advertising and marketing

- Consumer research shows that tobacco advertising has a powerful effect on smoking attitudes and behaviour of young people. The use of imagery and positive association in combination with brand consciousness in young people influences the young to smoke the most popular and well advertised product.

- Advertising functions as a "cue" to smoking (e.g. associating pleasure and fun with smoking may activate craving in smokers but it could also motivate young people to start smoking).
- Tobacco sponsorships promote brand association and makes it easier to start smoking. **Charlton et al. (1997)** found that boys who showed a preference for Formula One motor racing that was sponsored by cigarette manufacturers were more likely to start smoking.

Prevention strategies

Tobacco use is a leading cause of death according to The World Health Organization (WHO). Smoking kills about six million smokers per year worldwide. The health costs of smoking-related diseases are rising. The WHO and governments adopt various prevention strategies to prevent young people from starting to smoke or to help people quit smoking.

The WHO's Mpower strategy.

Monitor tobacco use and prevention policies (e.g. help to build strategies)

Protect people from tobacco smoke (e.g. smoke-free areas and smoke-free legislation)

Offer help to quit tobacco (e.g. counselling and national quit services)

Warn about the dangers of tobacco use (e.g. information and pictures on billboards)

Enforce bans on tobacco advertising, promotion and sponsorships

Raise taxes on tobacco

WHO's No Tobacco Day every year targets various aspects of primary prevention (e.g. children and adolescent smoking prevention (2008) or tobacco control (2011).

Primary and secondary prevention strategies

- **Primary prevention**: Strategies to prevent people from starting smoking (e.g. bans on smoking in public places, bans on tobacco marketing, and health promotion in the form of education about the dangers of smoking and anti-smoking campaigns.

- **Secondary prevention**: Interventions to help people stop smoking (cessation), such as nicotine replacement and therapy (i.e. treatment).

Hanewinkel and Wiborg (2002) Primary prevention campaign of smoking in Germany targeting adolescents: 'Be smart–Don't Start'.

- The aim of the study was to investigate the effectiveness of a school-based campaign in Germany with regard to primary and secondary prevention.

- The sample consisted of 131 classes with 2,142 pupils (mean age 12.9 years). Smoking status was assessed twice, once before a competition started and again six months after the end of the competition. The classes decided whether they wanted to be "a smoke-free class" for six months or not. The control group consisted of classes who did not enter the competition. The classes in which pupils did not smoke during the six months eventually participated in a prize draw with many attractive prizes. There were no differences in prevalence of smoking at baseline between the control (18.5 % smokers) and the experimental group (15.2% smokers).

- The results showed that pupils in the control condition showed significantly higher prevalence of smoking (32.9% smokers) compared to pupils in the experimental condition (25.5% smokers). More pupils stayed smoke-free in the experimental group than in the control group.

- The researchers concluded that participation in the competition could delay the onset of smoking in some adolescents (primary prevention) but the competition was not effective in smoking cessation (secondary prevention). This supports previous findings that it is very important to prevent young people from starting to smoke.

Effectiveness of primary prevention

- **Lemstra et al. (2008)** and **Gorini (2007)** found that a ban on smoking in public places in Italy and Canada decreased the prevalence of smoking (i.e. decreased number of people who smoke).

Ban on smoking reduces prevalence

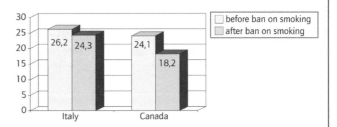

- **Willemsen and Zwart (2002)** found that the most effective strategies to prevent smoking among adolescents were a combination of a complete ban on tobacco advertising, increased prices, restricting tobacco product sales to specific shops, mass media education aimed at youth and intensified school-based education.

See units 7.8 and 7.9 on effectiveness of health promotion strategies in relation to smoking.

Treatments

Treatment for nicotine addiction is part of secondary prevention and typically based on nicotine replacement or drug therapy in combination with advice from health professionals.

Nicotine replacement therapy (NRT)

- Products such as nicotine chewing gum, patches, and nasal sprays contain low levels of nicotine and are used to relieve withdrawal symptoms and control cravings. Electronic cigarettes are a new form of NRT where people inhale nicotine in the vapour that comes from a device looking like a cigarette.
- NRT products do not produce the pleasurable effects of tobacco products and should in principle be less addictive.
- Nicotine gum is now one of the most used treatments but some smokers are unable to tolerate the taste and chewing demands.
- **Hughes (1993)** found that NRT is generally quite effective in smoking cessation but the problem is that some people become dependent on nicotine gum.

Bullen et al. (2010) Experimental research on electronic cigarettes on withdrawal

Aim investigate short-term effectiveness of electronic cigarettes on desire to smoke and withdrawal symptoms compared to inhalators.

Procedure The design was a single blind controlled randomized experiment. Participants were 40 smokers who smoke more than 10 cigarettes a day but had not smoked overnight. They were given either cigarettes, a nicotine inhaler or electronic cigarettes (either with 0 or 16 mg nicotine).

Results The electronic cigarette produced the same significant decline in the desire to smoke as the nicotine inhaler and had fewer side effects. Even the 0 mg cigarette suppressed the desire to smoke. This is interesting because it shows that simulation of smoking behaviour was enough to reduce craving.

Drug treatment

Zyban is a drug which is supposed to help people quit smoking. It should relieve withdrawal symptoms and block the effects of nicotine if people resume smoking.

Pisinger (2008) reviewed research on the effect of interventions at the individual level.

The study concludes that the most efficient methods are those that include consultations and participation in smoking cessation interventions, either alone or in groups. Nicotine replacement procedures as well as the drug Zyban are efficient, especially in combination with other interventions. Individualized treatments have higher success rates. Long-term cessation programmes are generally more successful in preventing relapse.

Jorenby et al. (1999) Controlled experiment on treatments for smoking cessation

- The aim was to investigate the effectiveness of nicotine patches and Zyban in smoking cessation.
- The experiment was a double blind, placebo-controlled study with 244 participants in the nicotine patch condition, 245 participants in the combined Zyban and nicotine patch group, and 160 participants in the placebo group. The treatment took place over 9 weeks. The participants were supposed to quit smoking at day 8 in the treatment.
- The results showed that 15.6% of the participants in the placebo group did not smoke after 12 months compared to 30.3% in the nicotine patch group and 30.3% in the combined treatment group.

MBSR

Davis et al. (2007) MBSR as a strategy to stop smoking

- The aim of the study was to investigate if MBSR could reduce smoking. MBSR is a stress reduction programme based on meditation principles from Buddhism (see more in unit 7.5).
- There were 18 participants in the study. They had an average smoking history of 19.9 cigarettes per day for 26.4 years.

- MBSR instructors trained the group in mindfulness in eight weekly sessions. Participants attempted smoking cessation in week seven without use of drugs or nicotine replacement. Six weeks after quitting the participants' breath was tested to see if they had stopped.
- The results showed that 56% of the participants had stopped smoking (the breath test). There was a positive correlation between compliance with meditation, smoking cessation and low levels of stress.
- The researchers concluded that MBSR could be useful for smoking cessation but this needs to be tested in a larger controlled study.

7.6 Discuss factors related to overeating and the development of obesity

Obesity is a growing health problem worldwide, including among children. According to the WHO (2004) obesity has reached epidemic proportions globally and problems with being overweight are now affecting more people than malnutrition and hunger.

The most frequently used definition of obesity is related to body mass index (BMI), which is a measure of excess body fat. BMI is a person's weight (in kilogrammes) divided by the square of his or her height (in metres).

Normal weight BMI 20–24.9
Overweight BMI 25–29.9
Clinical obesity BMI 30–39.9
Severe obesity BMI 40

Biological factors

Evolution

- The early humans were hunter-gatherers who lived as nomads for millions of years. Homo Sapiens appeared some 130,000 to 100,000 years BC and their bodies were adapted to the hardship of nomadic life.

- Our ancestors' diet was varied and the body's ability to store fat easily was advantageous for survival. The hunter-gatherers needed the fat to survive winters and the long journeys in search of food. The demand for energy was much higher than it is in modern societies with a sedentary lifestyle. The genetic predisposition to store fat could thus be a disadvantage today where food is abundant and people are no longer as physically active. The theory makes sense since it is at this point in human history that obesity is so frequent but it is impossible to test evolutionary theories.

Genetic predisposition

- **Stunkard et al. (1990)** performed a twin study based on 93 pairs of identical twins reared apart. The researchers compared the twins' BMI and found that genetic factors accounted for 66–70% of the variance in their body weight.

- The results indicate a strong genetic component in development of obesity but it is not really clear how genes operate here. One theory is that metabolism rates could be genetically determined but the evidence is still inconclusive. Another suggestion relates to the amount of fat cells in the individual.

- The obesity epidemic cannot be explained by genetic factors alone. Environmental factors play an important role (e.g. sedentary lifestyle and high energy foods). The increase in prevalence rates of obesity within the last 20 years has taken place over too short a period for the genetic makeup of the population to have changed substantially.

The neurobiology of food addiction (the theory of compulsive overeating)

- According to this theory, compulsive overeating shares many of the same characteristics as drug addiction. Food craving is related to secretion of dopamine in the brain's reward circuit.

- Dopamine is associated with motivation and goal-directed behaviour (anticipation) and the body's natural opioids are associated with the pleasure of eating the desired food (especially sugar and fat).

- People may become addicted to addictive substances such as nicotine and alcohol but research indicates that people can also become addicted to sugar. Sugar addicts experience the same withdrawal symptoms seen with those addicted to classic drugs of abuse when they are deprived of their drug.

- **Kesler (2009)** argues in his book *The End of Overeating* that manufactured food contains high amounts of sugar, fat, and salt that naturally stimulate the brain to release dopamine. Such foods are experienced as pleasurable and the brain gets wired so that dopamine pathways are activated by specific cues (or stimuli) such as smells, the sign of a fast-food restaurant or the mere thought of the preferred food.

- The cues cause craving (response). Craving is the motivation to seek out the food and the anticipation of pleasure stimulates the brain to release dopamine. Hunger is a natural cue for eating but in food addiction the urge to eat does not come from hunger but from cues associated with food. People who are addicted to food cannot control this urge to eat when they are not hungry, and this is one reason why they become obese.

- **Volkow et al. (2002)** used fMRI to study the brains of 10 obese people to investigate dopamine activity. The scanning showed that the obese participants had the same deficiency in dopamine receptors in the brain as drug addicts.

- The participants' brains showed a pattern of compulsive urge to eat when they saw their favourite foods. This indicates that people can become addicted to food.

- Volkow explains that most people's weight problems are not caused by food addiction. There are multiple causes of overweight and obesity, including unhealthy eating habits, lack of exercise, genetic vulnerability, and stress but in some individuals, food addiction could be an explanation.

Sociocultural factors

Sedentary lifestyle and change in eating patterns
- **Jeffery (2001)** argues that the current epidemic of obesity is caused by lack of physical activity (i.e. sedentary lifestyle due to the use of cars and increased television viewing) and eating behaviour (e.g. eating processed food high in energy).
- **Prentice and Jebb (1995)** examined changes in physical activity in a British sample. There was a positive correlation between increase in obesity and car ownership and television viewing. The data supports the idea of a relationship between sedentary lifestyle and increase in

obesity rates but correlational research cannot establish a cause-effect relationship.
- **Lakdawalla and Philipson** (2002) estimated that 60% of the total growth in weight could be due to a decrease in physical activity and around 40% to increased calorie intake. The dramatic increase in obesity among Pacific Islanders who are now among the fattest in the world could support the theory of change in lifestyle. The modernization of these islands has replaced traditional food with processed and ready made foods that are high in fat and sugar.

Food promotion and eating behaviour
Elliot (2005) argues a possible cause of obesity in the way the food industry use food packaging to present products as "fun food".
- The Food Standards Agency in the UK (**FSA, 2003**) reviewed 118 studies on how foods are promoted to children and how this might link to their eating patterns. The review found that food promotion for children is dominated by television advertising promoting food in terms of fun, fantasy, and taste rather than health and nutrition. This may have serious implications for eating behaviour: eating "for fun" and eating unhealthy food may contribute to food preferences, overeating and obesity.

Socioeconomic factors
Research shows a consistent link between low socioeconomic status and high rates of obesity.
- **Petersen (2006)** found an increased polarization in regard to health. People with higher education eat more healthy food and exercise more. They are also more likely to respond positively to recommendations from health campaigns on how to stay healthy.
- **Forslund et al. (2005)** performed a longitudinal study on the eating habits of obese and non-obese individuals. There was a link between the amount of television viewing and diet, obesity and cholesterol level but correlational data cannot say anything about cause-effect relationships. The researchers found that obese individuals tended to have a lower level of education than the non-obese.

Cognitive factors
- People who diet typically replace physiological hunger sensations with "cognitive restraint", i.e. they put a limit on what they can eat.
- Restraint theory predicts that extreme cognitive restraint is likely to make an individual more responsive to external cues (e.g. smell of food) or emotional events (e.g. stress or feeling down because weight loss is very small). They often experience a "loss of control" that ends in overeating.
- This is partly explained in terms of the **false hope syndrome (Polivy, 2001)**. It seems that obese dieters often set *unrealistic goals* and are overly optimistic as to how quickly they can lose weight. They may believe that weight loss will result in more radical changes in their lives than can rationally be expected. This cocktail of false hopes and unrealistic criteria for success could be an explanation for lack of success in dieting and ultimately obesity.

- Obesity rates in adults are very high in many countries and it is difficult to reduce excessive weight once it has become established. Therefore many prevention strategies aim to prevent children from becoming obese (e.g. targeting schools and after-school services as natural settings for promoting physical activity and learning about healthy eating.

- The promotion of healthy eating and regular physical activity is essential for both the prevention of future obesity (**primary prevention**) and for treating those who are already overweight and obese or just preventing them from gaining more weight (**secondary prevention**).

Prevention strategies for overeating and obesity

- Health promotion includes a number of prevention strategies to change unhealthy eating habits and promote health. One sugared soft drink daily could increase body weight by 50 kg over 10 years (**Ebbeling et al. 2002**).

- **Salmeron et al. (1997)** found that the most commonly eaten foods in the UK were white bread, savoury snacks, chips, other forms of potatoes, biscuits, and chocolate. All of these foods contain a high proportion of sugar, fat and salt. This study shows that there is reason to worry.

Education on healthy eating and physical activity

- Campaigns on healthy eating could in principle be a useful form of prevention when they focus on families because they could change the food preferences of both adults and children. Food preferences are established in childhood. Parents' food choice may influence what children eat and prefer for the rest of their lives. Education of parents of obese children has produced positive changes in the children's eating habits (**Golan et al. 1998).**

Examples of prevention strategies

The Eatwell Plate (UK prevention strategy from 2007)
A balanced diet requires a balanced intake of "macronutrients" (fats, carbohydrates, proteins) and "nutrients" (vitamins and minerals). The British Nutrition Foundation (2007) created "The eatwell plate", which gives an overview of a healthy diet showing the recommended proportion and types of food. The key message is the importance of a balanced diet with a variety of foods.

California Children's 5 a Day-Power Play! Campaign
This community-based campaign ran from 1993 to 1996. It used television spots and various initiatives to educate on the benefits of a diet and physical activity. It aimed to encourage low-income children to eat more fruit and vegetables at school and at home. The survey after the campaign showed that children who recalled television spots were more likely than others to report eating five or more servings of fruit and vegetables

Fat and sugar tax
Some countries (e.g. Denmark) have introduced taxes on unhealthy food such as fat and sugar in order to encourage a more healthy diet and reduce the costs of obesity. When the price of a food increases, the consumption of that food normally decreases. The fat and sugar tax is a way for governments to control people's diets and encourage them to eat more healthily (just like taxing cigarettes and alcohol to decrease consumption of these substances). This is called social engineering.

Treatments for overeating and obesity
Cognitive behavioural therapy (CBT)
CBT for obesity aims to change cognitions related to eating as well unhealthy eating behaviour.

The focus is on cognitions that lead directly to eating such as the client's permission-giving thoughts (e.g. "It's ok to eat now because I'm upset.")

The CBT programme involves:
1. **Focus on behaviours**: identify and adjust destructive eating patterns; monitor calorie intake; identify alternatives to social and emotional eating; start manageable exercise programme.
2. **Focus on cognitions**: identify and confront dysfunctional thinking that prevents healthy eating habits; improve body image and self-confidence; increase social support and adjust thinking to prevent feelings of shame and hopelessness.
3. **Focus on strategies to maintain weight loss**: maintain motivation and strengthen coping skills to deal with challenging situations and setbacks.

Stahre et al. (2007) Randomized trial of CBT to treat obesity
Aim To examine effectiveness of CBT in treating obesity.

Procedure Participants were obese women in Sweden (mean age 48.5 years and mean BMI 36.5). The experimental group joined a weight loss programme that included CBT. The control group did moderately intense physical activity. The treatment lasted for 10 weeks (two hours per week). Participants' weight was controlled periodically over an 18-month period. There was a small drop-out in both groups.

Results The results showed a significantly greater weight loss (5.9 kg) in the treatment group after 18 months compared to the control group who had gained 0.3 kg on average.

Conclusion The researchers concluded that CBT seems to be an efficient way of treating obesity and it is also a cost-effective alternative to many weight loss programmes.

Dieting
Obesity treatments always involves dieting in one form or another. It seems to be somewhat ineffective.

Wadden (1993) Meta-analysis of studies on effectiveness of dieting
- The study reviewed randomized control studies on the effectiveness of either moderate or severe calorie restriction on weight loss.
- The results showed that patients stayed in treatment for 20 weeks and that 50% lost around 9 kg or more. Modern approaches to diet with counselling were more effective in the short term compared to previous methods, which mainly focused on dieting and weight loss. The majority of obese patients in research trials tended to regain their lost weight.

- Wadden's findings are supported by data from a meta-analysis of 92 studies of interventions for the treatment and prevention of obesity **(NHS Centre for Reviews and Dissemination 1997)**. The conclusion of that study was that weight gain after treatment is the norm.
- Weight loss is not quick and this fact may result in many negative emotions and giving in to eat more than allowed. Many dieters are guided by all-or-nothing thinking. The belief that *one* little transgression (e.g. eating an ice cream) ruins the overall attempt to lose weight could make them stop the diet and indulge in food. This is described as the "what the hell effect" and it has been repeatedly demonstrated in chronic dieters.

Surgical treatments
Surgical treatments are used with severe obesity. The two most common are:
- **Gastric bypass**: a surgical procedure that cuts off part of the stomach to prevent overeating by limiting the ability to absorb food
- **Gastric banding**: a surgical procedure where a band is tied around the upper part of the stomach to reduce food intake and help the patient to feel full earlier.

Maggard et al. (2005) Meta-analysis of effectiveness of surgical treatments of obesity
- The study reviewed the results of 147 studies.
- The results showed that gastric surgery resulted in weight loss of 20 to 30 kg. The results were maintained for up to 10 years and patients reported an overall improvement in health. Gastric bypass was overall more effective than gastric banding.

Drug treatments
The National Institute of Health in the USA considers obesity to be a chronic disease. Two sorts of drugs are used:
- **Appetite-suppressant drugs:** decrease appetite or increase the feeling of being full because they act on neurotransmitters that affect mood and appetite (e.g. serotonin and adrenaline levels). There is some evidence for the effectiveness of these drugs although they have some side effects such as nausea, constipation, and dry mouth.
- **Lipase inhibitors:** reduce fat absorption. The drug has some unpleasant side effects, especially after eating fat. This may have a preventive effect since eating fat becomes associated with unpleasant consequences such as diarrhea.

Few studies have evaluated the safety and long-term effectiveness of drugs and some are concerned that they may be over-prescribed. Sibutramine has now been taken off the market in many countries because of its serious health risks (e.g. heart failure and sudden death).

Berkowitz et al. (2006) Randomized trial of effectiveness of an appetite-suppressant
- The aim was to test the effectiveness of the drug sibutramine in reducing weight compared with a placebo.
- The sample consisted of 498 obese adolescent boys and girls (age range 12–16, average weight 97.7 kg). The study was longitudinal. The drug sibutramine was given to 386 participants and 130 had the placebo. All participants had counselling about healthy eating, physical activity, stress reduction, and keeping track of how much they ate.
- The results showed that participants in the sibutramine group usually lost weight (6.4 kg) rapidly during the first eight months and then maintained their weight for the rest of the trial. The main side effect of the drug was an increase in heart rate. Those in the placebo group usually gained weight (1.8 kg).
- About one quarter of the participants left the study, which ran for only one year. There was no follow up on the long-term benefits or harm of the drug. The researchers did not control weight changes after the study, which makes it difficult to determine whether the weight loss was permanent.

The health belief model (HBM) (Rosenstock et al. 1988)

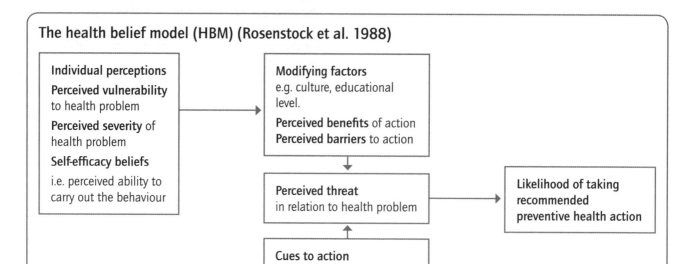

The model assumes that people make rational decisions on health-related behaviours and that people are ready to change if they:

- believe they are vulnerable to the health problem in question (**perceived vulnerability**)
- believe the health problem has serious consequences (**perceived severity**)
- believe taking action could reduce their vulnerability to the health problem (**perceived benefits**)
- believe the costs of taking action (**perceived barriers**) are outweighed by the benefits (**perceived benefits**).

- are confronted with factors (e.g. pain in the chest or a television programme) that prompt actions (**cues to action**).
- are confident that they are able to be successful in the action (**self-efficacy**) – if people believe they can stop smoking or eat healthier, they are more likely to listen to health promotion messages).

At the individual level there are **modifying variables**, i.e. individual characteristics such as culture, education level, past experiences, and motivation that can influence people's perceptions.

Quist-Paulsen and Gallefors (2003) Randomized controlled trial to investigate smoking cessation using fear messages after heart problems

Aim The researchers wanted to see if a longer intervention including *fear arousal* could promote smoking cessation and prevent relapse.

Procedure The participants (heart patients) were randomly allocated to a treatment group and a control group. All patients were offered group counselling sessions. Patients in the control group only received group counselling. Patients in the treatment group also got personal advice from trained nurses and information material stressing the risks of continued smoking (fear arousal) and advantages of cessation. They were advised to stop smoking and nicotine replacement was offered to those with cravings. Nurses contacted the patients in the treatment group by telephone nine times after they came home to encourage cessation and stressed the negative aspects of smoking on their condition.

Results In the intervention group 57% of participants and in the control group 37% had stopped smoking at the end of the programme.

Evaluation Using fear arousal is controversial but the researchers argue that it was justified since many more stopped smoking in the treatment group. The results indicate that cues to action and perceived threat can predict behavioural change. The study also provided additional help to support self-efficacy in the patients (e.g. by offering them medication to stop craving and by asking the spouses to stop smoking).

Strengths of HBM	Limitations of HBM
■ HBM has been applied successfully in health promotion. The model can help identify some of the important factors and cognitions involved in health behaviours. These factors can be applied to design health promotion strategies (e,g, as in **Quist-Paulsen and Gallefours (2003)** at an individual level. ■ HBM has suggested useful factors to address in health promotion (e.g. Janz and Becker (1984): "perceived barriers" seem to be the most significant in determining behaviour). Health practitioners could address this in one-to-one interventions and discuss how to deal with such barriers.	■ A limitation of the HBM is the focus on individual *cognitions*. It does not include social and economic factors, which are known to influence health behaviours as well (e.g. obese people may want to buy healthy food but they cannot afford it). ■ The main criticism of the model is the assumption that people are rational decision makers. People are sometimes "unrealistically optimistic" about their health and a threat is not always perceived as such by the individual.

Weinstein (1987) Unrealistic optimism

The researcher asked people to rate their risk of developing various disorders compared to other people like them. Individuals usually rate their chances of illness as less than those of other people. This is to a large extent the case in smokers. Weinstein suggested that the following factors affect "unrealistic optimism"

■ People tend to believe that if a problem has not appeared yet, then it is unlikely to happen in the future.

■ People tend to think that personal action can prevent the problem.

■ People believe that the problem is rare.

■ People have little or no experience of the problem.

Festinger (1975) Cognitive dissonance

■ Cognitive dissonance theory predicts that people are motivated to attend to information that supports their beliefs and to avoid information that contradicts them in order to avoid **cognitive dissonance** – an uncomfortable tension.

■ Smokers would tend to avoid information on the negative consequences of smoking (e.g. cancer) and focus on positive aspects of smoking (e.g. "It makes me relax.")

Stages of change model (transtheoretical model)

The model identifies five stages of change, which highlighted the processes involved in the transition from a smoker to a non-smoker.

1. **Precontemplation**: The person is not seriously considering quitting.
2. **Contemplation**: The person is aware that there is a problem and that something should be done but there is no commitment to quitting.
3. **Preparation**: The person is seriously considering quitting, perhaps by reducing the number of cigarettes or postponing the first one.
4. **Action**: The person has stopped smoking.
5. **Maintenance**: The person works to maintain non-smoking and prevent relapse.

Stages of change model

Prochaska and Di Clemente (1983) Processes of change in smokers

■ The aim of this cross-sectional study was to investigate stages of self-change in relation to smoking cessation.

■ Newspaper advertisements were used to recruit 872 smokers who wanted to change their smoking habits on their own. Participants were allocated to five different groups (long-term quitters, recent quitters, relapsers, immotives – no intention to stop smoking, and contemplators – thinking about quitting).

Participants answered a questionnaire to determine current stage of change. Saliva tests were taken to increase validity of self-reports on smoking stage. The study ran for two years.

■ The results showed 10 different processes of change. The researchers developed this into a model with five stages of change that are not necessarily linear but involved a shift across the five stages. The study showed that some of the smokers stayed in the contemplation stage throughout and that smokers often make a number of action attempts before they reach the maintenance stage.

West and Sohal (2006) Criticism of the stages of change model

- This large-scale cross-sectional survey compared ex-smokers and smokers who said they had made at least one attempt to quit.

- Many ex-smokers reported that they just decided to stop and then did it without making any plans. The results showed that unplanned attempts to quit were more likely to succeed for at least six months than planned attempts.

- The researchers argue that there is no process of change. Smokers simply react to a cue in the environment and decide to stop at once (catastrophe theory). Smokers have varying levels of motivational tension to stop and environmental triggers (e.g. a media campaign or friend quitting) can result in a change in the motivational state. This might lead to an immediate giving up of smoking and it seems to be a more complete transformation than if it involves a plan to quit at some point in the future.

- These results are more supportive of the HBM or at least some of the factors involved in behavioural change in that model.

Strengths of the stages of change model	Limitations of the stages of change model
■ The model is simple to use and it has generated a lot of research. It is a useful model because it can raise awareness of an individual's motivation to change and help to design appropriate interventions at the relevant stage of change.	■ Critics of the model argue that an individual may not necessarily contemplate stopping before he or she actually quits. People may be more likely to react to cues in the environment such as a friend quitting or a scary media campaign.
■ Many health practitioners find the model useful and robust in understanding smoking cessation. It has also been successfully applied in health promotion to stop alcohol abuse.	■ The model *describes* processes of change but does not explain them. The model does not take social and cultural factors that could influence motivation to change into account.

7.9 Discuss the effectiveness of health promotion strategies

Public health campaigns

- The *mass media* plays a crucial role in modern health promotion and all public health campaigns include the mass media. The media campaign can raise awareness about health issues, i.e. health risks of smoking or unhealthy eating habits, and it can use emotional appeals to promote change. This combination of cognitive and emotional appeals has proved very effective in modern anti-smoking campaigns.

- The media cannot change behaviour unless people have the necessary means to actually do something. The simple message such as "Smoking kills you" or "Exercise 30 minutes every day" must be supported by other health promotion strategies, i.e. offering easy access to smoking cessation clinics and restricted access to smoking in public areas.

Persuasive communication in the mass media

Some of the following factors characterize successful persuasion in the media:

- The source, i.e. the person who communicates the message must be credible (trustworthy or an expert).

- The audience (target group) should determine how the message is framed.

- The message should be short, clear, direct, and explicit. Fear appeals may backfire (e.g. "Smoking kills you") but they can be very effective if they are accompanied with specific information of *how* to change, (e.g. the address of a smoking cessation centre or information about how to increase self-efficacy in quitting). Indirect fear appeals, such as playing on emotions for loved ones can be effective.

- Attitude change is more likely to last if the target group actively participates in the communication rather than just passively receiving it.

The use of fear appeals in raising anti-smoking attitudes

- The National Tobacco Strategy (NTS) 2004–2009 in Australia used mass media anti-smoking advertisements based on fear appeals. The television spots were based on personal stories with extremely disturbing videos of people suffering from the consequences of smoking (e.g. mouth cancer or lung cancer).
- The same pictures were shown in advertisements in newspapers. Cigarette packages had warnings and scary pictures (e.g. of tumours). Real victims showed the negative consequences of smoking as a clear message that this could happen to others as well.

Peckmann and Reibling (2006) Effectiveness of fear appeals in promoting anti-smoking attitudes

- The researchers randomly exposed 1725 ninth-grade students in Californian schools to one of nine videotapes containing a television show that included a range of anti-smoking advertisements or control advertisements.
- The results showed that advertisements that focused on young victims suffering from serious tobacco-related diseases elicited disgust, increased negative attitudes towards the tobacco industry, and reduced intentions to smoke among all participating adolescents, except those with conduct disorder.

Evidence from the National Tobacco Campaign in Australia (**Woodward, 2003**) demonstrates that health campaigns can
- reach large amounts of people
- promote negative attitudes about smoking
- Increase knowledge about the health effects of smoking
- prompt calls to the quit line
- help smokers quit and reinforce successful quitters to remain ex-smokers.

According to Australian Smoking Statistics 2009, anti-smoking campaigns and health education have generally resulted in a decrease in smokers in Australia. For example, the proportion of Australian men who smoke fell from 40% in 1980 to 30% in 1989. The number of female smokers fell from 31% to 27% over the same period.

Beiner et al. (2006) studied a sample of nearly 800 Australian ex-smokers who had quit within the previous two years to find out what these ex-smokers perceived as the greatest help for them in quitting.
- 30.5% said anti-tobacco advertisements.
- 21% said conventional cessation aids and nicotine replacement therapy.
- 11% said professional help or advice.
- 8% said self-help materials.
- 7% said prescribed medications.
- Young ex-smokers found that the most effective anti-smoking advertisements were those that evoked strong negative emotion such as fear and sadness and conveyed a thought-provoking and believable message about the serious long-tem consequences of smoking.

The results indicate that media campaigns with anti-tobacco advertisements can be effective.

Community based anti-smoking promotion among teens

- The **TRUTH** anti-tobacco campaign (Florida) in 1998–99 was a grassroots movement targeting teenagers. The aim of this campaign was to prevent teen smoking by changing teens' attitudes and to encourage them to form groups and spread the message in the community.
- A core component of the campaign was adolescents confronting the tobacco industry and accusing them of manipulating them to smoke. The strategy of a youth movement against the tobacco industry was decided at the Teen Tobacco Summit in 1998 by teen delegates: "Truth, a generation united against tobacco".
- The campaign included the formation of a new youth anti-tobacco advocacy group called SWAT (Students Working Against Tobacco) who worked at grassroots level.
- The campaign used massive advertising including 33 television commercials, billboards, posters, the Internet (e.g. YouTube), programme sponsorships, merchandise and local youth advocacy groups.

Effectiveness of the campaign

- Effectiveness of the campaign was measured by telephone surveys with teens. Six months after launching the campaign 92% of teens were aware of the campaign.
- Teens' negative attitude to smoking had risen. Follow-up surveys showed that non-smoking teens were likely to say that they had been influenced by the campaign.
- The Florida Youth Tobacco Survey (FYTS) conducted in February 1999 found that the number of middle and high school teens defined as "current smokers" went down by 19.4% and 8% respectively. In total, it was estimated that 29,000 fewer Florida teens smoked after the campaign. This is one of the largest annual declines observed in the USA since 1980.
- **Sly et al. (2002)** carried out a survey 22 months after the campaign to investigate whether non-smokers had remained non-smokers. They found a positive correlation between amount of exposure to the key message theme (i.e. that the tobacco industry manipulates teens' attitudes to smoking) during the campaign and non-smoking.

(Schum and Gould, 2007) Why was the campaign effective?

- Youths were involved in planning the campaign. The youth guided model was effective because teens talked to each other about smoking. It became a true viral movement among them and gave them the opportunity to express concerns and fit in with their peers.

- Real teens served as the public voice of the campaign. Their passion for the issue was an essential element of the campaign. The Truth campaign became a "brand" that teens were proud of.

> The TRUTH campaign can also be used as an illustration of prevention strategies in unit 7.9, as prevention strategies are part of health promotion.

- The campaign created the social norm that kids don't smoke and made it public. Peer influence has a large effect on youth risk behaviour. Communicating that most kids don't smoke reinforces the idea that smoking is not the norm and that you can be cool without smoking.

- The campaign was a grassroots movement and the teens involved in it were passionate about it and spread the word to their local networks. This was before Facebook but the strategy of creating social networks and using them effectively was demonstrated in this campaign that was largely planned and executed by members of the target group who continued to recruit more teens.

8.1 Distinguish between altruism and prosocial behaviour

Altruism

- In evolutionary biology, altruism is defined as behaviour that benefits other organisms but has some costs. The costs and benefits are measured in terms of reproductive fitness (i.e. expected number of offspring).
- In social psychology altruism is a subcategory of helping behaviour. It refers to a behaviour that is meant to benefit another person rather than oneself (**Batson and Coke, 1981**).
- According to **Staub (1978)** altruistic acts may also result in reward for the individual (e.g. feeling good or virtuous.
- According to **Piliavin and Charng (1990)** psychologists have not been able to agree on a single definition of altruism.

> **Prosocial behaviour**
> Behaviour that benefits others or has positive social consequences.

Prosocial behaviour

- Prosocial behaviour refers to acts *intended* to benefit others. These are acts that are positively valued by society (**Hogg and Vaughan, 1998**). Aggressiveness and violent behaviour are not valued by society and this kind of behaviour is considered as "antisocial behaviour".
- Prosocial behaviour could be any behaviour that is initiated with the purpose of increasing another person's physical or psychological well-being and has positive consequences for that person (e.g. helping, comforting, sharing).
- Intentional prosocial behaviour is often called **"helping behaviour"**. Donating money to refugees in Somalia or doing voluntary work are examples of prosocial behaviour that aim to benefit other people.

> **Altruistic behaviour**
> Behaviour that benefits another person – sometimes at some costs.

8.2 Contrast two theories explaining altruism in humans

Kin selection theory (evolutionary theory)

- **Kin selection theory (Hamilton, 1963)** is based on the idea that individuals are more likely to sacrifice themselves for relatives than non-relatives. By sacrificing yourself for relatives (e.g. helping them at the cost of not having babies yourself) you still contribute to the survival of your genes by helping close relatives.
- **Dawkin's (1989)** selfish gene theory suggests that what could look as self-sacrifice could, in reality, promote one's own genes because it is not a question of individual survival but of the gene's survival. Kin altruism is in reality "egoism".
- The theory of reciprocal altruism (**Trivers, 1971**) suggests that helping behaviour among non-kin have evolved as an alternative system during evolution. This theory supplements kin selection theory. Reciprocal altruism is based on the strategy that altruistic acts are returned ("tit-for-tat" strategy) and therefore pays off long term.

Simmons et al. (1977): Kin and the likelihood of kidney donations

- The study investigated whether close relatives were more likely to be kidney donors.
- The results showed that 86% of parents said yes but only 47% of the siblings who could be donors agreed to donate a kidney to their relative when asked. The theory predicts that both should agree so the difference in agreement to make this sacrifice cannot be explained in terms of kin alone.
- Researchers asked potential kidney recipients to rate their emotional closeness to all possible donors before the choice of a donor was made. Generally, the recipients felt very close to 63% of the potential donors but only to 42% of the potential non-donors. It was found that when siblings were donors, the recipient and the donor were significantly closer in age and more likely to be of the same sex than were non-donors.

Strengths of kin selection theory	Limitations of kin selection theory
■ The theory is supported by empirical studies, which generally shows preference for helping close blood relatives (e.g. in organ donation). ■ Mathematical computer simulations demonstrate that kin selection is one of the possible selection processes in evolution together with reciprocity.	■ The theory cannot explain why people help individuals who are not relatives (e.g. cooperation among non-relatives, spontaneous acts of bravery, or the adoption of children who are not relatives. ■ Human kinship patterns are not necessarily based upon blood tie. Shared developmental environment, familiarity, and social bonding also contribute to kinship according to anthropologists.

Batson et al. (1981) The empathy-altruism theory

■ The **empathy-altruism theory** posits that some helpful actions are truly altruistic because they are motivated by the genuine desire to increase another's welfare. Batson's understanding of altruism is that it is the helper's *motives* that determine whether a behaviour is altruistic or not.

■ According to Batson the perception of a situation and the emotion that follows determines whether an individual will help or not. Altruism can only happen if another person's perspective is taken.

■ Observing another person's situation may either produce **empathic concern** (i.e. positive emotions like sympathy or compassion) or **personal distress** (i.e. negative emotions). "Empathy" evokes altruistic motivation to reduce another person's distress whereas personal distress evokes an egoistic motivation to reduce one's own distress.

■ According to **Batson (1991)** three factors facilitate perspective taking:

1. the observer has had similar experiences
2. the observer is attached to the victim
3. the person is instructed to imagine what it is like to be in the victim's position.

Perspective taking will produce the altruistic motive to reduce the other person's distress.

■ A major criticism of Batson's theory points to problems in finding out whether the **motive** is really empathic concern (altruistic) or just wanting to reduce personal distress (egoistic). **Cialdini et al. (1973)** suggested **the negative state relief model** as an alternative explanation. "Altruism" could rather be seen as a strategy to avoid feeling sad or upset (egoistic motive) and not a truly altruistic act.

Batson et al. (1981) Experimental testing of the empathy-altruistic theory

Aim To investigate participants' motives to help when they had the opportunity to escape.

Procedure Participants were students in an introductory psychology class at university. They were tested individually. Before they participated they filled out a questionnaire about themselves. Each participant was led to believe that he or she was an observer to a test where another student (Elaine) was being tested in recall of digit numbers. Participants read a short description of Elaine. Each description was manipulated so that the real participants could either identify with Elaine (high empathy) or not (low empathy). Participants then watched Elaine over a close-circuit TV (in fact a pre-recorded video). After two trials Elaine received electric shocks. She clearly expressed they were painful. Participants were asked if they would be willing to help Elaine by taking her place. Half of them heard that they could either take her place or fill out a questionnaire and then leave (easy escape situation). The other half were told that they could either take her place or watch Elaine go through the remaining eight trials (difficult escape situation). Then participants had to say what they wanted to do. When they had chosen, the experiment ended and they were debriefed.

Results High empathy condition: Most participants agreed to help Elaine. It did not matter much whether it was easy or difficult to escape. Low empathy condition: Most participants withdrew in the easy escape condition. When it was difficult some preferred to offer help. This could support the negative state relief model.

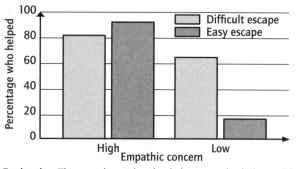

Evaluation The experiment involved clever manipulations with operationalized variables. This raises methodological considerations such as the possibility of demand characteristics. The participants were all psychology students and we cannot rule out that they guessed the aim of the experiment (demand characteristics and sample bias). **Cialdini et al. (1973)** argue that it is impossible to rule out that it is not true altruism but rather egoism that Batson's experiments demonstrate.

Oliner and Oliner (1988) interviewed rescuers of Jews during the Second World War and found that situational factors such as being asked to help increased altruism. Only 37% said they felt empathy with the Jews but 52% said they did it because of moral values (e.g. believing that all people are equal). The researchers argue that personality factors could also play a role in altruism. This is not considered in Batson's study.

Strengths of empathy-altruism theory	Limitations of empathy-altruism theory
■ The theory is supported by many experimental studies. ■ The theory can, to some extent, predict conditions under which altruistic behaviour will happen (e.g. the more people feel empathy the more likely they are to help other people and people who do not feel empathy will probably not help).	■ It is difficult to generalize findings from experiments such as this one in real life. ■ It is a problem that it is not possible to determine whether altruism is the result of empathic motivation or the motivation to escape one's own negative emotions. ■ It is clear that empathy does not always precede altruistic behaviour. People may help for other reasons.

Contrasting the two theories

Kin selection theory	Empathy-altruism theory
■ The focus is on genes that operate at a biological level without human consciousness. The theory is largely based on observation of animals and insects. Humans are much more complex.	■ The focus is on the human emotion empathy as the primary motivating factor in altruism.
■ Altruism is seen as a behaviour that has a cost to the individual (self-sacrifice).	■ The theory is based on altruism is seen as a behaviour that increases another person's welfare.
■ The theory is based on egoism (the genes are selfish and humans tend to favour kin because of genetic similarity).	■ Altruism (humans can be truly altruistic). The theory does not rule out the possibility of an altruistic personality.
■ The theory can explain observations of people who behave more altruistically towards kin but it cannot really explain why. It may not be for biological reasons. The theory cannot explain why people behave altruistically towards people who are not relatives.	■ The theory can explain why people tend to behave altruistically in situations that evoke empathy but there is not a clear linear relationship. People may feel empathy and choose not to help.
■ It is very difficult to test evolutionary theories as such but there is empirical support for kin altruism (kin selection), e.g. in research that involves organ donation or other situations that involve life or death.	■ It is relatively easy to test the theory under lab conditions but it is difficult to operationalize concepts like empathy.

Using one or more research studies, explain cross-cultural differences in prosocial behaviour

Sociocultural factors in prosocial behaviour

- Cultural norms, socialization practices in the family, and socioeconomic status are factors that influence *how* and *when* prosocial (or altruistic) behaviour is exhibited. Children learn cultural norms and practices from important others through observation and through reinforcement.

- Cultural dimensions such as **individualism** and **collectivism** seem to influence the degree to which prosocial behaviour is encouraged in children.

- Collectivist cultures value helping family members, for example when it is essential for the family's subsistence. In such cultures children exhibit higher levels of prosocial tendencies. In individualist cultures that value personal success and competitiveness, child-rearing practices encourage competitiveness and pursuit of personal achievement because this will enhance the child's likelihood of future social success.

Whiting and Whiting (1975) Comparison of prosocial behaviour in six cultures as a result of child-rearing practices

- This anthropological study was a systematic naturalistic observation of cultural differences in child-rearing practices and the consequence of that on prosocial behaviour.

- The researchers observed children between the ages of 3 and 11 years in six different countries (Kenya, the Philippines, Japan, India, Mexico and the USA) during their daily interactions with other people.

- Results showed consistent differences in the degree of prosocial behaviour in children among the studied cultures. Children from Mexico, and the Philippines generally acted more prosocially than those from Japan, India, and the USA. The most prosocial children were from the most traditional society, in rural Kenya. The most egoistic children came from the most complex modern society, the USA.

- One important difference was how much children participated in household chores and in the care of younger children. In the most prosocial cultures people tended to live together in extended families, the female role was important, and women's contribution to the family's economy was greater. In these cultures women delegated more responsibility to their children. In cultures (e.g. the USA) where children are paid to do household chores or don't participate at all, the same degree of prosocial behaviour was not observed.

- The results overall indicate that **degree of modernization** influences prosocial behaviour. This was attributed to different child-rearing patterns and cultural dimensions such as individualism and collectivism.

- According to the researchers the study also shows how different aspects of socioeconomic organization of a culture can promote or inhibit children's opportunities to acquire specific social behaviours. The findings also emphasize the importance of everyday practices in the promotion of concern for others.

Miller et al. (1990) Cultural norms and moral values influence the perception of social responsibility

- The researchers interviewed 400 individuals (adults and children) on what to do in hypothetical situations where a person had failed to help someone in need. The situations involved parents' obligation to help their child, friends' obligation to help a friend, and people's obligation to help a stranger. The situations were either life threatening, moderately serious, or a minor threat. The participants in this cross-cultural study were North Americans and Hindu Indians.

- Hindu Indians tended to see it as a moral duty to help in all situations. Their view of social responsibility was broader and more duty based compared to the American participants.

- North American participants tended to view social responsibility and helping as *personal choice*. This was particularly true if the danger was moderate or minor, or if the person was a friend or stranger. Adults in the USA were also more likely to say that *liking* the person in need affected their moral responsibility to help the person.

- Bystanderism can be defined as the phenomenon that an individual is less likely to help in an emergency situation when passive bystanders are present (**Darley and Latané, 1968**).
- The background for research on "bystanderism" was the Kitty Genovese murder in New York City in 1964. She was attacked, raped, and stabbed several times by a psychopath.

Later, a number of witnesses explained that they had either heard screaming or seen a man attacking the woman over a period of 30 minutes. None intervened or called the police until it was too late. Afterwards they said they said they did not want to become involved or thought that somebody else would intervene. This incident inspired social psychologists to explore factors that may influence whether people will help or not in an emergency situation.

Latané & Darley (1970) Theory of the unresponsive bystander

According to the theory the presence of other people or just the perception that other people are witnessing the event will decrease the likelihood that an individual will intervene in an emergency due to psychological processes like:

- **Diffusion of responsibility:** Responsibility is diffused when more bystanders are present and this reduces the psychological costs of not intervening.

- **Informational social influence (pluralistic ignorance):** If the situation is ambiguous people will look to other people around to see what they do.
- **Evaluation apprehension:** Individual bystanders are aware that other people are present and may be afraid of being evaluated negatively if they react (fear of social blunders).

Latané and Darley (1968) suggested a **cognitive decision model**. They argue that helping requires that the bystander:

1. Notice the situation (if you are in a hurry you may not even see what is happening).
2. Interpret the situation as an emergency (e.g. people screaming or asking for help, which could also be interpreted as a family quarrel which is none of your business.

3. Accept some personal responsibility for helping even though other people are present.
4. Consider how to help (although you may be unsure of what to do or doubt your skills).
5. Decide how to help (you may observe how other people react or decide that it is too dangerous to intervene).

At each of these stages, the bystander can make a decision to help or not.

Latané and Darley (1968) Experiment to investigate bystander intervention and diffusion of responsibility

Aim To investigate if the number of witnesses of an emergency influences people's helping in an emergency situation.

Procedure As part of a course credit, 72 students (59 female and 13 male) participated in the experiment. They were asked to discuss what kind of personal problems new college students could have in an urban area. Each participant sat in a booth alone with a pair of headphones and a microphone. They were told that the discussion took place via an intercom to protect the anonymity of participants. At one point in the experiment a participant (a confederate) staged a seizure. The independent variable (IV) of the study was the number of persons (bystanders) that the participant thought listened to the same discussion. The dependant variable (DV) was the time it took for the participant to react from the start of the victim's fit until the participant contacted the experimenter.

Results The number of bystanders had a major effect on the participant's reaction. Of the participants in the alone condition,

85% went out and reported the seizure. Only 31% reported the seizure when they believed that there were four bystanders. The gender of the bystander did not make a difference.

Ambiguity about a situation and thinking that other people might intervene (i.e. diffusion of responsibility) were factors that influenced bystanderism in this experiment.

During debriefing students answered a questionnaire with various items to describe their reactions to the experiment, for example "I did not know what to do" (18 out of 65 students selected this) or "I did not know exactly what was happening" (26 out of 65) or "I thought it must be some sort of fake" (20 out of 65).

Evaluation There was participant bias (psychology students participating for course credits) Ecological validity is a concern due to the artificiality of the experimental situation (e.g. the laboratory situation and the fact that bystanders could only *hear* the victim and the other bystanders could add to the artificiality. There are ethical considerations: participants were deceived and exposed to an anxiety-provoking situation.

Pilliavin et al. (1969) The cost reward model of helping

The theory stipulates that both cognitive (cost-benefit analysis) and emotional factors (unpleasant emotional arousal) determine whether bystanders to an emergency will intervene. The model focuses on *egoistic motivation* to escape an unpleasant emotional state (opposite of altruistic motivation; see unit 8.2 for an explanation of altruistic behaviour: the empathy-altruism model). The theory was suggested based on a field experiment in New York's subway.

Pilliavin et al. (1969) The subway samaritan

Aim The aim of this field experiment was to investigate the effect of various variables on helping behaviour.

Procedure

- Teams of students worked together with a victim, a model helper, and observers. The IV was whether the victim was drunk or ill (carrying a cane), and black or white.

- The group performed a scenario where the victim appeared drunk or a scenario where the victim appeared ill.

- The participants were subway travellers who were observed when the "victim" staged a collapse on the floor short time after the train had left the station. The model helper was instructed to intervene after 70 seconds if no one else did.

Results The results showed that a person who appeared ill was more likely to receive help than one who appeared drunk. In 60% of the trials where the victim received help more than one person offered assistance.

Conclusion The researchers did not find support for "diffusion of responsibility". They argue that this could be because the observers could clearly *see* the victim and decide whether or not there was an emergency situation. Pilliavin et al. found no strong relationship between the number of bystanders and speed of helping, which is contrary to the theory of the unresponsive bystander.

Evaluation This study has higher ecological validity than laboratory experiments and it resulted in a theoretical explanation of factors influencing bystanderism.

Based on this study the researchers suggested that **the cost-reward model of helping** involves observation of an emergency situation that leads to an emotional arousal and interpretation of that arousal (e.g. empathy, disgust, fear). This serves as motivation to either help or not, based on evaluation of costs and rewards of helping:

- costs of helping (e.g. effort, embarrassment, physical harm)
- costs of not helping (e.g. self-blame and blame from others)
- rewards of helping (e.g. praise from victim and self)
- rewards of not helping (e.g. being able to continue doing whatever one was doing).

Evaluation of the model
The model assumes that bystanders make a rational cost-benefit analysis rather than acting intuitively on an impulse. It also assumes that people only help for egoistic motives. This is probably not true.

> Most of the research on bystanderism is conducted as laboratory experiments or field experiments but findings have been applied to explain real-life situations.

The role of dispositional factors and personal norms in helping in an emergency situation – the Holocaust

- The Holocaust was an exceptional life threatening emergency situation for the European Jews. Witnesses to the deportation of Jews all over Europe reacted in various ways. Some approved of the anti-Semitic policies, many were bystanders, and a few risked their own life to save Jews. Within the context of the Second World War saving Jews was a risky behaviour because it was illegal in many countries and the Jews were socially marginalized (pariahs). In spite of this some people decided to help (act altruistically).

- Heroic helpers such as people who saved the Jews under Holocaust (e.g. Oscar Schindler or André and Magda Trocmé in the French Village Le Chambon-sur-Lignon) may have strong personal norms. Those who risk their lives to help others in situations like the Holocaust often deviate radically from the norms of their society.

Oliner and Oliner (1988) Dispositional factors and personal norms in helping

- The researchers interviewed 231 Europeans who had participated in saving Jews in Nazi Europe and 126 similar people who did not rescue Jews. Of the rescuers, 67% had been asked to help, either by a victim or somebody else. Once they had agreed to help, they responded positively to subsequent requests.

- Results showed that rescuers shared personality characteristics and expressed greater pity or empathy compared to non-rescuers. Rescuers were more likely to be guided by personal norms (high ethical values, belief in equity, and perception of people as equal).

- Rescuers often said that parental behaviour had made an important contribution to the rescuer's personal norms (e.g. the parents of rescuers had few negative stereotypes of Jews compared to parents of non-rescuers. The family of rescuers also tended to believe in the universal similarity of all people.

Exam Tip You only need to write about two factors in an essay. You could choose to focus on one of the theories (e.g. the cost–reward model) and a study and compare it with another theory (e.g. personal norms) and a study. This would give you enough material to examine factors influencing bystanderism.

Biological origins of attraction

Evolutionary explanation 1: Neurobiology of love

- According to **Fisher (2004)** love is a human universal and evolution has produced three distinct motivational brain systems in all birds and mammals to direct courtship, mating, reproduction, and parenting: **attraction**, the **sex drive**, and **attachment**. The three systems interact with each other to produce the combination of emotions, motivations, and behaviours associated with "love".

- **Attraction** is the equivalent to human romantic love in animals according to **Fisher (2004)**. Attraction is characterized by increased energy, focused attention on a specific mate, obsessive following, affiliative gestures, possessive mate-guarding, and motivation to win a preferred mating partner. Attraction evolved to motivate individuals to select and focus courtship attention on a favoured partner.

- The **sex drive** (libido) is characterized by craving for sexual gratification. In humans, this is associated primarily with testosterone in both men and women. The sex drive evolved to produce offspring.

- **Mutual nest building, grooming, maintenance of close proximity, separation anxiety,** and **shared parental chores** characterize attachment in animals. Animal research suggests that this brain system is associated primarily with oxytocin and vasopressin in the nucleus accumbens (the brain's reward centre). Attachment evolved to motivate individuals to stay with the preferred reproductive partner long enough to complete parental duties and experience this as rewarding.

Fisher et al. (2003) fMRI study of neurobiological mechanism of attraction

Aim To investigate the neural mechanisms associated with the attraction system (romantic love).

Procedure Participants were 10 women and seven men aged from 18 to 26, who reported being in love for an average of 7.5 months. The participants first filled out a questionnaire (The Passionate Love Scale) to investigate how they felt about their relationship. Then they were placed in the fMRI scanner. They first looked at a photograph of their beloved, then performed a distraction task of counting backwards, and finally they looked at a photograph of a neutral acquaintance. This was repeated six times.

Results There was increased activity in the dopamine rich brain areas associated with reward, motivation, and goal orientation (for example the ventral tegmental area and the caudate nucleus) when participants looked at their lover.

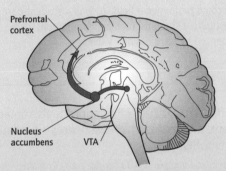

The results indicate the possibility of brain circuits dedicated to attraction (romantic love). The same brain circuits have been associated with "addiction", which could support the hypothesis that "romantic love is an addiction". Fisher argues that "romantic love" is universal and based on neurobiological factors.

Evolutionary explanation 2: Partner selection based on genes

Natural selection would favour couples that have genes which mutually enhance their offspring's chances of survival. This could be one way to select a "preferred partner".

Wedekind (1995) The sweaty T-shirt experiment – or investigating mate preference based on genetic makeup in relation to immune system functioning

- The experiment studied whether females would be able to identify males who had a genetic make-up which, in combination with her own, would boost the immune system of potential children. The study focused on a particular complex of genes (MHC genes) in the immune system known for the ability to protect against pathogens.

- A group of 94 students (half male and half female) participated in the experiment. The men were asked to sleep with a T-Shirt for two nights and keep it in a plastic bag.

- After two days the women were asked to rate how agreeable they found the smell of the T-shirts. The women had to smell seven different T-shirts. One was a control. Three of them contained T-shirts from men with an immune system similar to their own. Three contained T-shirts from men with an immune system that was dissimilar to the women's own – this should be the best match in terms of genes.

- Results showed that women preferred the odours of men with an immune system dissimilar to their own. This lends support to the evolutionary explanations of mate selection in humans.

- The experiment demonstrated that attraction was influenced by biological factors. The women preferred men with a genetic make-up that could increase the health of potential babies.

Evaluation of evolutionary explanations

- Research studies make it plausible that there are universal biological systems involved in attraction and love but this does not rule out that cultural factors may play an important role in attraction.

- Data from brain-imaging technologies show activity in specific brain areas involved in information processing and emotion but the brain is very complex and neuro-imaging data can describe but not really explain human attraction. Generally, it is very difficult to test evolutionary theories.

- Evolutionary theories cannot explain attraction and love between same-sex partners since such relationships are not formed to produce offspring.

Psychological origins of attraction

Burne (1971) Similarity-attraction hypothesis

The theory assumes that people are likely to be attracted to individuals who are perceived to be similar to themselves. This is because people who share our attitudes and values validate ourselves and boosts our self-esteem, which in turn leads to attraction. The theory is well supported by research.

Newcomb (1961) Field study of attitude similarity and liking

- Newcomb performed a field study in a student dorm to investigate if students' friendship formations were influenced by attitudes and values.

- For a semester, 17 male students were offered rent-free accommodation but in return they had to fill out questionnaires before they arrived and several times over the course of the semester. Newcomb predicted that in the beginning of the research period, people who were attracted to each other would *perceive* themselves as having similar attitudes.

- The study found that students with similar attitudes tended to become friends. Similarity in race and socioeconomic background also played a role.

Markey and Markey (2007) Romantic ideals, romantic obtainment, and relationship experiences – similarity or complementarity?

- A self-selected sample of 103 female and 66 male undergraduate students who were single but interested in finding a romantic partner (mean age 19.01) were recruited through advertisements.

- Participants first completed a questionnaire where they rated their own personality and then described the personality of their romantic ideal. They also completed filler questionnaires to disguise the true purpose of the study.

- The results showed that all participants wanted a romantic partner similar to themselves. Warm people were attracted to others who were warm. The same was found for dominance.

- The results indicate that people believe that similarity in a potential partner is important but maybe this ideal partner is difficult to find.

- A follow-up study with a new sample found that romantic couples who experienced high levels of love and harmony were more likely to consist of one individual who was dominant and one who was submissive. This indicates that complementarity on certain personality factors could affect harmony positively.

Morry (2007) Attraction-similarity theory

- When people are attracted to other people they tend to perceive them as similar (maybe because they project their own attitudes onto them).

- People prefer friends and partners who are similar in terms of attitudes and traits but the perceived similarity may not always be accurate.

- Perceived similarity is a main factor in attraction and relationship satisfaction and it has psychological benefits because it validates one's own views (reinforcement).

Dijkstra and Barelds (2010)
Aim Investigate if people would be likely to:

1. perceive *ideal partners* as similar to themselves (in line with the similarity-attraction hypothesis)
2. perceive *former partners* as different from themselves (in line with the attraction-similarity hypothesis).

This is based on the assumption that people change perception of a partner from similar to different when the relationship stops.

Results Their results were in line with the predictions. The participants' ideal partners were seen as similar to, and more positive than, the self. In contrast, former partners were seen as different from and more negative than the self.

Conclusion People tend to perceive their partner from their current perspective. If they are no longer attracted to a partner, he or she is seen as different from and generally not as positive as oneself.

Sociocultural origins of attraction

Proximity factor – physical closeness is important in attraction
The proximity theory of attraction suggests that simply being in the physical presence of another individual will enhance the probability of becoming friends.

Festinger et al. (1950) The role of proximity on friendship patterns
Aim The aim of the field study was to investigate formation of friendship patterns at Westgate Housing for student couples.

Procedure The researchers made observations and interviewed the residents regularly.

Results
- Results showed that proximity or opportunities to bump into each other on a daily basis increased chances for friendships. After some months more than 10 times as

many friendships had developed with people who lived in the same building, and even more with people who lived next door.

Conclusions
- The researchers suggest that physical proximity increases opportunities for interaction, which in turn increases *familiarity*. According to **Zajonc (1968)** the mere exposure effect is enough to increase liking. Also, we seem to be most attracted to people who are similar to us (see the similarity-attraction hypothesis) because people who resemble us or agree with us also reassure us **(Fiske, 2004)**.
- Geographical proximity may still be a factor in finding friends and lovers but with the Internet, dating sites, and chat rooms people at distance can now easily contact each other and develop friendships or romantic relationships. The Internet is thus creating a "psychological proximity" that can replace the "geographical proximity".

Cultural factors in attraction
Evolutionary theories claim that attraction is determined by biological factors. This implies that men and women should prefer the same in their partners (universal factors) but this is only true to some extent. Cultural factors seem to play a role as well (e.g. the role attributed to chastity).

Buss et al. (1990) Cross-cultural factors in attraction
Aim The aim of the International Mate Selection Project was to identify the characteristics that individuals valued in potential mates worldwide.

Procedure Participants were 9,474 individuals from 37 cross-cultural samples (33 countries and five islands on six continents; mean age 23.15). The data was collected through two questionnaires developed in the USA and translated.

Results
- Respondents in nearly all cultures rated **"mutual attraction and love"** as the most important in a relationship. This shows that the desire for mutual love in a relationship is not merely a Western phenomenon.
- **"Chastity"** showed the largest effect for culture (37% of the variance). Chastity was valued in China, India, Taiwan,

Palestinian Israel, and Iran. Respondents in the Netherlands and the Scandinavian countries did not care about chastity.
- **"Good financial prospects"**, **"good earning capacity"**, ambition, and social status are consistently valued more in a partner by women than men cross-culturally.
- **Youth"** is valued more by men than women. Men prefer wives that are younger but how much younger depends on the culture. In cultures that allow many wives, there may be large age differences.
- **"Physical attractiveness"** in a partner is valued more by men than women. Cross-cultural norms of physical attractiveness are, for example, clear and supple skin, regular features, full lips.

Evaluation The study suffered from problems of translation-back translation in the questionnaires, which could decrease validity of the results. The samples for each country were not representative so it is impossible to generalize the findings.

8.6 Discuss the role of communication in maintaining relationships

Role of attributions in the maintenance of relationships

Fletcher et al. (1987) Attributions in dating couples

Aim To study whether patterns of attributions were related to relationship satisfaction factors (happiness, commitment, and love).

Procedure Participants were 100 female and 31 male undergraduate students in a heterosexual dating relationship not living together. The study was conducted in the USA.

First participants completed various questionnaires. After two months 95 participants were still in their relationship. They were asked to write a free-response description of the relationship in their own words and fill out a questionnaire.

Results Individuals with the highest relationship satisfaction after two months attributed positive behaviour to themselves and their partner (dispositional) attributions) and attributed negative behaviours to situational factors. Participants in happy relationships tended to describe the relationship in more interpersonal terms ("we") in the free-response description. Participants who made more situational attributions for relationship maintenance reported significantly less happiness, less commitment, and lower levels of love.

Evaluation The study suffers from sampling bias (more females than males and all students) and there is a cultural bias as the study was conducted in the USA. This may limit generalizations.

Bradbury and Fincham (1990) Meta-analysis of research on attributions in married couples

- Spouses in *happy relationships* tended to focus on their partner's positive behaviour as part of the person's character. They were more likely to make attributions that locate the cause of

  1. positive events to dispositional factors in the partner (i.e. positive things happen because of the partner)
  2. negative events to situational factors (i.e. the partner is not to blame).

- Spouses in *unhappy relationships* tended to see their partner's negative behaviour as part of his or her character and downplay the partner's positive behaviour. They were more likely to make attributions that locate the cause of

  1. positive events to situational factors (i.e. positive events do not happen because of the partner)
  2. negative events to dispositional factors (i.e. the partner is to blame).

Discussion

- According to **Duck (1988)** some conflict is inevitable in all relationships. How people handle conflicts can promote growth of the relationship or end it. The important thing is not whether there is conflict but *how* conflict is handled.

- **Fincham (2004)** claims there is solid evidence for an association between attribution and marital satisfaction. *Happy couples* use a **relationship-enhancing pattern** ((e.g. not blaming the partner for negative events and giving credit for positive events). Unhappy couples use a distress-maintaining pattern (e.g. blaming the partner for negative events and not giving credit for positive events).

Role of communication of emotions in maintaining relationships

- Emotional expression and control seem to play a role in conflict resolution and marital satisfaction. Non-verbal factors (e.g. face, voice, gestures, and arousal of the autonomic nervous system) predicts emotional expressions according to **Gottman and Levenson (1986)**.

- **Gottman (1979)** found that dissatisfied couples displayed more negative affect and were more likely to return negative affect (negative reciprocity or retaliation). It was also relatively easy to predict how these couples would interact in conflict situations based on the spouse's behaviour.

Levenson and Gottman (1983) Observational study of relationship between marital dissatisfaction and negative affect

- In a laboratory 30 couples were observed while they had a **low-conflict discussion** of an event of the day and a **high-conflict discussion** on a major source of disagreement in their relationship. The discussions were videotaped and each spouse returned to the laboratory to make a self-evaluation of their communication (positive, negative, or neutral).

- Results showed that marital dissatisfaction was associated with higher levels of expressed negative emotions (negative affect) and return of negative affect (retaliation).

- The researchers took physiological measures during both sessions (e.g. heart rate, skin conduction) and found that the unhappy couples displayed similar physiological arousal (stress response).

- The researchers concluded that unhappy couples experience a negative spiral of expressed negative emotions that led to increased stress and mutual unhappiness.

- The observation was performed in a laboratory so it may be that the observed behaviour was not natural.

Gottman and Krokoff (1989) Comparison of data from two observations of couples

- The researchers compared data from two longitudinal observational studies of couples. The couples were observed in their home and in a laboratory discussion either on a low-conflict or a high-conflict issue. Conflict was only seen as a negative sign if couples could not resolve it constructively.

- Results showed that expressions of anger and disagreement were not necessarily associated with marital dissatisfaction

over time. Couples who solved their conflict with mutual satisfaction were more satisfied with their relationship.

- Couples who avoided conflict were less satisfied. According to the researchers this is because the couples do not have the opportunity to experience that they can solve conflicts together (relational efficacy).

- Three specific dysfunctional communication patterns (defensiveness, stubbornness, and withdrawal from interaction) were reliably associated with marital dissatisfaction over time.

Gottman's theory of the Four Horsemen of the Apocalypse – communication that predicts marital dissatisfaction

- **Criticism:** Making dispositional attributions (e.g. attacking the partner's personality or character with the intent of making the partner wrong).

- **Contempt:** Attacking the partner's sense of self with the intention to insult or psychologically abuse him or her (e.g. hostility, sarcasm, mockery).

- **Defensiveness:** Seeing yourself as a victim (e.g. making excuses by referring to factors out of your control, cross-complaining – listening to your partner's complaint but returning it with a complaint of your own).

- **Stonewalling:** Withdrawing from the relationship as a way to avoid (e.g. by silent treatment, monosyllabic response, or changing the subject.

Discussion

- Expressions of positive affect are generally associated with increased intimacy and relationship satisfaction. Positive affect seems to be particularly powerful in non-verbal communication (**Gottman et al. 1977**).

- **Noller and Gallois (1986)** videotaped standard content messages sent by married couples to one another with positive, neutral, and negative affect. They found that spouses who used more positive non-verbal communication (e.g. smiles and touching) also reported a higher level of marital satisfaction. Husbands who scored low on marital satisfaction used more eyebrow flashes on positive messages compared to happy husbands.

- Partners with communication problems can learn new positive communication patterns (e.g. validating the partner by verbal and non-verbal communication, taking responsibility for your own actions and learning from experience, avoiding being defensive, using empathy to understand your partner's expressed emotions and acting on these).

Exam Tip Research on the role of communication of emotions in relationships may also be used to answer questions on why relationships change or end (see unit 8.8).

Formation of relationships

- Individualist cultures assume that the free choice of a spouse is based on romantic love but they may in reality be "arranged" by social position, religion, wealth, opportunities, and class, according to **Duck (1999)**.
- **Moghaddam et al (1993)** argues that interpersonal relationships:
  - in Western cultures tend to be individualistic, voluntary, and temporary
  - in non-Western cultures tend to be collectivist, involuntary, and permanent.

Singh (2005) Arranged marriages in India

- The majority of marriages in India are still arranged by the parents or their representatives with or without the consent of the boy or girl involved. There is no room for romantic marriage in the Western sense. In the big cities, educated people now tend to seek the consent of their sons and daughters about the choice of preferred partners.
- In the past, young Indians trusted their parents in the process of finding a suitable match. A large percentage of the arranged marriages seemed to work, and if they did not very few knew about the dissolution of the marriage.

- In collectivist cultures, social networks motivate marriages. Families play an active and often decisive role in choosing marriage partners for the young. Love is supposed to be discovered after marriage (**Bellur, 1995**). In many parts of the world, arranged marriages are still the norm although modifications are now seen in some cultures.
- **Levine et al. (1995)** asked college students from 11 countries if they would marry someone who had all the qualities they desired even if they did not love the person. In the USA 4% said yes. In Australia 5% said yes. In the UK 8% said yes. These are individualist countries. In India 49% said yes and in Pakistan 51% said yes. These countries are collectivist.

Buss et al. (1990) Cross-cultural study of mate preferences in 33 countries

- This study investigated the effects of culture and gender on heterosexual mate preferences in a sample of 9,494 adults from 33 countries.
- In all cultures, men and women agreed that love and mutual attraction are primary factors in mate selection.
- In countries with traditional values (collectivist countries such as China, India, Iran) men placed high value on a woman's chastity, her desire for home and children, and her ability as a cook and homemaker. In the same societies, women valued men with good financial prospects, high social status, and ambition.

Maintenance of relationships

- A large proportion of marriages in the Western world end in divorce (in some countries up to 50% of marriages). In some cultures, divorce is non-existent or rare (e.g. in China).

- Arranged marriages usually last longer than romantic marriages (**Fiske, 2004**). Marriage in traditional societies is a contract between families and often involves economic and social engagements that create powerful bonds between the families and makes divorce impossible. This could be a reason for stability of marriages.

Are arranged marriages happier?

- **Gupta and Singh (1982)** interviewed 50 Indian couples who had married for love or lived in an arranged marriage. The couples who married for love reported diminished feelings of love after a few years of marriage. Those who lived in arranged marriages reported higher levels of love.
- **Yelsma and Athappilly (1988)** compared 28 Indian couples in arranged marriages, 25 Indian couples in love marriages, and 31 American couples. Individuals in arranged marriages scored higher on marital satisfaction compared to the couples in love marriages.

- **Xiaohe and Whyte (1990)** investigated the prediction of defenders of arranged marriages that "love matches start out hot and grow cold, while arranged marriages start out cold and grow hot". A sample of 586 married women in the Sichuan province in China participated. The data showed that the role of parents had declined and young people were more involved in matchmaking. The researchers found that wives in love marriages were more satisfied with their marital relationship than the wives who were in arranged marriages. This was found regardless of the length of the marriage. The researchers concluded that their data does not support the idea that arranged marriages are happier than love marriages.

According to **Hogg and Vaughn (1998)** in spite of the focus on love in relationships in the West, there is general agreement among psychologists that a relationship that survives over time is one in which the partners adapt and change with respect to what they expect of each other. Love that involves friendship, caring, respect, and mutual sharing of experiences could result in the powerful bonding of lasting relationships as in the ideal of the Western "love marriage".

- Sternberg (1986) suggested the **triangular theory of love** with three components that many psychologists believe are important in close relationships:
  - ☐ **intimacy** (feeling close, connected, and bonded)
  - ☐ **passion** (romance and physical and sexual attraction)
  - ☐ **commitment** (desire to maintain the relationship in spite of adversity and costs).
- Partners begin to develop an **interdependent** relationship from the beginning of their relationship and they gradually increase their mutual involvement. Successful couples tend to develop more commitment and intimacy over time than less successful couples.
- According to **Buunk (1998)** one of the most prominent features in which happy and unhappy couples tend to differ is the way they communicate with each other. Couples are happier when their interaction is characterized by problem solving and open communication (see unit 8.6).

Building intimacy is dependent on being able to communicate openly.

Buunk (1998) Characteristics of happy and unhappy couples

Happy couples	Unhappy couples
■ Express their feelings openly and disclose their thoughts. ■ Show affection and understanding of each others' feelings (empathy and perspective taking).	■ Show conflict-avoidance (e.g. not wanting to discuss problems). ■ Demonstrate soothing (e.g.ignoring or covering up differences). ■ Take part in destructive communication (e.g. criticizing, disagreeing, complaining).

Equity theory and relationship satisfaction

- According to **equity theory** there must be a *balance* between the two partners in a relationship, i.e. the relationship should be perceived as fair. People compare their own *gains* compared to that of the partner's and may look for alternatives if they are not satisfied.
- **Buss and Shackelford (1997)** found that sexual dissatisfaction and specific sources of conflicts (for example partner's complaints about jealousy) were linked to thinking about extramarital sex in the first year of marriage. This could support the theory.

- **Clark and Mills (1979)** argue that romantic relationships are based on sharing and belonging - not equity principles. Partners respond to each other's needs because they want to feel close to each other. The study found that individuals interpreted a partners' tendency to reciprocate as a sign that he or she was not really interested in a romantic relationship. The researchers argue that the level of rewards (not equity) is more likely to predict satisfaction in love relationships.

Investment model of commitment (theory)

- **Rusbult et al. (1991)** suggested the **investment model of commitment** with the concept of accommodation as an important strategy to maintain a relationship (i.e. ensure longevity of the relationship).
- **Accommodation** means that a person is willing to adopt a constructive approach and inhibit the impulse to react destructively (i.e. retaliation) when a partner displays destructive behaviour. High levels of accommodation are consistently associated with well-being.

- **Murray and Holmes (1997)** found that over time partners in committed relationships created "positive illusions" of their partners. The **idealization** of the partner was positively associated with relationship satisfaction and fewer conflicts. Confidence in the partner seems to foster a sense of trust and security (secure attachment), which in turn promotes accommodation in conflicts. Idealization could also be a potential threat to a relationship if the partner cannot live up to the high expectations.

Flora and Segrin (2003) Analysis of young couples' satisfaction and stability of relationship
Aim To investigate the extent to which shared interests and spending time together was a predictor of perception of quality of the relationship.

Procedure The participants were young dating couples (dating for at least six months) and married couples (married for around four years). The study was a longitudinal study and data collection took place through questionnaires and interviews

At the beginning of the study the participants described positive and negative feelings, disappointment, and contentment with their partner. After 12 months the participants filled out questionnaires to measure well-being and satisfaction with the relationship. All married couples were still together but 25% of the dating couples had split up.

The researchers also looked into factors that could predict break-up of the relationship in the first interview with *dating couples*.

Results The first interview showed that preference of shared interests and spending time together was important in marital satisfaction, especially for the men. Positive and negative feelings were not considered very important. For women the amount of their own negative feelings and disappointment with the partner predicted break-up.

After one year men's satisfaction with the relationship still depended on shared interests and spending time together. Experiences of positive and negative feelings played a role but only if their partner showed negative feelings. For women, the amount of their own negative feelings about the partner was associated with less satisfaction. Shared interests and spending time together was only the second most important factor for women.

Evaluation The study was conducted with a sample from the USA so it may not be possible to generalize the findings. Self-reports may be biased.

> **Exam Tip** You may include studies and theories from unit 8.7 in your discussion on relationships. Patterns of communication could be one factor in your analysis of why relationships may change or end.

Sprecher (1999) Longitudinal study on development of love over time

Aim To investigate whether people in close relationships reported increased love over time. The second aim was to study how beliefs about relationships could change.

Procedure A self-selected sample of 101 romantic heterosexual student couples was surveyed five times over four years. Each time they completed questionnaires to measure love, commitment, and satisfaction. They were also asked to report changes since previous surveys. Only 41% of the couples were together at the end of the study.

Results Individuals in *intact relationships* said they felt an an increase in love, commitment, and satisfaction over time but this was not supported by the data. This indicates that happy couples wanted to see increases in positive affect (positive illusions). Individuals in *broken relationships* were likely to say they felt a decrease in commitment, love, and satisfaction in the time before the break-up. Satisfaction decreased the most in this group. This suggests that people end their relationships because of dissatisfaction rather than the disappearance of love.

The results support the idea of "positive illusions" as beneficial for a relationship.

Evaluation The study was conducted with a sample of young students in the USA so it may not be possible to generalize the findings. Self-reports may be biased.

8.9 Evaluate sociocultural explanations of the origins of violence

Bandura (1977) suggests that people learn to behave violently (including violent attitudes and norms) through direct experiences and through observing models.

- Social learning theory focuses on **observational learning** and **modelling**. The theory proposes that children learn to be violent due to exposure to violent models and because violent behaviour is rewarded. The support for this proposition comes from the results of the classic Bobo doll experiment (**Bandura et al., 1961**) showing that children who watched an aggressive model being rewarded for aggression were likely to imitate the aggression later.

- Social learning theory (SLT) has been applied to explain the development of aggression and intergenerational transmission of violence through **socialization**. Children are influenced by socialization factors such as the family, the immediate environment (including peers), and the media.

- Social learning can be *direct* via instructions or *indirect* (e.g. role models and no direct instructions). Children who grow up in violent families and neighbourhoods where they watch models use violence and obtain benefits from it (e.g. power) may be likely to see violence as a legitimate means to get what they want or exert power over other people. They may even justify the use of violence.

Totten (2003) Qualitative study on girlfriend abuse among violent marginal male youth in Canada

Aim To explore how young girlfriend abusers used violence to construct their masculinity. The study focused on how families and peer groups contributed to learning and identification with violent norms as part of establishing a masculine gender role.

Procedure A purposive sample of 30 abusive adolescent males from a large city in Canada participated in the study. They all had pro-abusive beliefs, masculine ideals, and admitted to using violence towards their girlfriends.

The mean age of the boys was 15.6 years, six belonged to an ethnic minority and the rest were white. Many were gang members and most had dropped out of school early. The researchers used semi-structured interviews to collect data.

Results The adolescents' background had similar features. They had all been exposed to violent behaviour in the family and they saw this as justified and even necessary. The fathers all had rigid authoritarian beliefs (e.g. rigid gender roles). The fathers all used violence to control family members or to defend their honour.

Out of 30 adolescents, 21 had adopted violent behaviour. They were all abusive and used physical and sexual violence for the same reasons as the fathers. The boys said that they had the right to use violence if girlfriends did not behave. In some cases the fathers had given them instructions on how to abuse women in particular situations.

Evaluation The study used a small and purposive sample so it is not possible to generalize. The qualitative data gave an in-depth insight into how the violent adolescents experienced the use of violence themselves. This could be used as a starting point to design interventions to prevent violence, such as by providing positive role models (mentoring) as well as education and job opportunities.

Strengths of SLT in relation to violent behaviour	Limitations of SLT in relation to violent behaviour
<ul><li>Social norms of violence can be transmitted from parents to children as predicted by SLT.</li><li>SLT can also explain that adolescents use violence in marginalized social peer groups because it pays off in the form of status (reinforcement).</li></ul>	<ul><li>SLT cannot explain how structural factors such as poverty contribute to establishing the social norms of male superiority.</li><li>The theory does not take individual factors such as intelligence and personality into account.</li><li>Some people may be more prone to violence (e.g. due to brain damage as a result of childhood abuse).</li></ul>

Subculture of violence theory (Wolfgang and Ferracuti, 1967)

- According to the theory violent behaviour results from a *commitment* to subcultural norms and values. Individual violent values lead to violent behaviour because subcultural values act as a mechanism of **social control** among group members.

- Violence is used as a means to defend honour and maintain status (e.g. within the group, in the family, or in relation to other groups). If members of subcultures perceive threats to reputation or honour they will defend their honour with violence if necessary, even if it threatens their life.

- The theory was developed based on work in an inner-city African-American neighborhood in Philadephia. It was suggested that the subculture of violence phenomenon was a lower-class masculine phenomenon related to race. This is now contested.

Evaluation of the theory of subculture of violence

- The theory can explain how violence may be used to establish and maintain power within a social group (i.e. to establish social hierarchies). Dominance and power could also be one explanation of school bullying (e.g. **Gest et al., 2003**, found that bullies are seen as popular and "cool").

- The theory does not explain what sociocultural structural factors could lead to violence because the primary focus is on social norms and values as the origin of violence. High rates of violence could be the result of poverty and class oppression rather than a culture of honour (Anderson, 1999).

- **Nisbett and Cohen (1996)** found support for the theory's proposition that violence is used to maintain honour in the Southern states of the USA where there are high rates of violence. They argue that a "culture of honour" seems to have survived from the herding economies brought to the area by Irish and Scottish settlers between the 17th and 19th centuries.

Berburg and Thorlindsson (2005) Subculture of violence influences aggressive behaviour

Aim This was a large-scale survey of adolescent boys and girls at public schools in Iceland. The research was carried out to investigate whether pro-violent values influenced group conduct norms as predicted by the subculture of violence theory.

Procedure Data was collected in a large-scale survey in Iceland with adolescent boys and girls in 49 public schools. Participants were between 15 and 16 years old. The sample was a racially homogenous group.

Participants answered questions on how often they engaged in various threatening and physically violent acts (e.g.fighting, kicking, punching).

Results Results showed a significant impact of conduct norms on aggressive behaviour. The most violent students said they conformed to group conduct norms. Boys were more likely to behave aggressively than girls.

Group pressure to respond to personal attacks with aggression or violence could act as a form of social control.

The predictions of the subculture of violence theory were supported by these cross-cultural data. The conclusion was that group adherence to values and norms encourage aggressive behaviour through:

1. internalization of values encouraging violence
2. social control processes ensure adherence to conduct norms (i.e. conformity).

Evaluation The survey was based on a large sample of adolescents from Iceland so the findings could be generalized to similar age groups in Iceland. An equal number of boys and girls participated so there was no gender bias.

The data was collected through self-reports so there may be a bias. People do not always tell the truth, especially in a socially sensitive study like this one.

Conclusion

The two psychological explanations of violence (SLT and the theory of subculture of violence) suffer from the same limitations of mainstream theories of violence that tend to focus on either **internal causes** (i.e. locate violence within the person) or **external causes** (i.e. locate violence within the social environment). Such one-dimensional explanations of violence mostly acknowledge the importance of other variables SLT biological factors) but these are often not included in the explanations.

Critical thinking: could biological factors cause violence?

Testosterone and violence
- Testosterone is a steroid male sex hormone secreted in the testes of males and in the ovaries of females. Men produce ten times more testosterone than women.
- Testosterone has been linked to aggression and dominance behaviour because castration of a male usually has a pacifying effect on aggressive behaviour in males.
- The relationship between aggression and testosterone is complex and difficult to test scientifically because measurement of testosterone levels from blood or saliva is not reliable.

McAndrew (2009): Evolutionary explanation of the link between testosterone, aggression, and dominance
- Evolution has shaped hormonal responses in males that are particularly sensitive to situations that involve challenges to status or competition with other males.
- Testosterone is secreted to prepare the body to respond to competition or challenges to one's status. Any situation that is perceived as a threat or a challenge to a male's status would result in an increase in testosterone levels.
- The hormonal changes in such situations are important factors in explanations of aggression. Explanations that do not include biological factors are incomplete at best.

Nisbett and Cohen (1996) Quasi-experimental study to test relationship between "culture of honour" and physiological responses to an insult

Aim To test whether male participants from the South (assumed to belong to a culture of honour) would be more likely than male participants from the North of the USA to respond with aggression to insults. The researchers also measured cortisol and testosterone levels. The participants were all university students.

Procedure
- The researchers predicted that southerners from a "culture of honour" would be more aggressive and have higher levels of cortisol and testosterone than northerners.
- Participants were experimentally insulted publicly. Cortisol and testosterone levels were measured before and after the insult through saliva and blood test.

Results After the experimental insult, cortisol levels rose 79% for the southerners and 33% for northerners. Testosterone levels were higher in southerners who were insulted. They were generally more aggressive and showed more domineering behaviour than any other group.

Conclusions
- The researchers argued that southerners who were insulted in front of others saw themselves as *diminished* in masculine reputation and status. This could explain why they exhibited more aggressive and domineering behaviour.
- In a culture of honour males who do not retaliate to insults risk their masculine reputation. Culture of honour norms dictate retaliation. Such norms have become embedded in social roles, expectations, and shared definitions of masculinity.

Exam Tip Studying two explanations with related research and evaluation is enough for the exam. Critical thinking means that you could consider alternative explanations of violence than the sociocultural explanations. You could use the biological explanation of aggression here to argue that sociocultural explanations in isolation do not offer a full picture. The theory of testosterone and violence presented here could lend some support to the propositions of "culture of honour" theory.

Discuss the relative effectiveness of two strategies for reducing violence

8.10

The Olweus Bullying Prevention Programme (OBPP)

- The programme includes all staff, parents, and students in the school (universal programme). The aim is to change the school environment as a whole while targeting individual students. Teachers receive training so that they can recognize and deal with bullying and implement cooperative learning strategies in the classroom. Includes supervision of the playgrounds and lunchroom. Students fill out questionnaires.

- The aim is to identify bullies in elementary, middle, and high schools and help them and their victims. Adults should be positive role models and set firm limits to unacceptable behaviour.

Olweus (1993) Longitudinal study on the effect of OBPP on bullying

- The study was conducted in the Bergen area in Norway after three adolescents had committed suicide as a result of bullying. A sample of 2,500 children from fifth to eighth grades participated in the programme over two years. Data collection took place through observations and questionnaires (teachers, students).

- Results showed an overall 50% reduction in self-reported bullying incidents (victimization or bullying other students) and a general improvement of the social climate of the classes.

- Students' self-reports showed higher satisfaction with school life, improved order and discipline, more positive social relationships, and a more positive attitude toward schoolwork and the school in general.

- This indicates a high level of effectiveness of the programme but not all studies find the same. **Roland (1993)** could not replicate the findings in another part of Norway. **Olweus (2003)** only found a 21–38 % reduction in observed bullying in a later study and the same was observed in the USA.

Black (2007) Implementation of OBPP in the USA

- Participants were 13 inner city schools in one urban school district. The programme ran for four years but only nine schools completed.

- Results showed that not all schools followed the programme as it is intended (average fidelity to programme was 48%).

- Observed bullying incidents decreased 25.5% in all schools. The drop could perhaps be explained by the fact that all schools implemented increased supervision. On average, students' self-reported bullying incidents increased from 39% to 43% in year 4 of the programme but schools that implemented the programme most rigorously actually had a decrease in self-reported bullying.

- **Black (2007)** argues that the mixed results in terms of reduction in bullying could be due to less rigorous implementation, lack of resources, and cultural differences between Norway and the USA. OBPP was developed in Norway, where social responsibility for all is a core value. This value is perhaps difficult to translate into the American culture of individual independence.

MACS (Metropolitan Area Child Study) for prevention of aggressive behaviour and violence in children

- The programme consists of:
  - **A classroom programme** with focus on empathy training and social problem-solving skills.
  - **Training in social skills**, which takes place in small group sessions where students meet and discuss peer relations and adequate social problem-solving strategies.
  - **Family counselling**, which place in small groups with other families. The meetings start with lessons and then families discuss specific issues in relation to family-specific problems.

MACS Research Group (2002)

Aim To investigate whether the violence prevention programme could reduce aggression and violence.

Procedure

- This was a longitudinal, quasi-experimental field study with 2,181 elementary school students classified as high risk from two inner-city areas in the Midwest of the USA. The intervention ran over eight years. Participants mostly belonged to ethnic minority groups and many were poor (i.e. participated in the free lunch programme).

- The study included four conditions:
  1. control group (no intervention)
  2. full programme
  3. only the classroom programme
  4. the classroom programme and social skills training for high-risk children.

Results Overall there was no effect of the programme on levels of aggression but there was an impact in some of the subgroups.

- Students who had participated in the full programme either early or late and came from low-risk schools showed less aggression compared to the control group.

- Students from high-risk schools showed a higher level of aggression after the programme compared to the control group. The study showed that early intervention is most effective if the full programme is offered.

Guerra et al. (2006) Relative effectiveness of MACS

- Normally aggressive behaviour has negative consequences in the peer group but it seems that some aggressive children are able to maintain a popular status among peers. Youth who began the MACS late intervention program and already had high levels of popularity were able to increase in aggressiveness while in the programme.

- If aggression and violence is seen as normal (normative) in the peer group (e.g. because you live in a violent neighbourhood) and it pays off (e.g. in increased attention from teachers or increased peer status) it is likely to continue in spite of intervention programmes, according to **Guerra et al. (2006)**.

- There are general problems in precise measurement of effectiveness. Most effect studies look at average scores (e.g. how many children become delinquent) but do not include how various factors could affect outcomes for different groups. This means that programmes may be effective sometimes and with particular groups but not in other situations.

Discussion of relative effectiveness of school-based programmes

- It seems that school-based strategies to reduce violence are not always very effective. It is probably because violence is a complex phenomenon that must be addressed at social, cultural, individual, and socioeconomic levels. It is necessary to look at what works when and with whom as well as what does not work (**Guerra et al., 2006**).

- **Ferguson et al. (2007)** performed a meta-analysis of effectiveness of school-based anti-bullying programmes and found that overall they were not very effective in reducing bullying or violent behaviour in schools. The programmes targeting at-risk youth were slightly better. The reason for this could be that bullying may allow some bullies to climb the social dominance hierarchy among children at the expense of other children. For such bullies the anti-bullying programmes offer no incentives.

Exam Tip The learning outcomes require you to study two strategies for reducing violence.

8.11 Discuss the effects of short-term and long-term exposure to violence

Stress and coping

- Individuals who are exposed to violence short-term (e.g. in terrorist attacks, natural disasters, school shootings, or other traumatic events) or long-term (e.g. victims of bullying) will typically exhibit a stress response that includes fear and physiological arousal partly due to secretion of stress hormones and activation of the amygdala (fear centre). See more on this in unit 3.8.

- The fight or flight response (**Cannon, 1932**) is a pattern of physiological arousal that prepares humans (and animals) to react to emergency situations. Normally stress responses are short-lived but with long-term exposure to stressors humans are not able to return to normal physiological functioning. This could develop into chronic stress and post-traumatic stress disorder (PTSD).

- **Lazarus (1975)** suggested the cognitive appraisal model of coping. According to this model cognitive appraisal can influence stress responses (see unit 3.8).

Effects of short-term exposure to violence (terrorism)

The case of terrorism

Terrorism includes attacks on civilians with the purpose of injuring or killing as many as possible. Being exposed to violent terrorist attacks may result in depression and long-term PTSD partly because terrorist attacks could lead to a perception of continuous threat to one's safety and well-being.

Shalev (1995) Stress responses to direct exposure to a terrorist attack in Israel

Aim To investigate PTSD after terrorist attacks in a sample of 12 hospitalized survivors of an attack on an Israeli bus.

Procedure

- Victims were interviewed after the attack and after 10 months. The researchers used a specific questionnaire (Impact of Event Scale) to assess symptoms of PTSD.

- In the first interview the victims were extremely upset and had intrusive thoughts about the event but they showed no sign of avoidance coping (i.e. avoiding to think of or talk about the traumatic event).

- In the second interview intrusive thoughts had decreased but avoidance coping had increased. Overall, victims showed significant levels of PTSD in the last interview.

Evaluation The study was a case study with a small sample so it is not possible to generalize the findings.

Schuster et al. (2001) Stress responses to direct and indirect exposure to terrorism during 9/11

Aim To investigate the extent to which adult Americans suffered from stress symptoms in the immediate aftermath of the terrorist attacks.

Procedure Participants were 560 adults living in the USA who were randomly selected. The researchers collected data through telephone interviews three to four days after the attacks. Five of the questions were related to PTSD.

Results Even *indirect exposure* to the terrorist attack could result in stress reactions – 90% of respondents said they experienced a little bit of stress, 68% said they were moderately stressed but 44% said they were very stressed. People who lived close to New York suffered from higher levels of stress overall.

Conclusions

- The study found that 36% of the respondents considered terrorism to be a very serious problem where they lived and 44% anticipated terrorist attacks in the next five years.

- The study found that, for some people, the level of stress was associated with how much they watched television. Extensive television watching correlated with high levels of stress because people perceived what they saw as a threat to personal safety. They appraised the situation as being dangerous to them personally and reacted to this perceived threat. This is consistent with the cognitive appraisal model of stress (**Lazarus, 1975**).

Effects of long-term exposure to violence (bullying)

The case of bullying

- **Cyber bullying and depression: Wang et al. (2010)** found that victims of cyber bullying had higher levels of depression than victims of face-to-face bullying. About 14% had experienced cyber bullying. Boys and girls are equally vulnerable. Cyber bullying seems to be particularly hurtful because the abuse is spread much wider through the social media and victims do not know how many people may have seen it.

- **Long-term exposure to bullying and depression: Hyman (1990)** argues that long-term exposure to school victimization (bullying) can severely affect a child's daily functioning, including school performance. It affects the child's future psychological health and may lead to depression and PTSD.

Carney and Hazler (2007) Cortisol levels and bullying

Aim To investigate changes in cortisol levels in relation to bullying.

Procedure The researchers took saliva tests from 94 sixth-grade students between the ages of 9 and 14. Students also filled out questionnaires on their experience of being bullied or watching somebody being bullied (being a bystander). Cortisol levels were tested in the morning and before lunchtime (a period associated with bullying).

Results Anticipation of bullying was associated with high levels of stress and anxiety in both victims and bystanders. Long-term exposure to bullying was related to lower levels of cortisol (hypocortisol). This condition is associated with chronic fatigue syndrome and post-traumatic stress disorder.

Evaluation

- The researchers argue that cortisol levels increase when a person experiences a short-term exposure to bullying. This affects learning and memory. Long-term bullying and low levels of cortisol may have more enduring negative consequences on physical, social, and psychological health.

Bullying and PTSD

- **Mynard et al. (2000)** studied the effects of long-term exposure to bullying and posttraumatic stress (anxiety disorder).

- They gave a questionnaire called "the victim scale" to 331 British pupils. Bullying was defined as physical victimization (e.g. hitting or punching the victim), verbal victimization (i.e. name calling), social exclusion (e.g. excluding the victim from taking part in games or being part of the peer group in general), and attacks on property (e.g. ruining the victim's mobile).

- Results showed that around 40% of the students had experienced some kind of bullying during their schooling. All types of bullying were perceived as stressful but the results indicate that different types of aggression may have different effects. Social exclusion is more likely to lead to PTSD. Overall, bullying had a very negative impact on the victims' psychological health.

- Experiences of peer victimization may lead to serious long-term psychological problems such as powerlessness, helplessness, poor self-confidence, and social isolation, which are all linked to PTSD.

Intrinsic motivation	Extrinsic motivation
■ Intrinsic motivation comes from *within* the person (e.g. feelings of competence, control, or the satisfaction of being able to run a marathon).	■ Extrinsic motivation comes from external rewards (e.g. winning a trophy or money, social prestige, or a coach's praise).

Bandura (1977) Theory of self-efficacy

■ The theory suggested that people who gradually come to master a task develop a feeling of self-efficacy, i.e. an expectation that they are competent and successful in that particular task. This serves as intrinsic motivation. According to Bandura, self-efficacy can be individual but a sports team may also have self-efficacy and this could influence team performance.

■ The theory is based on the assumption that people's engagement and persistence in a task are determined by beliefs in their own competence and expectations of success or failure. People high in self-efficacy set higher goals, try harder, and persist longer. People low in self-efficacy tend to give up in the face of difficulty.

■ Self-efficacy refers to situation-specific confidence. Self-efficacy is related to a specific task and may differ in training and competitive situations (e.g. athletes may believe they can perform a jump shot in basketball in practice but may still apprehend a good defender in a game).

■ Bandura (1997) argues that people's level of motivation and performance in sport are based more on what they *believe* than on what is objectively true. Self-efficacy beliefs can be manipulated (e.g. by a coach, and a person's self-efficacy can be measured).

Self-efficacy beliefs are influenced by four factors that interact to affect efficacy expectations and performance:

■ **Previous experience:** Experiences of success increase self-efficacy and experiences of failure may reduce self-efficacy. If an athlete has developed self-efficacy in a specific domain, he or she is more likely to be able to cope with setbacks and make appropriate attributions.

■ **Modelling (vicarious experiences):** Watching other people perform the task successfully may increase an athlete's perception of being able to do it also, especially if the model is similar to the athlete.

■ **Verbal persuasion:** Athletic performance could increase if another person encourages the athletes to believe they can do it (e.g. a team member or a coach). Positive feedback from a coach may also increase perceptions of self-efficacy.

■ **Emotional and physiological arousal:** The way an athlete interprets emotional and physiological arousal will affect self-efficacy beliefs in relation to own performance. If a weightlifter interprets increased pulse rate as anxiety it could reduce self-efficacy but if it is interpreted positively it can boost self-efficacy.

Hochstetler et al. (1985)

Aim To investigate if it is possible to manipulate expectations of success in a cycling task using different models.

Procedure A sample of 40 females took part in a study they thought measured physical performance in a cycling task. Participants were divided into two groups and saw a video before the task. Group 1 saw a video of a woman who had great problems doing the task and showed signs of distress. Group 2 saw a video of a woman who had no problems doing the task and seemed to cope well with it.

Results Participants in group 1 found the task much harder than those in group 2. Manipulation of expectations and modelling had an effect.

Evaluation The study was a controlled experiment with issues of ecological validity but the findings are important. Slight deception was used in this experiment but it would not have been possible to run the study without the use of deception. The participants were all females so the findings cannot be generalized to males. The results indicate that it is possible to manipulate beliefs of self-efficacy and this could be applied in sport.

Bandura and Banfield (1991) studied self-efficacy beliefs in athletes and how this affected performance. They found that athletes who believed that *effort* made a difference were more likely to develop self-efficacy than athletes who believed in innate ability. The researchers argued that self-efficacy beliefs are not the only factor in success. Having the necessary skills, being able to set realistic goals, and being physically and psychologically ready are also important factors in successful performance in sport.

Feltz et al. (1989) performed a field study of changes in individual and team self-efficacy in a hockey team over a season. At the beginning of the season measures of individual self-efficacy were correlated to how the team performed. After eight games this correlation had changed and self-efficacy was more closely related to how the team performed. The results show that it takes some time to develop team self-efficacy and indicates that coaches should focus on how to develop team self-efficacy as it could be very important for team cohesion and team performance.

Strengths of self-efficacy theory	Limitations of self-efficacy theory
■ The theory has been successfully applied in sport psychology (e.g. in coaching where the four sources of self-efficacy can be manipulated to increase individual or team self-efficacy). ■ A number of self-efficacy measurements have been developed and applied in sport psychology. Perceived self-efficacy is a strong and consistent predictor of individual athletic performance.	■ Self-efficacy alone cannot explain success or failure in sport. Athletic performance is based on a complex interaction of psychological and physiological factors as well as skills. ■ Some studies are correlational so it is difficult to establish a cause-effect relationship between self-efficacy beliefs and performance. ■ It is not really clear how self-efficacy affects performance and motivation.

Harter (1978) Competence motivation theory

- The theory has been used to explain differences in sport.
- The theory is based on the assumption that humans have an innate motivation to be competent and that *feelings of competence* are the primary determinants of motivation. Perception of competence is linked to one's affective state. Positive feelings (positive affect) follow success in mastery attempts whereas negative feelings (negative affect) follow lack of success.

- According to Harter "perceived competence" is a predictor of **cognitive** (i.e. self-efficacy and control), **affective** (i.e. enjoyment or anxiety), and **behavioural** (i.e. achievement) outcomes. According to the theory, motivation is influenced indirectly by feelings of control, competence, and self-worth.

Harter's competence motivation theory

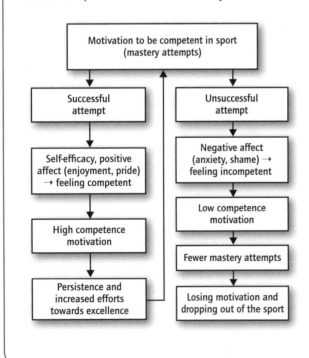

- According to Harter difficult but realistic goals provide the greatest positive feelings and intrinsic motivation. Successful mastery attempts promote self-efficacy and feelings of personal competence and this leads to higher motivation.

- Research shows that perceptions of competence are stronger in athletes who receive more opportunities to demonstrate physical competence. Therefore coaches should provide opportunities for mastery attempts and give focused feedback on performance.

- According to the theory unsuccessful mastery attempts result in perceived failure (negative affect) and less mastery attempts. The end result is low competence motivation and the athlete may loose motivation and drop out.

- Socializing agents (parents, coaches, and peers) play a role in the development of children's self-perception and affective responses. Harter claims that positive and contingent feedback should be given for effort and improvement to nurture children's perceptions of competence and enjoyment of sport. This will increase feelings of control, positive affect, and intrinsic motivation, which are important factors in success in sport.

Ommundsen et al. (1991)

Aim To examine the relationships between low perceived soccer and social competence with dropout from soccer. The researchers also examined the potential influence of negative affect.

Procedure Personal interviews were done with 223 boys, between 12 and 16 years of age, who played soccer in an organized league in Norway. Data were collected in two interviews with an interval of 16 months.

Results The older soccer players (14–16 years) who scored low on perceived soccer competence and low on perceived peer popularity showed the least soccer persistence. They also reported low soccer enjoyment (negative affect). For the younger players (12–13 years) lack of successful peer interaction meant low sense of belonging to the team. This had a negative influence on their motivation to continue. In the older soccer players perceived soccer competence was more important in predicting persistence in soccer than perceived social competence. In the younger players perceived social competence predicted persistence.

Evaluation The longitudinal design with interviews at the beginning and at the end made it possible to test whether perceived competence correlated with achievement motivation. There is a gender bias as only boys participated in the study.

Strengths of competence motivation theory	Limitations of competence motivation theory
■ Empirical research such as **Ommundsen et al. (1991)** has supported that competence beliefs are important and have predictive value in young athletes' participation in sport. ■ The theory and its concepts have been widely applied to establish successful coaching practices to establish strategies for enhancing perceived competence, enjoyment, and social support in sport and physical activity.	■ The theory cannot fully account for all factors that influence perceived competence and participation behaviours over time (e.g. why participation in sport tends to decline dramatically during adolescence for both boys and girls). This area needs more research. ■ The exact role of how the social and interpersonal factors in the sport context influence adolescents' motivation are not fully explained in the theory.

Using one or more research studies, explain the role of goal setting in the motivation of individuals

Three basic goals have been identified in sport psychology:

- **Outcome goals (or competitive or ego goals):** These focus on winning (e.g. receiving a medal a medal or beating an opponent).

- **Performance goals (task or mastery oriented):** These focus on individual performance independent of other sportspeople and the team. A typical performance goal for an athlete could be to serve five aces in a tennis match or run the 100-metre sprint in under 10 seconds.

- **Process goals:** These focus on improving form, strategy, or skill techniques that are required to achieve success (e.g. keeping the elbow down and wrist firm in the tennis backhand or keeping the back erect during dead lifts in body building).

Filby et al. (1999) did a field experiment to investigate how goals alone or in combination affected performance in college-age soccer players. The participants were assigned to five different goal groups based on scores on a soccer wall volley test. Group 1 had no goals (control group); group 2 had outcome goals only; group 3 had process goals only; group 4 had outcome and process goals; and group 5 had outcome, performance, and process goals in combination. The soccer players trained for five weeks based on their specific goal-setting strategy and were then tested again. The results showed that groups 4 and 5 outperformed the other groups and the control group had the lowest performance. This shows that a multiple goal strategy is the most effective. A goal setting strategy that uses all three types of goals has generally proved best for athletes in terms of increasing motivation by dealing with psychological development and performance improvement.

Nicholls (1984) Achievement goal theory of motivation

- According to this theory, an individual's internal sense of ability (competence) is a central achievement motive. The goals people adopt and how they define success and failure in relation to those goals will influence their motivation.

- Nicholls suggested two achievement goal orientations:

Task-goal orientation	Ego-goal orientation
■ The goal is mastery of a particular skill (task oriented) and mainly focused on development of skills.	■ The goal is to win and to outperform others.
■ There is higher intrinsic motivation because individuals enjoy participation in sport and experience situations as providing positive information about their performance.	■ There is lower intrinsic motivation because participation in sport is a means to obtain extrinsic rewards.
■ Perceived competence and self-efficacy is related to learning a new task, improving, or trying your best but not related to how others perform.	■ Individuals are more likely to experience pressure to perform well to show that they are better than others.
	■ Perceived competence is based on social comparison and not self-improvement.

- The theory predicts that individuals who adopt a task goal orientation are likely to be motivated Coaches could use this knowledge to promote intrinsic motivation in athletes by creating a motivational climate that is performance oriented rather than outcome oriented, i.e. emphasis on learning, improvement, and effort as keys to success **(Newton et al. 2002).**

Ntoumanis et al. (1999) found that task goal orientation was associated with the use of adequate problem-solving coping strategies such as trying harder, seeking social support, and cutting down on competing activities. Athletes high in ego goal orientation were more likely to use emotion-focused coping strategies such as becoming upset and letting out negative feelings. Other studies have shown that athletes with a strong ego goal orientation tend to show a maladaptive pattern with increased concern over personal mistakes and perceived criticism, which could affect motivation negatively.

Four reasons why goal setting results in improved performance and motivation:

1. Goals direct attention toward goal-relevant activities and away from goal-irrelevant activities (concentration).

2. Goals have an energizing function. High but realistic goals lead to greater effort than low goals. Achievement goals (task goal orientation) should be the essential part of the training programme for athletes.

3. Goals affect persistence. When goals are realistic and achievable motivation is increased. Persistent athletes are more likely to be high achievers and this influences self-efficacy and thus motivation.

4. Goals affect action indirectly by leading to the arousal and discovery of relevant strategies.

At top sporting levels there is little difference in the skill levels of athletes and it is often their ability to handle arousal and anxiety that makes the difference between winning and losing. According to **Gould (2000)** skilled athletic performance is not just a matter of physical competence but reflects a close coordination between mind and body (i.e. psychological and physical skills). Participation in competition tends to cause some degree of arousal and precompetitive anxiety. This is normal and may be beneficial if the athlete can control it and use it as a facilitator. If not anxiety may be detrimental to sporting performance.

Arousal	Anxiety
■ A state of physiological and psychological alertness and anticipation that prepares the athlete for action. ■ The physiological activity in arousal is similar to stress (increased heart and respiration rates, sweating, and butterflies in the stomach). Arousal is thus activation of the body. ■ Arousal contributes to optimal performance but too much of it can have a negative effect on performance.	■ A negative emotional state with feelings of nervousness, worry, and apprehension as a consequence of arousal of the body (**Weinberg and Gould, 2007**). ■ Anxiety involves cognitive anxiety, somatic anxiety, state anxiety, and trait anxiety.

- **Cognitive anxiety:** Anxious thoughts such as apprehension, doubts about competence, or fear of failure before a competition. Researchers believe that when cognitive anxiety increases performance declines so it is perhaps the most important factor in determining outcome.

- **Somatic anxiety:** Perceived physical arousal such as increased respiration and heart rate. Physical arousal is the body's stress reaction and it is how this stress is perceived and interpreted that makes a difference.

- **State anxiety:** An immediate emotional state characterized by apprehension (e.g. feeling somewhat nervous before a race and very nervous during the final seconds of the race). State anxiety and physiological arousal may be difficult to distinguish.

- **Trait anxiety:** Some people are more anxious than others (personality or acquired trait) and trait anxiety predisposes the athlete to perceive situations that are not objectively dangerous as threatening.

The inverted-U theory

The theory is based on the **Yerkes-Dodson law (1908)**, which states that there is an optimum level of physiological arousal (optimal point) for every task and after this level is reached, arousal either levels off or rises above the optimal level.

- The inverted-U theory predicts that the relationship between arousal and performance is curvilinear and takes the form of an inverted U if the level of arousal and quality of performance are plotted into a graph. Arousal and anxiety are seen as interrelated in the theory.

  - The optimal level of arousal for a task depends on factors such as the complexity of the skill required to perform the task. Tasks such as putting in golf require fine motor skills and low levels of arousal. Less complex tasks such as weightlifting require higher levels of arousal.

- There is support for the theory's suggestion of an inverted-U relationship between arousal and performance in relation to types of skill, level of expertise, personality, and audiences in sport performance. However, there is also criticism of the theory for lack of clarity of what is understood by arousal.

- There are individual differences in what constitutes optimal levels of arousal and this should be taken into consideration in coaching. For example, research shows that an elite sportsperson generally needs higher levels of arousal in order to produce optimal performance. This is not clearly explained in the theory.

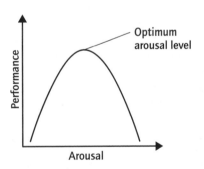

Oxendine (1970) examined the inverted-U theory in relation to various sports and found that levels of arousal for optimal performance varied according to the nature of the skill needed. The researcher suggested that more complex skills (e.g. putting in golf) need less arousal for optimal performance whereas less complex skills (e.g. tackling in football and weightlifting) require high arousal.

Klavora (1998) studied the relationship between pregame state anxiety and performance in 95 male high-school basketball players throughout a season. Levels of anxiety were measured using a standardized test. The coaches evaluated players' game performance in comparison with their usual ability. Results supported the prediction of the inverted-U theory. Optimal performance was usually associated with moderate pregame state anxiety and worse performance was associated with either high or low state anxiety before the game.

Strengths of the inverted-U theory	Limitations of the inverted-U theory
■ The theory has been successfully applied in sport psychology, for instance in trying to optimize arousal levels (relaxation or "psyching up" exercises) depending on what skills are required in a particular sport. ■ The theory has predictive value and has been supported by a number of research studies even though arousal is not clearly defined. ■ The theory can explain why expert performers sometimes make errors under pressure.	■ The theory can describe the nature of the relationship between athletic performance and arousal in an inverted-U but it is not really clear why this happens. ■ The theory is general and does not take individual factors into account. ■ The theory cannot clearly explain the nature of the arousal or the exact effects of psychological factors such as cognitive anxiety or self-efficacy on performance.

Hanin's theory of individual zone of optimal functioning (IZOF)

■ According to the theory the relationship between anxiety and sport performance is best explained by *individual differences* in optimal pre-competition anxiety, which varies considerably among athletes. The theory predicts that athletic performance can be increased if an athlete's pre-competitive state anxiety can be determined and a zone of confidence can be placed around it. Arousal control techniques (e.g. relaxation or thought stopping) can then be used to control anxiety levels.

■ Hanin criticized the inverted-U theory for not taking individual factors into account. Athletes are different and so is their response to arousal and anxiety. Athletes have individualized zones for optimal functioning, which are unique to them.

■ Pre-competitive state anxiety levels can be measured before the competition or after the competition (the recall method). In both cases self-report measures are used. Critics argue that the recall method is not very precise.

■ Hanin has developed the theory and now focuses upon emotions in general rather than just anxiety. This seems a useful addition to the theory as it makes sense that both positive and negative emotions should be in an optimal zone prior to competition. Peak performance probably depends on a number of distinct emotions.

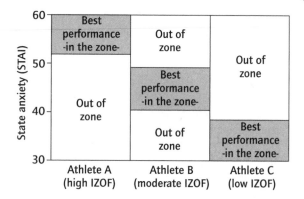

Amnesi (1998) performed a study with three elite tennis players. The IZOF of each athlete was established and they were instructed in techniques to reduce anxiety. In the second part of the study, athletes measured their anxiety level before competitions and used the learned techniques to move pre-competitive anxiety into their individual zone of optimal functioning so that anxiety could serve as a facilitator. The results showed an increase in the quality of performance. The study was important because it showed that Hanin's theoretical concepts could be applied in a real-life setting.

Raglin and Morris (1994) studied volleyball players in college and found that they tended to perform within their IZOF when they played matches against highly skilled volleyball players but not when they played against less skilled players. It seems that it is not necessary that athletes be in their IZOF when they compete against weaker opponents or teams because they will probably win anyway. The results of the study could also explain why weaker teams sometimes win over a stronger team because the strong team did not take the game seriously enough. The unexpected loss will probably make them adjust their arousal level in future matches.

Strengths of the IZOF theory	Limitations of the IZOF theory
■ The theory has been successfully applied in sport psychology. An athlete can learn to identify his or her own IZOF so that relevant interventions can be applied to increase or decrease arousal (emotions). ■ The theory has been supported in a number of research studies although some studies have found only weak support (e.g. **Raglin and Morris, 1994**).	■ It is very time consuming to establish athletes' IZOF and it is quite complicated and perhaps not very exact (retrospective data and self-reports). ■ Apparently athletes do not always need to be in the IZOF to function optimally. The theory cannot explain why elite athletes do not need to be in the IZOF when they compete against less skilled athletes.

Techniques in motor skill development: massed practice versus distributed practice

- Athletes need to have sufficient knowledge of their sport stored in their memory (**declarative**, e.g. facts, rules, and strategies, and **procedural**, e.g. how to perform a movement).

- Practising skill development is an important part of an athlete's training. Once the basic motor skill is learned, the athlete needs to practice in order to reach expert performance (**Fitts and Posner, 1967**).

Massed practice

- This is continuous practice without rest between practice trials. The skill is practised repeatedly over an extended period of time to learn the skill to perfection.

- Massed practice is mostly used to train "discrete tasks" such as a tennis serve, a golf swing, shooting a basketball, or striking a match (a discrete task is a single unit of action with a clear beginning and end).

- An elite tennis player may choose to use massed practice to improve the footwork on his or her backhand drive to reach the skill level where the drive can be performed accurately and automatically under pressure.

Distributed practice

- The skill is practised with intervals of rest periods and usually the practice time is less than the rest time.

- Distributed practice is often used to train "continuous tasks" such as swimming, a gymnastic floor exercise, cycling, and running, which are likely to build up to fatigue (a continuous task has no clear beginning or end and can continue as long as the athlete wants).

- An athlete may watch another athlete doing a movement or a shot (modelling) and then have a short practice session with feedback from the coach. Then the athlete might practise on his or her own for 10 minutes, rest, then start again.

Variable practice

- This is a combination of the massed and distributed practice. This is most often used for skill development.

- Time constraint, fatigue, number of participants, and type of motor skill being learned are factors that influence the making of practice schedules.

- It is important that the coach thinks of varying the content and sequence of practice drills to keep up motivation and avoid fatigue. This could be particularly true with children and adolescents. Mental training sessions could also come in between motor skill practice.

Singer (1965)

- The researcher performed an experiment to study the effects of massed and distributed practice on participants performing a novel basketball skill (i.e. bouncing a basketball off the floor and into a basket).

- Participants were allocated to (1) a massed practice group (shot 80 consecutive shots with no rest), (2) a distributed group who shot four sets of 20 shots with five minutes of rest between sets, and (3) a second distributed group who shot four sets of 20 with a 24-hour rest between sessions over four days. The participants did two tests.

- Results showed that the third group had learned the skills best but performance did not differ significantly between the other groups in the first test. In the second and final test groups 1 and 2 performed better than in the first test. This was perhaps because the participants had the opportunity to rest between the first and second test.

Lee and Genovese (1988)

- The researchers performed a meta-analysis of 116 studies on the development of motor skills using massed and distributed practice and found that distributed practice had a better effect on performance than massed practice in experimental research.

- They also suggested that distributed practice results in better learning than massed practice conditions but the problem in many of the studies they reviewed is that there is not a clear distinction between "learning" and "performance".

Strengths of massed practice	Limitations of massed practice
■ It works best when practising discrete tasks that demand a high degree of precision (e.g. a tennis forehand). ■ It works best for highly motivated and highly skilled athletes.	■ There is a possibility of fatigue and boredom, especially in novice athletes. ■ It is less efficient in team sport and in open skills (e.g. goal keeping).
Strengths of distributed practice	**Limitations of distributed practice**
■ It works best in improving performance because it allows for feedback from the coach. ■ It works best for the novice or less-motivated athlete and in sports where energy demands are high or where the task is boring or dangerous.	■ It can be more time consuming than massed practices. ■ Athletes may forget parts of the skill learned during the rest

Imagery technique – training mental skills

Imagery activates "pictures" in the brain as if they were real. The brain cannot really tell the difference. Imagery can be used to create mental pictures of athletic situations (e.g. a movement or competition) to enhance performance and skills

Neuroimaging shows that the brain uses the same neural mechanisms to imagine movements (motor imagery) as those used in preparation and programming of actual movements. This is called "functional equivalence".

According to **Callow and Hardy (2001)** it is not the content of imagery in itself that is important but rather what it means to the athlete.

Monroe et al. (2000) The four Ws of mental imagery

■ **Where** do athletes use imagery? The majority of imagery research has focused on its use in training but it is perhaps more often used during pre-competition (e.g. to increase concentration). **DeFranceso and Burke (1997)** found that imagery techniques were the most common strategies used by professional tennis players.

■ **When** do athletes use imagery? Imagery is used during practice and competition to control psychological factors and focus. Some athletes use it when they are injured.

■ **Why** do athletes use imagery? Imagery is used to promote confidence and self-efficacy and development of specific motor skills.

■ **What** imagery do athletes use? Imagery could involve the setting of a competition, positive images of performance or emotion.

Martin et al. (1999) Applied mental imagery model

A framework with five dimensions for imagery research and application used to develop the SIQ (Sport Imagery Questionnaire).

1. **Cognitive specific:** Skill learning and development, skill execution, and performance enhancement. "I can easily change an image of a skill."

2. **Cognitive general:** Strategy learning and development and strategy execution. "I imagine executing the entire programme just the way I want it to happen in a competition."

3. **Motivational specific:** Enhancing motivation. "I imagine myself winning a medal."

4. **Motivational arousal:** Regulating stress and arousal, getting psyched up, and calming down. "I imagine myself being 'in the zone' and ready to run."

5. **Motivational general mastery:** Gaining or maintaining confidence and staying focused. "I imagine myself focused on my breathing and in control."

Moritz et al. (1996)

- The researchers explored the relationship between imagery and confidence using the SIQ, which measures the relationship between utilization of the five types of imagery. The participants were all from individual sports (e.g. roller skating, gymnastics).

- Results showed that highly confident elite roller skaters were more likely to use imagery related to mastery and emotion (motivational general mastery and motivational arousal) compared to less confident athletes.

- The study was correlational so a cause-effect relationship could not be established. The study is important in spite of this because it showed that specific imagery types are associated with specific variables and this could be further investigated.

Callow and Hardy (2001)

- The researchers studied the relationship between imagery type and confidence in 123 female county netball players. Participants answered the SIQ and a week later a test related to sport confidence.

- Results showed that netballers of differing skills used different types of imagery. Lower skilled netballers high in confidence used more imagery dealing with challenging situations (motivational general mastery) and imagery related to strategy (cognitive general) but less related to emotion.

- The higher skilled netballers high in confidence used more goal achievement related imagery than their less confident opponents.

Strengths of imagery	Limitations of imagery
■ Imagery seems to be a powerful technique for many athletes to rehearse aspects of skill learning, visualize sport performances and get "psyched up". ■ Effectiveness of imagery is perhaps supported by neuroimaging studies showing that imagining activities or emotions activate the same brain processes as in actual experiences. This could explain why it works.	■ Not all athletes can use imagery. Sport psychologists do not really know why the technique is effective for some athletes and not for others. ■ Athletes with low confidence (self-efficacy) tend to imagine failure scenarios and that can impede performance. ■ It is difficult to validate athletes' self-reports of imagery experiences. This means that it is difficult to make general conclusions.

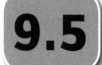

9.5 To what extent does the role of coaches affect individual or team behaviour in sport?

Why do coaches' beliefs and expectations affect athletes' perceptions and behaviour? The self-fulfilling prophecy

Horn and Lox (1993) formulated **"the expectancy theory in sport"** and created a four-step model to explain the process of the self-fulfilling prophecy:

1. The coach forms expectations of each athlete (or team) based on available information such as physical appearance, skills tests, and past performance in practice and competitive events.
2. Expectations can affect treatment of individual athletes on the team (e.g. with regard to the quality and amount of feedback given.)
3. The differential treatment of individual athletes influences the athletes' perceptions of competence as well as performance in a positive or negative manner.
4.   The athlete's behaviour and performance conforms to the coach's original expectations and this reinforces the coach's original assessment.

Chase et al. (1997) Coaches' efficacy beliefs and team performance

Aim To investigate coaches' efficacy beliefs for their teams in relation to team performance.

Procedure Four female coaches of Division III women's basketball teams answered questionnaires about confidence in their teams' abilities to perform specific basketball skills (e.g. shoot field goals, free throws, and commit turnovers) and "playing well" before each game.

Results Coaches were only able to reliably predict team performance for the skills of free throw shooting and committing few turnovers. Good performance preparation also contributed to high efficacy expectations in their teams.

The researchers found that coaches' efficacy expectations were to a large extent linked to skills. This may be because free skills like throw shooting and committing few turnovers can make the difference between losing and winning games so coaches may focus on proper execution of these skills and practise them more. The researchers recommend that coaches focus on self-improvement and effort because these factors are controllable and influenced by coaching techniques. If players are aware of a coach's low efficacy expectation for their team, a self-fulfilling prophecy effect might occur, i.e. these expectations may inadvertently contribute to low player efficacy.

Weinberg and Gould (2007) Coaching behaviour
Coaches who behave differently according to high or low expectancies typically fit into one of these categories:
Frequency and quality of coach-athlete interaction (e.g. spending more time with and showing more positive feelings towards "high-expectation" athletes).

Quantity and quality of instruction (e.g. lower expectations for "low-expectation" athletes, thus creating a lower standard of performance; less persistence in the instruction of difficult skills; and allowing less practice time).

Type and frequency of feedback (e.g. providing more praise after a successful performance from "high-expectation" athletes and providing more instruction and information feedback to them).

Solomon et al. (1996) investigated the relationship between actual coach feedback and player perception of feedback. They found that coaches primarily provided mistake-contingent feedback and attended to high expectancy athletes. These players perceived the received feedback as more adequate than did low expectancy athletes. Overall, high expectancy athletes received more feedback.

Alfermann et al. (2005) Coaches' influence on skill development in athletes

The study investigated how coaches' leadership styles (democratic or autocratic) and feedback affected athletes' skill development.

Study 1:
Aim To investigate the relationship between:

1. athletes' skill development and perceived coach behaviour
2. athletes' skill development and perceived motivational climate.

- Participants were 119 competitive swimmers (61 male and 58 female) from various clubs (mean age 12.5 years). They were placed into three skill levels (called "career phases") based on their age, year of practice, and level of competition.

Procedure
- Participants completed the same questionnaires (on coaches' leadership style and ability to establish positive motivational climate) twice with an interval of 12 months.

Results
- The results showed that the coaches' behaviour was rated as positive and encouraging. Participants perceived their coaches as providing a "mastery climate" with democratic leadership where "performance climate" was downplayed.

- There was a positive relationship between perceived coach behaviour (instruction and positive feedback) and swimmers' skill development.

Evaluation

A limitation of this study was that a third of the participants dropped out during the year but this is not unusual in the field of voluntary youth sport. Another limitation was that skill level and age could be confounded. A third limitation is the lack of exact definition of "skill level".

Study 2:

Aim To investigate if there was a difference between team and individual sports and to estimate the impact of coach behaviour and motivational climate on skill development.

Procedure Participants were were 212 junior athletes (136 male and 76 female) of individual and team sports (mean age 15 years). They completed the same questionnaires twice within four months to prevent loss of data due to dropouts as in the first study.

Results These showed opposite patterns of relationships for individual and team sports. Skill development of team sport athletes was associated with higher perceived social support and less instruction whereas individual sport athletes' skill development was associated with less perceived social support, more instruction, and a higher mastery climate.

The results in study 2 indicate that team sports require more group-oriented behaviour from the coach. Coaches' instructions should focus both on the team and individual development as well as give social support.

Garcia-Bengoechea (2003) performed a qualitative study with 12 adolescent athletes (aged 13–17) to investigate how they perceived the influence of factors other than the coach on their sport motivation. The data was collected with semi-structured interviews and analyzed using inductive content analysis.

The overall findings indicate that the coach is a central socializing factor together with parents but also that the adolescents perceived them as their main source of pressure and control (see more on motivation in unit 9.1).

9.6 Explain the relationships between team cohesion and performance

An athletic team is a group and therefore subjected to group dynamics. From the moment the team is formed, athletes begin to interact with each other. One of the things a coach must attend to in team sport is building a team spirit (or to form team cohesion) so that team members cooperate to reach common goals. Team cohesion is assumed to be positively related to greater team success.

Carron (1982) defines cohesion as "a dynamic process that is reflected in the tendency for a team to stick together and remain united in the pursuit of its goals and objectives". An indicator of team cohesiveness is that team members use terms like "we" and "us" instead of "I" and "me" (see more on social identity in unit 4.4).

Team cohesion depends on four key factors

1. **Individual factors:** For example athlete satisfaction with membership. This is one of the strongest determinants of team cohesion.

2. **Team factors:** For example communication, having clear team and role goals, individual perceptions of importance of achieving goals, gender, and previous success. This is important factor as it indicates team efficacy, i.e. collective efficacy).

3. **Leadership factors:** For example coaches' effort and success in establishing a "we" mentality (cohesion) and communicating clear goals (coach efficacy, such as the team's perception of the coach's efficacy and the coach's self-efficacy).

4. **Environmental factors:** For example the size of the group and external pressures to win. Small groups are more likely to experience cohesion while elite teams are more likely to be cohesive if they have success.

Carron et al. (1985) developed the Group Environment Questionnaire (GEQ) to examine perceptions of task and social reasons in being with the team. The two main dimensions in the model are:

- **Task cohesion:** the degree to which members of a team are committed to work together to achieve specific and identifiable goals
- **Social cohesion:** the degree to which members of a team like each other and enjoy being a member of the team.

The GEQ measures four dimensions of cohesion:

- individual perception of the group as a social unit
- individual attraction to the group as a social unit
- individual perception of the group's task
- individual attraction to the group's task.

Carron et al. (2002)

Aim To examine the relationship between team cohesion and team success in elite sport teams.

Procedure

- Eighteen university basketball teams and nine club soccer teams participated. The 294 Canadians (154 females and 140 males) all had considerable competitive experience.
- The teams were assessed for perceptions of *task* cohesiveness (group integration task and individual attraction to group task using the GEQ) and team success (operationalized as the team's win-loss percentage).

Results The results demonstrated a strong relationship between task-related dimensions of cohesion and success.

Conclusion The researchers concluded that one reason for the relationship between cohesion and team performance could be that greater team cohesion contributes to greater collective efficacy that, in turn, contributes to enhanced team performance.

9.7 Describe aids and barriers to team cohesion

Aids to team cohesion

- **Team building:** Building a team spirit and mutual goal setting are crucial to building team cohesion. These involve minimizing the status differences of team roles and emphasizing team goals. The focus on team identity and a common task often leads to satisfaction with the team. **Carron and Dennis (2001)** found that the most important personal factor for task and social cohesion was *member satisfaction*.

- **Focus on performance and process goals to promote collective efficacy:** If the team and coach formulate team goals together it is more likely that the team will develop a sense of ownership and commitment to the goals. Collective efficacy is positively related to perceptions of team cohesion.

- **Democratic leadership style:** More likely to promote cohesion. Coaches should also set challenging group goals, prevent formation of social cliques, and know the team climate and something personal about each group member.

- **Clear communication:** Clear, consistent and unambiguous communication from coaches with regard to team goals, team tasks, and individual team members' roles are important to avoid ambiguity.

Kesthan et al. (2010) found a relationship between the coaches' leadership styles and team cohesion in professional Iranian football teams. Athletes' perception of team cohesion correlated positively with perceptions of the coach exhibiting higher levels of training, social support, positive feedback, democratic behaviour, and lower levels of autocratic behaviour.

Barriers to team cohesion

Weinberg and Gould (2008) argued that the following factors could influence team cohesion negatively:

- **A clash of personalities in the group:** Some athletes may not be able to control their anger (e.g. when a team member makes a mistake).

- **A conflict of task or social roles among group members:** Individual athletes may not want to spend as much time on training as required to reach common goals or they may not be happy with their own role in the team.

- **A breakdown in communication among group members or between the group leader and members:** A respectful and clear communication between team members and between the coach and the team is important to maintain team cohesion.

- **One or more members struggling for power:** Athletes who are too ego goal oriented may see their membership as a way to achieve personal success rather than success for the team.

- **Frequent turnover of group members:** The team does not have a chance to interact and get to know each other.

- **Disagreement on group goals and objectives:** If the team and coach formulate team and task goals together, it is more likely that the team will develop a sense of ownership and commitment to the team. (See more on goal setting in unit 9.2.)

9.8 Discuss athlete response to stress and chronic injury

- Sport psychologists have identified stress as a critical factor in individual and team performance as well as social functioning. Athletes use a number of coping strategies to deal with stress. The inability to manage stress adequately in sport is linked to performance problems, decreased enjoyment, anxiety, aggression, burnout, and injury.

- The chances of a sportsperson being injured are statistically high. According to Finch et al. (1998) 20–30 per cent of total injuries in a population are related to sport and the economic costs of injury are high. Basketball, bicycling, and soccer are sports that are particularly likely to cause injuries.

The stress process in sport

Stressor →	Stress response →	Coping
■ **Major life-events (Holmes and Rahe, 1967)** ■ Too much training, injury ■ Failure to meet academic standards, financial problems ■ Problems with coach or team selection ■ Expectation to perform (parental, coach, own) ■ Competition or game	■ Arousal (stress hormones) → increased heartbeat, sweating, and nausea ■ Muscle tension, problems of coordination and fatigue ■ Problems with **attention and/or peripheral vision** (peripheral narrowing) ■ **Cognitive appraisal** – cognitive interpretation of stressor **(Lazarus and Folkman, 1984)** major key to understanding athletes' behaviour (coping)	■ Use of various coping strategies to manage stress such as imagery and relaxation ■ **Problem-focused, emotion-focused (Lazarus and Folkman, 1984)** ■ Problem-focused coping (change the stressful situation): increase effort, goal setting, seek advice ■ Emotion-focused coping: relaxation techniques, meditation, seek social support, or using drugs ■ Avoidance coping

Two theoretical approaches to stress from general psychology: Holmes and Rahe's (1967) theory of major life events and Lazarus and Folkman's (1984) cognitive appraisal

1. **Holmes and Rahe (1967):** The original social and readjustment rating scale has been modified to fit the athletic environment including items like "problems with the coach".

2. **Lazarus and Folkman (1984):** Cognitive appraisal is a key concept in Lazarus and Folkman's transactional model of coping. The athlete's *perception* of the situation in relation to coping resources and goals is critical to how he or she behaves.
   - Perceived imbalance between own abilities and demands may result in negative feelings such as self-doubt, worry, and apprehension. This could lead to competitive stress with an increased risk of injury.
   - Perceived balance between own abilities and demands results in positive feelings and competence beliefs.

Athlete response to stress

- According to **McGrath (1970)** an athlete is stressed when there is a substantial *perceived imbalance* between physiological and psychological demands and the athlete's capability and when failure to meet the demand has important consequences.

- **Wilson and Pritchard (2005)** found that students who were athletes reported more stress in meeting academic demands and relationship stress compared to non-athlete students. The athletes also reported lack of sleep as a source of stress. There seemed to be an imbalance between the demands and the athletes' perceived abilities.

- Competitive stress is defined as the negative emotions, feelings, and thoughts that an athlete might have with respect to his or her experience in a competition. This could include feelings of apprehension, anxiety, muscle tension, nervousness, physical reaction, thoughts centered on worry and self-doubts, and negative statements (**Scanlan et al. 1991**).

Gould et al. (1993) Coping strategies in elite athletes to manage stress

Aim To investigate which coping strategies successful athletes used.

Procedure The study gave questionnaires, with open-ended questions, to Olympic wrestlers and National Champion figure skaters to find out which coping strategies they had used to manage stress in the past. The wrestlers reported 39 different coping themes that could be organized into four dimensions:

1. thought-control strategies such as positive thinking and self-talk
2. attentional focus strategies such as concentration control
3. behavioural strategies such as fixed routines and rest
4. emotional control strategies such as relaxation and visualizations.

Results Generally the coping strategies were a mix of problem-focused and emotion-focused. The female figure skaters also reported using social support as a coping mechanism. Other research studies have confirmed that females use social support to a larger degree than males.

Evaluation A methodological problem is the use of retrospective data, which may be less reliable due to memory issues.

Two hypotheses on the role of stress in injury

- Stress disrupts attentional processes and concentration (e.g. narrowing peripheral vision). This results in less vigilance to cues signalling physical danger (**Andersen and Williams, 1988**). For example a football player who focuses exclusively on the ball may miss an opponent's position and run into the opponent or he or she can be tackled.

- Stress produces physiological arousal that increases muscular tension and reduces coordination of movement (**Nideffer, 1983**).

Anderson and Williams (1999) Athletes' responses to stress

- The researchers tested athletes' stress responses (visual perception, reaction time, and anxiety) under laboratory conditions and compared the results with incidents of injuries over the competitive season. They tested 196 collegiate athletes from 10 sports.

- The athletes also completed measures of life events and social support at the beginning of the season. The researchers used these and changes in reaction time and perception to predict injury incidents.

- Results showed that the only significant predictor of injury was negative life-event stress for all athletes. For athletes who scored low in social support, peripheral narrowing during laboratory stress, and major negative life events together were associated with higher injury rates (26%). This seems to support a possible association between life events stress, perceptual deficits, social support, and injury.

- **Smith and Smoll (1991)** argue that psychosocial factors such as social support and coping skills could influence the extent to which athletes are affected by stressful life events. Stressful life events should be seen as a risk factor but protective factors such as adequate coping skills and social support can prevent stress-related injuries in sport.

- **Johnson (2011)** conducted a qualitative study with 20 competitive athletes. The aim was to describe athletes' experiences of psychosocial risk factors associated with risk of injury. Data were collected with interviews. The results showed that four risk factors emerged:

  1. history of stressor
  2. person factors
  3. fatigue
  4. ineffective coping strategies.

These findings support Andersen and William's stress-injury model although fatigue was not included there.

Athlete response to chronic injury

- Injuries, whether acute or chronic, are a significant source of stress for athletes and may seriously affect their well-being. Injured athletes experience **physical stress** (for example pain and physical inactivity), **social stress** (for example social isolation and lack of social support), and **psychological stress** (for example anxiety and fear that they will not be able to continue in their sport).

- Chronic injury appears as a consequence of overtraining and overuse. Physical treatment may help for a while but the pain and swelling will often return. It is difficult for others to see that an athlete has a chronic injury but it is often very painful. Despite pain many athletes continue training to avoid losing training and competition time. For some athletes, the injury may be so serious that they cannot continue in their sport.

- The most used models within sport psychology are based on stress and coping theories such as **Lazarus and Folkman (1984)**. The focus on cognitive appraisal shows the importance that psychologists attach to individuals' *interpretation* of their situation. This approach could explain why many studies on athletic injury are qualitative in nature.

Wiese-Bjornstal et al. (1998) Integrated model of psychological response to sport injury and the rehabilitation process

- The model incorporates the concept of cognitive appraisal but also includes personal and situational factors as well as emotional and behavioural responses as mediating factors. The model is more complex than Lazarus and Folkman's model and it has been developed specifically to explain injury and recovery within a sport context.

- At the centre of the model is **cognitive appraisal** integrated with emotional and behavioural response. The model illustrates the dynamic nature of injury and the recovery process.

- An injured athlete's cognitive appraisal affects emotional response, which in turn affects behaviour, which in turn affects cognitive appraisal again. The model assumes that cognitive, emotional, and behavioural responses have implications for physical and psychological outcomes. Personal factors (e.g. how much the athlete has tied his or her identity to the sport) also influence the recovery process in this model.

- The model can also illustrate the consequences of not adhering to the rehabilitation process if the arrows are followed in reverse order (e.g. the athlete takes a risk by not attending to the injury so that it becomes chronic).

- Limitations of the model include that it does not explicitly take into account that total recovery may not happen (chronic injury) and that the athlete continues to practise sport in spite of the injury.

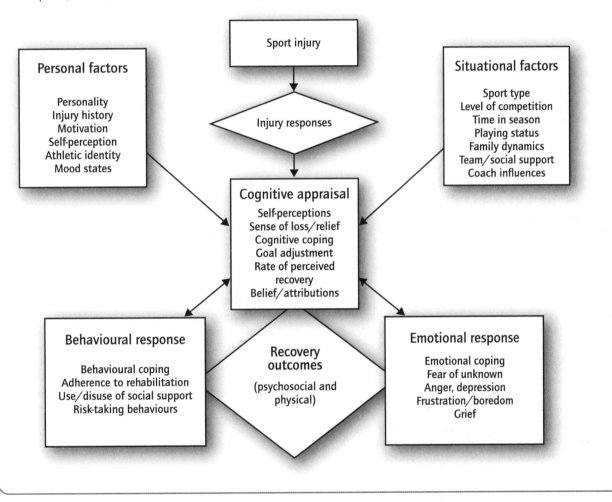

Sport injury

Personal factors

Personality
Injury history
Motivation
Self-perception
Athletic identity
Mood states

Situational factors

Sport type
Level of competition
Time in season
Playing status
Family dynamics
Team/social support
Coach influences

Injury responses

Cognitive appraisal

Self-perceptions
Sense of loss/relief
Cognitive coping
Goal adjustment
Rate of perceived recovery
Belief/attributions

Behavioural response

Behavioural coping
Adherence to rehabilitation
Use/disuse of social support
Risk-taking behaviours

Recovery outcomes

(psychosocial and physical)

Emotional response

Emotional coping
Fear of unknown
Anger, depression
Frustration/boredom
Grief

Shuer et al. (1997) Psychological response to chronic injury

Aim To investigate the psychological responses and coping strategies used by athletes with chronic injuries.

Procedure Participants were 280 elite collegiate athletes from various sports (e.g. tennis, water polo, swimming, volley ball). The mean age of the participants was 19.5 years. Half of them were female. Full scholarships were held by 26% and 20% were on partial scholarship. Of the athletes, 134 (48%) were injured and 117 met the criteria for chronic overuse injuries. They all continued training in spite of the injury. The researchers measured **coping responses** with instruments measuring subjective distress for life events, **intrusive thoughts** (involuntary entry of thought of the injury into awareness which are common when people have experienced traumatic events), and **avoidance coping** (trying actively not to think of the injury).

Results The results showed that athletes who suffered from chronic injury scored very high on avoidance coping (e.g. 81% endorsed "I avoided letting myself get upset when I thought about it or was reminded of it."). Intrusive thoughts were only high in athletes with acute injury. Female athletes scored higher on avoidance coping than male athletes.

Discussion of results High avoidance scores indicate *denial* according to the researchers and the consequence is that the injury is not treated appropriately. The researchers argue that elite athletes have been trained from early childhood to endure pain and discomfort and they have difficulty distinguishing the pain of training from pain signalling the onset of a possibly serious injury. Denial, minimization, and distortion are cognitive strategies to avoid facing the seriousness of an injury and this may present a potential threat to the health of athletes.

Cultural considerations: culture of risk?

- Shuer et al.'s findings are in line with **Nixon (1992)** who argues that elite sport is a *"culture of risk"* because athletes routinely risk their physical health for their sport. It seems that athletes conform to norms of the sporting culture, which normalizes pain and injury at the expense of athletes' short-term and long-term health. This culture's norms and beliefs makes athletes willing to play in pain, return from injury before they are fully recovered, and even criticize athletes who do not conform to such expectations.

9.9 Examine reasons for using drugs in sport

- The use of performance enhancing drugs is called "doping". Performance enhancing drugs (PED), such as anabolic steroids, growth hormones, amphetamines, and painkillers, have been used by elite athletes and Olympians for many years.

- The professionalization of sport, sponsor money, and intense public interest in competitive sport have increased the pressure on athletes to perform at their optimum level. The performance level of top athletes has become very similar in most sports and this contributes to the pressure to train even harder and perhaps "cheat" in order to win.

- **Goldman (1984)** asked 198 elite athletes from a variety of sports (e.g. sprinters, swimmers, and power lifters) if they would take a "magic drug" that would allow them to win an Olympic gold, but with the drawback that they would die within five years. A majority of the athletes (98%) said they would use illegal performance enhancing drugs if they could win without getting caught, even at the expense of their lives (52%).

Some reasons for athletes to use drugs

Physical reasons	Psychological reasons	Social reasons
<ul><li>Enhance performance</li><li>Cope with pain and injury rehabilitation</li><li>Control weight</li><li>Develop a stronger and more attractive body</li></ul>	<ul><li>Control emotions (anxiety, depression, aggression)</li><li>Control stress responses</li><li>Enhance self-confidence</li></ul>	<ul><li>Pressure from coaches and parents to perform</li><li>Social pressure from peers and the need to gain acceptance in the team</li><li>Pressure to perform in order to get scholarships or obtain financial gains</li></ul>

Anshel (1991)

- This was a survey to investigate the causes of using performance enhancing drugs and recreational drugs among elite athletes. Participants were 126 male and female athletes from the USA representing nine sports.

- The data was collected through personal interviews and the focus of the interview was to explore reasons for the use of drugs.

- Results showed that 64% were aware of drug use on their team, 72% of males and 40% of females indicated that a team-mate took an illegal drug, and 43% acknowledged that athletes use drugs for the purpose of enhancing performance as opposed to recreational use.

- The primary reasons for using drugs in sport included:

  1. the need to be competitive, increase strength, and control weight.

  2. the need to reduce pain, relax, cope with stress, and overcome boredom.

- The study gives insight into various reasons for drug use. The information comes from athletes themselves but self-reported data may not always be reliable. The researchers avoided questions about personal use to avoid effects of under-reporting (e.g. because of social desirability effects or because of the controversial nature of drug use).

Wadler and Hainline (1989)

- The researchers suggested that athletes may be more likely to experiment with performance enhancing and recreational drugs than non-athletes. Athletes use drugs to cope with the pain of injury rehabilitation, to cope with the psychological stress from the competitive demands of sport, and to handle a decrease in self-confidence because of lack of success.

- The researchers pointed at five possible categories of athletes who use drugs:

  1. Athletes at risk of not reaching the desired level of performance.

  2. Athletes approaching the end of their career who want to maintain their level of performance.

  3. Athletes with weight problems (either desire to increase or decrease weight).

  4. Injured athletes who try to recover faster.

  5. Athletes who feel external pressure (e.g. from coaches, team mates, or parents) or who believe that performance-enhancing drugs are widely used so they have to use them as well to be competitive.

Game theory

Game theory was developed in mathematics but has been applied to sport psychology to explain why it seems rational that athletes use drugs.

Two partners in crime who are arrested and held in separate prison cells can illustrate the game of "Prisoner's dilemma". Neither of them wants to confess or betray the other but the police give them the following options:

1. If you confess but the other prisoner does not, you go free and he or she gets three years in jail.

2. If the other prisoner confesses and you do not, you get three years and he or she goes free.

3. If you both confess, you each get two years.

4. If you both remain silent, you each get a year.

The logical thing to do would be to confess and betray your (partner (e.g. prisoner 1 would go free and prisoner 2 would get three years if he or she does not confess). However, prisoner 1 does not know what prisoner 2 will do. The options are (seen from prisoner 1's perspective):

- If prisoner 2 remains silent and prisoner 1 does the same, they both get a year. That's the *high payoff* situation.

	Prisoner 2 stays silent (cooperates)	**Prisoner 2 confesses (defects)**
Prisoner 1 stays silent (cooperates)	Each get a year in jail (high payoff)	Prisoner 1 gets three years in jail (sucker payoff) Prisoner 2 goes free (temptation pay off)
Prisoner 1 confesses (defects)	Prisoner 1 goes free (temptation payoff) Prisoner 2 gets three years in jail (sucker payoff)	Each get two years in jail (low payoff)

- If prisoner 2 confesses and prisoner 1 remains silent, prisoner 2 goes free (*temptation payoff*) while prisoner 1 gets 3 years. It is better to confess and take the two years (*low payoff*) than remaining silent and take the three years (*the sucker payoff*).

It seems that each prisoner is better off confessing no matter what the other prisoner does.

Game theory applied to the use of EPO in the Tour de France (the doping game)

- According to **Shermer (2008)** the cyclists compete according to certain rules (e.g. that performance enhancing drugs are prohibited). However, the drugs are very effective and at this point difficult or impossible to detect. The payoffs for success are high so the motivation to use banned drugs is powerful. He calls this "the doping dilemma" because the athlete is placed in a situation similar to the one in the prisoner's dilemma.

- If some of the elite cyclists do not abide by the rules ("defect") and take drugs to gain an advantage, the other cyclists have to do the same to have a chance. This leads to a cascade of cheating through the ranks.

- The penalties for using drugs are high (e.g. exclusion from the team or disqualification) and therefore a *code of silence* reigns among the cyclists ("high payoff") and doping becomes a reality in most professional sports. It is this "code of silence" that prevents an open communication about how to reverse the trend and return to abiding by the rules.

Real-life examples
- Bjarne Riis – Tour de France winner, 1996 – confessed to the use of doping in 2007. Riis was called Mr. 60% because of his high level of red blood cells (due to EPO).

- Floyd Landis won the Tour de France in 2006 but was disqualified because he tested positive for testosterone.

Strengths of game theory	Limitations of game theory
■ The theory is intuitively appealing with its focus on rational decision making based on a cost-benefit analysis. ■ It can, to some extent, explain why it seems a rational choice for sportspeople to use banned drugs in spite of the risks. ■ Real-life examples and empirical studies support the theory.	■ The theory focuses primarily on the material incentives and legal aspects of getting caught and not so much on other factors (e.g. the mental and physical risks) but this is taken into account in the sport deterrence model. ■ People are not always rational decision makers and it may be that pressure rather than deliberate rationalization leads to the use of drugs.

Smith et al. (2010)

- This was a qualitative narrative-based case study with 11 young Australian elite and non-elite athletes to investigate their attitudes to the use of drugs in sport and to explore the contextual factors that could influence these attitudes.

- Participants all said that the use of banned performance enhancing drugs was cheating but they also found legal performance enhancing drugs essential. The results indicate that attitudes to drugs were, to a large extent, shaped by two factors:

1. the legality of the drugs
2. the drugs' impact on performance.

- Smith et al. concluded that attitudes are shaped by early sporting experiences, sporting cultures, influential people, and commercial pressures rather than an individual athlete's desire to use drugs. If drug use is common within a sporting environment, the chances are that young athletes will also use them even though they are illegal.

9.10 Discuss the effects of drug use in sport

- The WADA (The World Anti-Doping Agency) has made a list of banned substances and if an athlete is tested positive on these drugs the person risks being stripped of any medals and his or her career. This can explain the "code of silence" that reigns in professional sport with regard to the use of performance enhancing drugs.

- Drugs are classified by their purpose:
  - performance enhancing drugs (e.g. **anabolic steroids**, EPO, human growth hormones, beta-blockers, and stimulants.
  - recreational drugs (e.g. alcohol, cocaine, marijuana, and tobacco.

Consequences of drug use in sport

- **Legal and ethical implications** of taking performance enhancing drugs: First, it is illegal and, second, it is cheating and unsportsmanlike to try to get an unfair advantage over opponents. Athletes risk prison sentences and losing their career.

- **Risk of getting addicted:** Many drugs are potentially addictive (both performance enhancing and recreational drugs).

- **Health effects:** Most drugs have side effects that could affect the health of the athlete and even cause death.

Anabolic steroids

- Anabolic steroids are probably one of the most used drugs in sport (e.g. in weightlifting, baseball, shot put, cycling). These steroids are a synthetic version of the male hormone testosterone that has been modified so that it stays longer in the blood stream.
- Known health effects are increased risk of heart diseases, kidney and liver problems, death from certain cancers, and psychic changes (e.g. psychotic symptoms and aggression).
- **Franke and Berendonk (1997)** had access to classified documents of the DDR hormone doping programme and found severe effects of the large doses of steroids given to male and female athletes. This report shows some of the serious adverse effects of anabolic steroids, especially when taken by adolescents and in large doses.

Biological effects

- Increased muscular size and strength increase body weight; increase number of red blood cells (anabolic effect).
- There is a masculinizing effect (androgenic effect) related to development of primary sexual characteristics in males:
  - males: risk of shrinkage of testes, enlarged breasts, and sterility
  - females: risk of shrinking breast and uterus, irregular menstruation, enlarged clitoris, increased facial and body hair, deepened voice.

Psychological effects

- High levels of testosterone have been associated with increased aggression and psychological problems (e.g. irritability and mood swings) but the evidence is inconclusive.
- **Sharp and Collins (1998)** argue that there is not yet a clear link between use of anabolic steroids and aggressive behaviour. There may be a number of psychosocial factors that could interact with the steriods (e.g. expectancy effects).

Olrich (1999) Athletes' own perceptions of the effects of taking anabolic steroids

- Olrich studied athletes' perceptions of the effects of drug use in a small sample of male bodybuilders. He performed qualitative interviews with 10 males (age range 18–57) about their *perceptions* of use and discontinuance of steroids. Five of them had taken steroids but had stopped and five of them were still taking steroids.
- Only one had experienced minor unpleasant side effects and feelings of guilt. Most of the participants were very positive about using steroids, for instance perceiving that they had more energy, libido, had increased feelings of being well in their body, increased self-confidence, and increased aggressiveness (seen as positive) as well as increased peer recognition and enhanced sexual attraction.
- All stated that they were dependent on the extra mental edge provided by steroids. This was interpreted as a form of psychological addiction by the researchers. Participants also stated that they wanted to maintain the benefits that came from the use of steroids and avoid the negative consequences of losing muscle mass.
- The researchers concluded that it is probably not possible to prevent anabolic steroid use by referring to negative short-term effects but the long-term effects are unknown.
- The sample was small and not representative so it is not possible to generalize from the results. The study describes the experiences of these bodybuilders, which is a valuable contribution to the study of athletes in context.

Yesalis et al. (1993) reported that there are an estimated one million or more steroid users in the USA and only a small percentage of users appear to have mental disturbances that result in clinical treatment. A small number of the users who experience significant psychological changes will probably recover without additional problems once they stop using steroids. This could indicate that steroid use is quite common and most of it goes unnoticed in the general population who are not in elite or professional sport.

Case study: Heidi Krieger, a victim of anabolic steroids

- Heidi Krieger (now Andreas Krieger) was a victim of a state-sponsored programme in DDR (former Eastern Germany) to produce athletes that could prove the superiority of the Communist state by beating the USA.
- From age 16, Heidi Kruger was given anabolic steroids without her knowledge. The coaches told her that the pills were vitamins. She was able to throw the shot a distance of around 14 metres when she was 16 but this increased to around 20 metres at the 1986 European women's shot-put championships.
- By the time she was 18 she weighed 100 kilograms, had a deep voice, increased body and facial hair, and appeared masculine. She had wild mood swings, from depression to aggression to euphoria. She felt out of place in her own body and had problems with her sexual identity but she became the European Champion in her sport.
- Heidi's career ended in 1991 because she had problems with her knees, hips, and back because of her big muscles and strenuous workouts. When she heard that her achievements were due to hormone doping she would not accept it at first and felt betrayed by the coaches and trainers.
- Heidi became depressed and felt lost without her sport and no future job together with an increasing despair and ambiguity about her sexual identity. She even considered suicide. She eventually had a sex-change operation and is now Andreas Krieger.

Compare models of the causes and prevention of burnout

Smith (1986) gave the following characteristics of burnout:

- Physical and emotional exhaustion that takes the form of lost energy, interest, and trust.

- Feelings of low personal accomplishment, low self-esteem, failure, and depression. This manifests itself in decreased performance levels.

- Depersonalization and devaluation where the individual becomes impersonal and unfeeling towards the sport and others. This means that athletes stop caring about their sport (sport devaluation).

How to detect burnout?

Burnout can be identified through symptoms using various questionnaires, for example:

- **Maslach Burnout Inventory** (developed for the workplace but also used in sport).

- **The Athlete Burnout Questionnaire** – the ABQ (**Raedeke & Smith, 2001**) is a standardized test specifically developed to measure burnout in a sporting environment. Once symptoms of burnout are identified preventive measures should be taken to help athletes start coping adequately and to reverse the symptoms.

Smith (1986) Cognitive-affective model of stress and burnout in sport

- According to this model, burnout is the result of a process that involves physiological, psychological and behavioural factors that interact and progress in four predictable stages. Each of these factors is influenced by level of motivation and personality.

- **Stage 1:** The athlete is confronted with situational demands that are too high or which conflict with other demands (e.g. high amounts of physical training or pressure to win).

- **Stage 2:** The athlete interprets and appraises the situation (cognitive appraisal). For some, the situation seems more threatening than it actually is. This results in feelings of helplessness (e.g. an athlete may be afraid of losing his or her place in the team.

- **Stage 3:** The athlete focuses on the physiological responses as a result of the cognitive appraisal. If the situation is appraised as threatening the physiological response may be anxiety, tension, insomnia (sleep disruption), fatigue, and reduced immune functioning.

- **Stage 4:** The physiological processes lead to specific types of coping behaviours (e.g. decreased performance, interpersonal difficulties, and inappropriate coping strategies).

Gould et al. (1996, 1997)

This was a longitudinal study of elite youth tennis players, aiming to detect possible causes of burnout.

The researchers found a number of personal and situational factors linked to burnout:

- **Physical concerns:** (e.g. overtraining, feeling tired all the time, lack of physical development, irregular performance, losing).

- **Logistical concerns:** (e.g. demands on time, leaving little or no time for alternative activities, friends, and school).

- **Social or interpersonal concerns:** (e.g. dissatisfaction with social life, negative parental pressure, negative team atmosphere, cheating by competitors, dissatisfaction with coaches).

- **Psychological concerns:** 50% of the reasons for burnout were psychological concerns (e.g. unfulfilled expectations, realization that a professional career was unlikely, feeling no improvement, and lack of enjoyment due to pressures to win or maintain a scholarship).

The results of Gould et al. indicate that there are two different lines of stressors in burnout:

- A combination of social and psychological stressors (athlete perfectionism and situational pressure stressor). *Perfectionism* could predispose young athletes at risk of burnout. *Environmental pressure* from others (parents and coaches) is another risk factor. Stress comes from having the expectations to win, to please others, and feel worthy. These results could be due to the young age of the tennis players.

- A physical driven stressor comes from external demands for physical training that the athlete is not able to meet but this stressor was found to be less frequent in this study.

Raedekes (1997) Investment model of burnout (or entrapment theory)

- The investment model is based on an assumption that athletes consider cost and benefits associated with athletic participation. The model is a *motivational theory* where burnout is seen as a lack of motivation and commitment due to an imbalance between the *perceived* costs and benefits.
- The model includes five determinants of commitment (rewards, costs, satisfaction, investments, alternatives) and how the athlete evaluates these will determine whether commitment is based on *enjoyment* or *entrapment*.
  - **Commitment because of enjoyment** means that athletes will participate because the sport is rewarding in itself relative to the time and energy put into it.
  - **Commitment based on entrapment** means that the athlete participates but has low satisfaction and perceive more cost than benefit. The athlete may continue for some time without commitment but this could end with burnout sooner or later.

Raedeke (1997)
- Radeke investigated athlete burnout in a sample of 236 female and male swimmers aged 13–18. The researcher was interested in the reasons for participation in sport with a focus on sport attraction ("want to be involved") and sport entrapment ("have to be involved").
- The participants completed a questionnaire that assessed possible determinants of commitment and burnout (emotional and physical exhaustion, swim devaluation, and reduced swim accomplishment).
- The data were analysed and swimmers were grouped according to determinants. Results showed that athletes who scored high on sport entrapment scored higher on burnout scores compared to athletes who scored high on attraction-related reasons for participating in the sport.
- The results indicate that a commitment perspective could be a useful framework for understanding athlete burnout but it is a bit simplistic.

Comparison of the cognitive-affective model and investment/entrapment model

	Cognitive-affective model	Investment/entrapment model	Similarities
View of burnout	Burnout is viewed as a response to chronic stress caused by overtraining (overload and helplessness)	Burnout is viewed as a lack of motivation and commitment due to a perception of imbalance between investment and reward	Both models focus on perceptions and emotions.
Key concepts	■ Deindividuation ■ Physical and psychological exhaustion ■ Cognitive appraisal	■ Deindividuation in the form of sport devaluation ■ Enjoyment/entrapment ■ Cognitive appraisal implied	Both models include "estrangement" from the sport in the form of deindividuation as a sign of burnout
Strengths of the model	■ The model has been empirically tested and supported ■ The model is useful to determine specific antecedents to stress – this could help in the treatment of athletes with burnout	■ The model has been empirically tested and supported ■ Raedeke's model has contributed with the concept of "entrapment", which has been incorporated in other models	There is not much empirical research yet but both models have been tested (especially Smith's model) and supported
Limitations of the model	■ It is a relatively complex model and not all dimensions are properly operationalized	■ It is a relatively simple model that does not specify dimension of the conceptual framework (e.g. what is understood by "cost" and "benefit") ■ Motivation is but one of many factors in burnout	Both models have limitations in relation to clear operationalization of concepts
Application of the model in prevention of burnout	■ Changes could be made to environmental demands ■ Appropriate coping strategies could be learned to address the various dimensions of the mode (e.g. if coping resources and social support are high the chance of burnout is reduced)	■ Stress management techniques could be used, such as cognitive-affective stress management (emotion-focused coping strategy) but also problem-focused coping (e.g. more free time between training)	Both models encourage stress management techniques to prevent burnout but also to investigate antecedents of stress/burnout in the individual athlete in an attempt to minimize stressors

Prevention of burnout

- The aim of studying overtraining and burnout is to develop programmes and strategies that help the people involved in training athletes to detect and treat burnout.

- Prevention of burnout focuses on the early identification of signs of burnout, stress monitoring by changes in environmental factors and teaching appropriate coping strategies to athletes and coaches.

Kennta and Hassmen (1998) argue that mental and physical fatigue results from a general overload of practice and competition in combination with the feeling of having no life. They suggested a recovery strategy for athletes in danger of burnout that matches the overload-stress source (physical, social, or psychological).

- If the overload is *physical* (e.g. through heavy weightlifting or overload of running practice) the recovery process could focus on physical strategies such as nutrition, hydration, massage, and sleep.

- If the overload is *psychological* and *social* (e.g. through heavy weightlifting anxiety or fear of failure) the recovery process could focus on taking some time off, dissociation (e.g. through heavy weightlifting watching a movie), techniques of muscle relaxation, visualization, and "cognitive restructuring" through cognitive therapy.

Raedeke (2002) Study on how to detect burnout signs in athletes

Radeke performed a qualitative study with 13 swimming coaches to determine what coaches identified as signs of burnout in young swimmers. Coaches mentioned possible signs of burnout:

- Withdrawal (e.g. not showing up for training).

- Reduced sense of accomplishment (e.g. perceiving imbalance between desired goals and physical ability).

- Devaluation of the sport (e.g. expressing hate or general dislike of the sport. This is a sure sign of burnout).

- Exhaustion (feelings of having no physical or psychological resources left, this is a sure sign of burnout).

- Loss of control (feeling an imbalance between the sport and "having a life").

Raedeke (2002) Suggestions of coaching strategies to prevent burnout

- Coaches should create a supportive training environment, be empathic, provide individualized feedback, encourage team cohesion and friendship in the group, and cooperate with parents to support the athletes.

- The training should be exciting and fun.

- Coaching and training should be flexible so that athletes can get time off from swimming to prevent feelings of exhaustion and meaninglessness.

- Coaches should help athletes set realistic but challenging goals and provide various training techniques.

Interventions to prevent stress and burnout

Cognitive-affective stress management training (SMT)

- A cognitive-behavioural approach of psychological and physical coping strategies to deal with stress (based on the cognitive-affective model of stress and burnout).

- Incorporates relaxation training (physical), imagery, and "self-talk" strategies.

- The technique includes three phases:

  - **Conceptualization of stress:** Focus on assessing situations that produce stress and understanding the athlete's response to stress and their use of coping strategies.

  - **Skill acquisition:** Focus on learning and practising integrated coping responses (relaxation, imagery, deep breathing, and cognitive restructuring techniques). The athlete learns to identify stress-inducing self-statements like "I can't let my team down" and replace them with adequate coping strategies.

  - **Skill rehearsal:** The athlete practises the coping skills under conditions of high emotional arousal (e.g. imagining a stressful situation).

Crocker et al. (1988) Test of the effectiveness of SMT

- Researchers carried out a field experiment to investigate the effectiveness of SMT in helping youth elite volleyball players to control dysfunctional stress processes in relation to emotion, cognition, and performance. The players were all under 19 years of age.

- The team members were assigned to either an experimental group (SMT) or a waiting-list control group. The SMT programme consisted of eight modules each separated by a week.

- The results indicated that the treatment group had fewer negative thoughts in response to videotaped stressors. This group also demonstrated superior service reception performance in a controlled practice session compared to the control group. There was no difference between the two groups in measured state anxiety or trait anxiety.

- The cognitive measures and the performance results provide support for the SMT. The study was performed under real-life conditions, which increases ecological validity.

Distinguish between qualitative and quantitative data

Quantitative data	Qualitative data
■ Data in quantitative research (quantified data): **numbers.** ■ Operational definition of research and "closed" data in the form of numbers (generally not open to interpretation). ■ Analysis of data relatively easy: **statistical tests.** ■ Data from many participants (probability sampling) and inferential statistics → generalization of findings to populations.	■ Data in qualitative research: **text** (transcripts and field notes, also pictures). ■ Naturally occurring and **rich data** (open ended, i.e. open for interpretation). ■ Analysis of data often difficult and time consuming: **no single approach to data analysis** but, for example, thematic analysis such as interpretative phenomenological analysis (IPA) or grounded theory. ■ Data from few participants (non-probability sampling) → difficult to generalize.

Explain the strengths and limitations of a qualitative approach to research

■ The purpose of qualitative research is to understand the world as the participants sees it. "Reality" is seen as dynamic as it changes with people's perceptions. This is linked to a constructionist approach (people construct realities and there is no single objective reality) or a phenomenological approach (people's subjective reality is important) to understanding humans.

■ The focus is on design and procedures that makes it possible to study behaviour in everyday situations and to obtain rich data.

■ The topic of research is influenced by the research process, the participant and the researcher. This means that factors such as "participant expectations" and "researcher bias" may influence the results.

■ Research takes place "in the real world", and it intends to "in the real world", what goes on in the real world.

Strengths	Limitations
■ This approach generates rich data (in-depth and subjective information open for interpretation). ■ It is useful for investigating complex and sensitive issues. ■ People are studied in real-life settings so there is more ecological validity. ■ The approach generates new ideas and theories to deal with real-life problems. ■ Researcher(s) and participants are often interacting with each other for longer periods of time.	■ There are often large amounts of data to analyse. ■ It can be very time consuming, especially if triangulation is used, as research often takes place over a prolonged period. ■ It is usually difficult to generalize results to other settings because of the few participants in qualitative research (but generalization is possible under certain conditions). ■ Interpretation of data may be subjective but reflexivity and credibility checks can reduce bias. ■ "Participant expectations" and "researcher bias" may influence the research process. Reflexivity and credibility checks can reduce bias.

To what extent can findings be generalized from qualitative studies?

Generalization of results from qualitative research is often not possible because:

- Most studies have few participants.
- Sampling is based on selection criteria and not representativeness (e.g. purposive, snowball or volunteer sampling).
- The goal of data analysis is to understand the subjective experience of participants in the study.

The question of generalization of qualitative research findings is a continuous object of discussion in qualitative research.

- Some qualitative researchers argue that it is important to generalize findings from qualitative research studies as this contributes to application of its results outside the research itself (ecological validity).
- They argue that under some conditions generalization may be possible.

Lewis and Richie (2003) distinguish between three forms of generalization:

Representational generalization	Inferential generalization or transferability	Theoretical generalization
■ Findings from a study can be applied to populations outside the study. ■ If findings from similar research studies corroborate findings, some degree of generalization may be possible.	■ Findings from a study can be applied to settings outside the study. ■ The findings can be "transferred" to similar settings (transferability).	■ Theoretical concepts developed in the study can be used to develop further theory.
Example: Interview data from a study with homeless people in city X and in city Z have generated similar findings.	Example: Results from a pilot study on victims of domestic violence towards women to test the effectiveness of a service to help them cope and develop resilience could be transferred to similar settings (e.g. shelters for abused women).	Example: The theory and theoretical concepts developed on what might be effective problem solving in a particular area (e.g. as developing resilience in homeless adolescents, could be effectively applied in policies to establish help centres for people).

Exam Tip You will be asked to consider if the findings from the study in the stimulus material can be generalized. You can address this question with general knowledge from this chapter but you need to make reference to the actual study and give examples.

Discuss ethical issues in qualitative research

According to Silverman (2008), qualitative researchers should ask (1) why they are doing the study, (2) if the findings can be of value to the common good, (3) if it will help or protect the people in the study, and (4) what are their own moral, political or personal interests in the study.

Generally the same ethical considerations are made as in quantitative research particular ethical considerations are often also made in qualitative research because:

- The small number of participants in qualitative research may result in difficulties with anonymity.
- Research topics are often sensitive (e.g. domestic violence, homelessness, health issues) and require particular consideration for the participants in the study.

- There is often a long-term research process with close personal contact between the researcher and participants so participants may reveal very personal information and it can be difficult to maintain researcher objectivity at times.
- The research process may result in obtaining sensitive information such as participants' criminal activity. The researcher needs to consider this in advance, decide if the researcher will inform the authorities and if participants should be informed about this before they participate.
- Informed consent cannot always be obtained (e.g. in covert participant observations). Some research projects may involve danger to the researcher (e.g. covert participant observations in prisons or street gangs).

Ethical issue	How to deal with it
Informed consent	■ Participants must understand what the study will involve and they must agree to participate. Participation is voluntary. ■ Participants should be able to understand the information given before, during, and after the study. The researcher could, for example, translate information sheets or discuss the results with participants. ■ An ethics committee must give permission if informed consent cannot be obtained because of the nature of the research. ■ In **covert participant observations**, the researcher(s) should carefully consider whether the data from the research is so important that the study is justified – especially if the research could be dangerous for the researcher or some of the participants.
Protect participants from harm	■ Consider whether the research could potentially harm participants in any way. ■ Questions should be clear and direct if the topic is sensitive. ■ Consider whether the interview or observation if participants show signs of discomfort or distress. ■ Protect participants from the consequences of participation (e.g. in research on domestic violence). ■ Follow-up in research to ensure participants' well-being.
Anonymity and confidentiality	■ Full anonymity is the rule, but in cases where this is not possible the participants should be fully informed. ■ Research material (e.g. videotaped interviews) should be destroyed and transcripts anonymized.
Potential exploitation of participants	■ The researcher could use reflexivity and consult other researchers when researching socially or psychologically vulnerable people who are not able to protect themselves. ■ The researcher must seriously consider whether findings based on deception and covert observations in research on sensitive issues can be justified. The degree to which "invasion of privacy" is acceptable should be critically evaluated and the study abandoned in some cases.

Exam Tip The ethical issues mentioned here are general. You must try to see which ones would be most appropriate to mention in relation to the specific study you have in the stimulus material and argue why this could be relevant by giving examples from the study.

Discuss sampling techniques appropriate to qualitative research

■ The goal of qualitative sampling techniques is to select participants who are particularly informative about the research topics under investigation (i.e. information-rich participants) and generalization of findings is less important.

■ The objectives of the research project and the characteristics of the population of interest will influence the choice of sampling method.

■ Possible ways to sample participants in qualitative research are: purposive sampling, snowball sampling, convenience sampling.

Purposive sampling
Characteristics of individuals are used as the basis of selection in order to reflect the diversity of the sample population. The number of participants in the study may not be decided in advance so recruitment of participants can continue throughout the research project until the researchers find that they have enough data to generate theory (data saturation). Participants are selected based on salient characteristics (selection criteria) relevant to the research topic such as:

■ socioeconomic status, gender, age, attitudes, social roles (e.g. mother)
■ specific experiences (e.g. domestic violence, being homeless, having lost a child, being a nurse working with cancer patients, being a sport coach, HIV status)
■ purpose of the study.

Strengths of purposive sampling	Limitations of purposive sampling
■ Participants represent the research topic because they are selected specifically based on salient characteristics relevant to the research. ■ It is a relatively easy way to select a sample. The sample may be supplemented with more participants during the research.	■ Sampling may be biased. If the sampling process is based on objective selection criteria, documented, and explained the bias is limited. ■ It is difficult to generalize from a small purposive sample.

Snowball sampling (snowballing)
Snowballing is considered a type of purposive sampling. Participants who are already in the study can help the researcher to recruit more participants who could potentially participate in the study through their social networks. This sampling technique may be used when it is difficult to recruit participants (e.g. because the research is socially sensitive, involving people such as drug addicts or the homeless).

Strengths of snowball sampling	Limitations of snowball sampling
■ It is a cost-efficient and easy way to recruit participants. ■ It is useful in sensitive research where participants are not easily accessible (e.g. research on drug abuse or criminal offenders).	■ It is likely to be biased because participants know each other and may have same attitudes or experiences. ■ Ethical issues (anonymity and confidentiality are difficult to maintain since participants know each other).

Convenience sampling (volunteer)
Participants are chosen based on availability. People at hand (for example the first 10 obese people you see in a shopping mall, social workers in a resilience project, a group of co-workers in an organization, students present at a lecture) are simply asked if they are willing to participate in the research. Some may refuse to take part in the research but those who accept are "volunteers".

The advantage for the researchers is that they don't need to search for participants since they are at hand. The problem is that they are not recruited based on any population so it is very difficult to generalize.

Strengths of convenience sampling	Limitations of convenience sampling
■ It is an easy and cost-efficient way to recruit participants. ■ It is a quick way to collect data and do research.	■ It is likely to be biased. ■ It is likely to generate research with low credibility and poor in information.

Exam Tip The stimulus material in the exam question will give some information about the nature of the study and you should use this to discuss why a particular sampling technique is used or could be used in that particular research. Your argument could, for example, include reasons in regard to the topic under investigation or the difficulty in recruiting participants. You may also point at relevant strengths and limitations of a relevant sampling technique but you always need to refer to the stimulus material.

Explain the effects of participant expectations and researcher bias in qualitative research
"Reality" is often seen as co-constructed by the researcher and the participants in the qualitative research process.

- **Participant expectations** (or participant bias, expectation bias) can be described as participant factors that influence the outcome of the research (e.g. the participants' ideas of what happens in the research, how they should behave or what they expect to gain from participation in the research).
- **Researcher bias** (or expectation bias) can be described as researcher factors such as the researcher's beliefs or values that could potentially bias the research process. For example, a gay researcher could focus too much on data that shows discrimination towards gay men and ignore data indicating the contrary.
- **Strauss and Corbin (1998)** state that bias in qualitative research is not only inevitable but also desirable (e.g. researcher bias may add to the richness of knowledge about a complex problem). It is important that the researcher and the participants are both actively involved in the research process and bring their ideas, beliefs and values into the research.

Potential effects of participant expectations
- Participants' ideas of the research could lead them to behave in ways that are not natural in order to please the researcher or because they have an idea of getting advantages of participating (e.g. in research on coping with a fatal disease they could think that they may recover).
- Participants may not agree with the researcher's interpretation of the data if it is presented to them. This could, for example, due to 'self-preservation' (if the research reveals sensitive things that the participant will not accept or recognize).
- Participants in qualitative research bring individual perceptions, or ideas that influence the research process and the results, (e.g. participants in a study on managers' communication styles in an organization may be more likely to give biased answers if they perceive that their responses could harm them.
- Participants may behave in ways that they feel is expected of them (socially desirable) or they may conform to other participants' ideas because they want to be accepted or not appear as different.
- Participants try to be consistent in their answers and sometimes a previous statement influences a later one. This means that some must be untrue. The researchers should not uncritically believe everything the participants say but rather cross-check for credibility.

Potential effects of researcher bias
- The researcher's own ideas, beliefs, values, and attitudes may bias the research process and the outcome so that the results are a reflection of the researcher's subjective expectations rather than a reflection of the participants' ideas.

- The researcher is the primary instrument of research and has a major influence on the research process (e.g. choice of research topic and participants, analysis and interpretation of data). The researcher therefore needs to be aware of subjectivity in the research process (self-bias) and apply reflexivity.
- The researcher may not give enough attention to the social process and the participants' experiences (e.g. in a focus group on coping with divorce the researcher may not pay enough attention to how participants influence each other's statements).

- If the research process takes a long time the researcher may change attitudes to the project and the participants and this could affect the data (e.g. a researcher doing a participant observation in a prison may come to dislike the participants).
- The researcher could influence the outcome of an interview by nodding and smiling more when participants respond as expected and frowning or looking astonished when participants give unexpected answers. This could bias data collection.

Explain the importance of credibility in qualitative research

- Credibility is based on an evaluation of whether or not the research findings represent a "credible" interpretation of the data drawn from participants' original data (Lincoln and Guba, 1985). This means that the investigation must present a true picture of the phenomenon under investigation and it should be possible to check how the results of the study were obtained. Credibility check is one of the most important factors in establishing **trustworthiness** (i.e. that the results can be trusted) in qualitative research.
- Different strategies are used to ensure scientific rigour and credibility.

What is credibility?

- Credibility in qualitative research is the equivalent of internal validity in quantitative research where the focus is on whether or not the study (or test) measures what it actually intended.
- Credibility is a criteria used to judge the quality of qualitative research. The conclusions of the study must give a true picture of the phenomenon under study and be 'true' in the eyes of those being studied (be credible from the perspective of the participants in the study).

- Credibility is linked to participant expectations and researcher bias. The researcher's training, experience, status and particular interests should be reported. All information that may have affected data collection, analysis and interpretation should be noted. This is called reflexivity, which means that the researcher should use self-awareness and critical self-reflection as to how his or her potential biases could affect the research process and conclusions.

Credibility within a study depends on factors such as:

- Triangulation – the use of alternative data collection methods, alternative methods of analysis or use of other researchers. If a similar picture emerges from triangulation the findings give a consistent and credible picture of the phenomenon under study.
- Researcher reflexivity – the researcher explains how individual bias could influence the research process and how this has been prevented.
- Cross-checking facts and discrepancies in the participant's accounts.
- Having the results checked by other people (e.g. peer review and consulting the participants in the study).
- The researcher leaves a "decision trail", documenting every decision taken in the collection, analysis and interpretation of the data.

Explain the effect of triangulation on the credibility/trustworthiness of qualitative research

- **Triangulation** is used to increase the credibility of the conclusions in a qualitative study. Researchers can use different procedures or sources in the study to ensure that the conclusion gives a *true* picture of the phenomenon under investigation.
- **Credibility** is based on an evaluation of whether or not the research findings represent a "credible" (true) interpretation

of the data drawn from the participants' original data (Lincoln and Guba, 1985).

- Triangulation is based on the assumption that by *comparing* data obtained from different methods or different researchers in the same setting it is possible to overcome potential biases from using a *single* method or a *single* researcher. The purpose is to establish credibility/ trustworthiness.

Researchers could use the following triangulation procedures to enhance credibility/trustworthiness in their research:

	Method triangulation	Data triangulation	Researcher triangulation	Theory triangulation
How?	Use of different methods (observation and interview or two ways of interviewing) in the same study, etc.).	Comparison of data from multiple sources (from different participants, observations from different days, pictures and texts, etc.).	Use of more than one researcher to collect and analyse the data.	Use of several and perhaps competing theories to analyse the data.
Effect	Bias is reduced and credibility increased. The use of several methods takes advantage of strengths of the different research methods and compensates for their methodological limitations.	Bias is reduced and credibility increased. It provides additional sources to describe the phenomenon under investigation.	Bias is reduced and credibility increased. It is particularly effective to counteract researcher bias because interpretations are discussed.	Bias is reduced and credibility increased. It promotes a deeper and more credible understanding of the topic under investigation. This could reveal contradictions in the data and protect against researcher biases.

Explain reflexivity in qualitative research

Reflexivity is a strategy used by qualitative researchers to explain how a researcher's subjectivity contributes to the findings. This approach acknowledges that a researcher may be biased towards the findings because he or she perceives and interprets through his or her own individual lens (subjectivity). This is in contrast to the assumption of the "objective researcher" in quantitative research.

Reflexivity is linked to the validation of qualitative research, for example credibility and trustworthiness. The researcher is seen as an *instrument* and he or she should be able to document the phenomenon under study as it is experienced by those under investigation. This is of major importance in qualitative research studies.

In order to achieve credibility the researcher is dependent on factors such as training, experience, status, and presentation of the self. A qualitative research report should include some information about the researcher as well as information about the researcher's relation to the topic or the people under investigation. All information that may have affected data collection, analysis, and interpretation should be noted. This is called **reflexivity**. The researcher demonstrates self-awareness and critical self-reflection by explaining how his or her potential biases could have affected the research process and conclusions.

10.2 Interviews

Evaluate semi-structured, focus group, and narrative interviews

Semi-structured interview	Strengths of the semi-structured interview	Limitations of the semi-structured interview
This is one of the most used methods of data collection in qualitative research (Willig, 2001). *Characteristics of the semi-structured interview* ■ There is an interview guide giving themes to explore (a checklist to ensure standardization of interviews so all participants give the information but there is flexibility in terms of order, wording and depth of questions). ■ Open and closed-ended questions can be used. ■ These interviews are informal and conversational in nature. ■ They are mostly face-to-face interviews.	■ Themes to explore are decided beforehand and noted in the interview guide. ■ The researcher can ask the interviewee to elaborate on answers and get in-depth knowledge. ■ It is useful in socially sensitive issues because themes can be fully explored.	■ There is only limited space to explore themes that have not been planned beforehand. ■ The one-to-one situation can appear somewhat artificial and may raise issues of ecological validity. ■ Data analysis is very time consuming

Focus group interview	Strengths of the focus group interview	Limitations of the focus interview
The focus group interview is often used as an alternative to semi-structured interviews (e.g. to explore a group of participants' understanding of particular issues such as health behaviour, parenting, treatment or coping with stress). **Characteristics of the focus group interview** ■ A group of around 6-10 people (the focus group) are interviewed at the same time. ■ A facilitator introduces the participants to each other, asks questions and leads group interactions. ■ Participants are supposed to interact with each other as they would in real life. They use their own language and even people who are illiterate can participate. ■ Participants discuss and respond to each other's statements. This gives the special dynamic to the interview and generates rich data.	■ It is a quick way to collect data from several participants at the same time. ■ It provides a natural setting for interactions between participants and the conversational approach may result in better ecological validity than the semi-structured interview. ■ It may be useful in socially sensitive issues because people may be more likely to reveal how they think and why they experience what they do.	■ It may raise ethical issues when participants are not free, for example in institutions like prisons or nursing homes. ■ The presence of other participants may result in group dynamics such as conformity. This could result in data that do not really represent the individual participant's beliefs. ■ If the topic is particularly sensitive participants may not want to disclose private information.

Narrative interview	Strengths of the narrative interview	Limitations of the narrative interview
Narratives are individual *interpretations* of the world and such narratives influence people's behaviour (e.g. in coping with difficult issues like infertility, loss or being terminally ill). **Characteristics of the narrative interview** ■ A narrative is a mix of *facts* and *interpretations* of experiences that help the individual to create meaning and identity. ■ A narrative is often constructed like a real story with an opening, a middle and an ending. It can be based on a life story or a story of a particular situation. ■ Interviewer stimulates narratives by asking questions such as: "Could you tell me more about the time when you were told that you would never be able to have children?" ■ The interviewer does not interrupt during the narrative interview but may show interest through eye contact or other physical signs of attention or invite for further narrating by asking questions such as: "And then what happened?"	■ It is a useful way to gain an in-depth understanding of how people construct meaning in their lives. ■ It can be used with all people because they can use their own language and can talk freely without being interrupted. ■ It may be useful in exploring socially sensitive issues because it gives insight into how people think and why they experience what they do.	■ It is time consuming to transcribe and analyse the huge amount of data from narrative interviews ■ The narrative may go in all directions beacuse it is the participant who decides what to tell. Not all data can be used in the research. ■ Ethical issues involved in having people tell about traumatic experiences – especially if they experience a major life crisis

Exam Tip The exam paper will contain an example of a study using one of the three forms of interviews mentioned here. You could be asked to explain or evaluate the use of the interview and this means that you should look for possible reasons for using an interview in the context of the study.

If you are asked to evaluate the use of a specific form of interview, you could point at strengths and limitations in relation to the character of the study.

Discuss considerations involved before, during, and after an interview

Considerations before an interview

	Considerations before an interview	**Discussion**
1	Data collection method and establishing an interview guide	■ The choice of interview method is based on aim, time, and resources, etc. ■ The interview method should be capable of capturing the quality of people's ideas, interpretations, and understanding of the situation.
2	Interviewer – choosing the right one and training the person	■ Consider gender, ethnicity, language and age. ■ It is important that participants feel comfortable and that the interview can be conducted in a language they understand. Training of interviewers to have a professional approach is very important.
3	Sampling and sampling method	■ Consider the selection criteria for participants (e.g. parents of children with conduct disorders or homeless female adolescents). ■ Decide the sampling method (e.g. purposive, snowball, convenience). Sampling depends on the research topic but in qualitative research a purposive sample is often chosen because the focus is on how people experience specific situations.
4	Data recording	■ Decide the sampling method (e.g. advantages and limitations of the recording methods must be considered (e.g. it may be best to audiotape a semi-structured interview so that the researcher can concentrate on the interaction with participants).
5	Transcription of the data	■ A verbatim transcript is the word-by-word text of the interview. This is often enough to perform thematic analysis. ■ A post-modern transcript includes features such as pauses, laughter, incomplete sentences, and interruptions. It is more difficult to analyse.
6	Ethical considerations	■ Is the research socially sensitive? ■ Does the research involve emotional stress? ■ How will informed consent and briefing be addressed?
7	Reflexivity	What is the researcher's interest and position in the research – and how could it be addressed?

Considerations during an interview

	Considerations during an interview	**Discussion**
1	Establishing rapport between interviewer and participant(s).	■ A trusting and open relationship is the best way to have participants talk freely.
2	Data recording	■ Make sure that technical equipment (e.g. a video recorder) functions properly from the start so that the interviewer can concentrate on the participant.
3	Active and neutral listening	■ Ask questions clearly and be an active listener. Don't interrupt the respondent and be neutral. ■ Ensure that participants have the possibility to explain their own views to prevent bias such as "participant expectation" or researcher bias .
4	Professional approach	■ If participants want to withdraw in the middle of the interview, they should be allowed to leave (even though data is lost).

Considerations after an interview

	Considerations after an interview	Discussion
1	Debriefing	Participants must be informed about the results of the research. They should also have the possibility to withdraw their data.
2	Confidentiality and anonymity	Make sure that participants cannot be identified. Since participants' own words are used as documentation for interpretation, names of participants can be changed.
3	Credibility check	Ask for peer review to check interpretations. Consult participants about the analysis and interpretation of the data.
4	Specific consent to use data, photos, etc.	All data produced in the study including videos, photos, etc. should only be used if there is specific consent from participants. It is a norm to destroy videos and photos after a study to ensure anonymity but there are exceptions.

Explain how researchers use inductive content analysis (thematic analysis) on interview transcripts

The goal of inductive content analysis is to give a credible representation of the social world under investigation. In the research report, there should be a balance between description and interpretation.

The process of inductive content analysis involves the following:

- Collecting data and making an initial analysis.

- Preparing the data for content analysis (will transcription be verbatim or post-modern?).

- Reading and re-reading the material. Identification of initial themes based on first readings of the raw data (for example, grounded theory approach). This first attempt at coding prepares for analysis.

- Analysing. This starts early in the data collection process and moves back and forth between data collection, analysis, and concept development.

- analysis, and low-level themes into higher-level themes.

- Checking whether interpretations are credible (e.g. consistent with the raw data and in line with the participants' perceptions.

- Structuring emergent themes and making a summary table of themes. Include relevant quotations to illustrate each theme.

- Inferences and conclusions are formed based on the summary table. At this stage the researcher tries to identify relationships between themes. This very important part of the process may reveal specific patterns in the themes which may lead to formulation of theory.

The process of inductive content analysis

153

Evaluate participant, non-participant, naturalistic, overt, and covert observations

- Participant observation is sometimes referred to as 'ethnography' and it is used in sociology, anthropology and psychology.
- Participant observations are used when first-hand information about people (for example, a sports team, a street gang, homeless adolescents or abused women) is needed.

- The researcher participates actively in the participants' life, observes, listens, and produces field notes. Participation can for example be as a co-worker, voluntary work in shelters or sports clubs in order to describe beliefs and experiences of the participants (their own 'theories of the world').
- The researcher could include reflexivity in the research process to increase credibility, for example if own experiences influence choice of topic or how relationship with participants could influence data collection and interpretation.

Characteristics of participant observations:

- The researcher becomes part of the target group under investigation.
- The focus of the study is on *natural* behaviour in its *natural* context.
- The researcher enters the field (the place where the research takes place) and act as the instrument of data collection. The aim is to obtain a close and intimate familiarity and empathy with participants through personal involvement with people in their own environment.

The researcher needs professional and interpersonal skills to stay as objective as possible in the research process. He or she must be able to initiate and maintain relationships with the people under investigation.

Strengths of participant observation	Limitations of participant observation
■ It generates detailed and in-depth information of a topic, which cannot be studied by other methods. ■ It is useful in exploring socially sensitive issues because the researcher can take many different aspects of a topic into consideration (holistic approach). ■ It is a good method to avoid researcher bias because the aim is to understand social processes from the perspective of participants.	■ Data collection and analysis is very time consuming, especially in long-term projects. Often groups are small so it is difficult to generalize findings. ■ It is a highly invasive research method: can influence people's lives and environment. ■ The researcher may lose objectivity. It is difficult to keep a balance between involvement and detachment. Reflexivity can increase credibility.

Evaluate non-participant observation

- Non-participant observation is sometimes used in combination with participant observation (e.g. in research on gambling where researchers may decide to gamble themselves (participant observation) and combine that with observations of gamblers in a gambling setting).

- Qualitative data from field observations can be combined with data from interviews or quantitative data (triangulation).

Characteristics of non-participant observation

- The researcher does not take part in the participants' life and interactions, instead merely observes and records behaviour in the setting, so it is considered to be a method that does not interfere much with participants' normal life (an unobtrusive method).
- Non-participant observation can take place in a naturalistic setting and the researchers records natural behaviour (e.g. recording if gamblers engage in specific behaviours that they think may bring luck).
- The researcher will inform participants about the observation in general terms but not about the exact behaviours being studied to avoid increase in those behaviours (reactivity or demand characteristics).

Non-participant observation can also be used to study children or parent-child interactions (e.g. in controlled observations in laboratories using one-way mirrors). This is not a natural setting and the question is whether it is natural behaviour.

Strengths of non-participant observation	Limitations of non-participant observation
■ It is easier to collect data because the researcher does not interact with participants but only observes. ■ The researcher can observe natural behaviour. ■ It is a useful way of observing the behaviour of small groups or interaction between individuals. ■ Observational data can be cross-checked with other observers to establish credibility.	■ There is a risk that the presence of the researcher influences data (reactivity). ■ Deception may be necessary to avoid reactivity. ■ Consider artificiality. It is difficult know that natural behaviour is recorded, especially in laboratory observations. ■ Coding of observational data can be difficult if it is not a structured observation. ■ Analysis can be time consuming and costly.

Evaluate naturalistic observation

- Observations in qualitative research mostly take place in a naturalistic setting and focus on the context and natural behaviour (e.g. a study on how a mother and her infant interact in their own home or a prison where inmates are studied). Naturalistic observations are more likely to be high in ecological validity.

- Observations can also take place in a laboratory setting (controlled observation). In qualitative research the researcher is not normally interested in behaviour in a deliberately set-up situation. He or she will record natural behaviour in the laboratory (e.g. mother-child interactions).

Characteristics of naturalistic observations

- Data are collected by the researcher who observe and record how people (or animals) behave. The aim is to collect information in a natural environment (the context) to provide an account of the interactions in a particular social group.
- The researcher often spends a long time "in the field" in order to become familiar with participants' natural environment. The researcher collects data and writes field notes used for analysis.
- Observations in the field can be complemented with, for example, interview data or quantitative data from questionnaires (triangulation).

Strengths of naturalistic observation	Limitations of naturalistic observation
■ The researcher can observe natural behaviour in a natural environment. Qualitative researchers prefer naturalistic observations because it increases ecological validity. ■ It can be combined with controlled laboratory observations and data from other qualitative methods (triangulation to increase credibility). ■ Observational data can be cross-checked with other observers to establish credibility.	■ Ethical issues are involved if the naturalistic observation is covert. ■ Analysis of data can be time consuming and costly – especially if the observation is unstructured.

Evaluate overt and covert observations
- Observations may be overt (participants know they are being observed) or covert (participants do not know they are being observed).

- The researcher decides in advance which technique to use for the qualitative research. It depends on the topic of the study. For example, research in religious cults or street gangs could be conducted as covert because the researcher wants to be sure that the data genuinely describes the world as the participants sees it.

Overt observations: Participants know they participate in the research		Covert observations: Participants do not know they participate in the research	
Strengths	**Limitations**	**Strengths**	**Limitations**
■ Participants can be informed about the topic and give informed consent. ■ Data collection can be triangulated with interview data.	■ The researcher may lose objectivity and become too involved. ■ The researcher's presence is a potential source of bias (reactivity).	■ It is possible to study groups that cannot be studied otherwise; or when it is vital to avoid reactivity. ■ There is limited or no reactivity since participants don't know about the research.	■ Participants are not informed about the research and cannot give informed consent. ■ It can be dangerous if participants find out about the study.

Exam Tip Researchers will decide before the observation whether it should be covert or overt depending on the research topic. You could be asked to evaluate the use of covert observation in the context of the study in the stimulus material. Take a close look at the study and try to make a reasoned argument on why the researchers have used that approach, using examples from the stimulus material.

Discuss considerations involved in setting up and carrying out an observation
- Researchers enter the social world of the people they are studying and participate in that world – overtly or covertly.

- Researchers must be able to put themselves "in the shoes" of the people they are studying to experience events in the way participants experience them.
- Researchers should be objective (e.g. avoid letting personal beliefs and values interfere with the research process).

Considerations in setting up and carrying out an the observation

	Considerations	**Discussion**
1	Methodological considerations	■ Overt/Covert; participant/non-participant observation and how choice of method could influence the data (e.g. increase participant expectations).
2	Ethical considerations	■ Informed consent. For covert observation the group's permission to study them has not been obtained. ■ Debriefing of participants after the study – gain retrospective consent in covert observations if possible. ■ Ensure anonymity of participants (e.g destroying videotapes or material after the study that can reveal participants' identity.
3	Sampling method	■ Consider the sampling method (e.g purposive, snowball, convenience). Sampling depends on the research topic but in qualitative research a purposive sample is often chosen because the focus is on specific people or specific situations.
4	Data recording	■ This could include decisions of how to make field notes in covert observations (e.g. if it would be possible to make entries in a field diary every day). ■ In overt observations, data collection is expected by participants but the researcher should decide what to note observations (e.g. conversations, interaction between group members, norms, and power relationships). ■ In socially sensitive areas videos or audiotapes cannot be used for ethical reasons as it would reveal participants' identity.

	Considerations	Discussion
5	Observer characteristics	■ Match observers to the target group. For example, a female researcher could not do covert observation in a street gang or a young male researcher could not covertly join a convent to study nuns. The success of participant observations depends on the researcher's ability to 'blend in' with participants.
6	Degree of involvement in the group	■ In overt observations the degree of involvement may be rather superficial. ■ In a covert observation of a street gang involved in criminal activities it could be necessary to accompany group members on their criminal expeditions but this would be ethically problematic and even dangerous.
7	Objectivity of researcher	■ The researcher often stays a long time "in the field" and could become more subjective as time passes. It is an advantage if more observers work in the field and compare data. ■ The researcher needs to be attentive to potential biases (participant expectancy and researcher bias). Credibility checks and reflexivity could control for this.
8	Analysis of data	■ Consider conductive content analysis and thematic analysis. ■ The researcher should decide how to analyse the data from observations and field notes.

Discuss how researchers analyse data obtained in observational research

■ The field notes in observational research (or transcripts of audio or videotaped observations) can be analysed using qualitative content analysis (inductive content analysis).

■ The field notes contain raw data as well as researcher comments and inferences to the observation. These are entered continuously and should be seen as preliminary analysis and attempt to identify possible themes.

■ The purpose of inductive content analysis is to identify categories (themes) that can be organized in lower-level and higher-level themes in the data. It is assumed that inductive content analysis can describe the social world as it is seen by participants.

Field notes can be compared with data from other sources (e.g. interviews, pictures, narratives) to increase credibility (triangulation).

Possible content of field notes
* Description of the physical context (e.g. the buildings, the environment, the rooms).
* Description of people (e.g. their role, how they behave, how they interact, how they dress).
* Dialogue (e.g. what people say to each other).
* Special events (e.g. meetings, coaching sessions, visits of specialists, excursions).
* A diary where all events are registered chronologically in the field and before entering the field if relevant.
* A reflective/analytic diary including comments to what happens in the field, reflections on own life experiences (reflexivity) and preliminary attempts of analysis and emerging themes.

Inductive content analysis could include the following steps:

■ **Reading and re-reading of field notes, transcriptions, etc.** to provide a complete description of the topic of interest (includes context, intentions of participants, processes in which behaviour is embedded). The more description the "thicker" the description (detailed) and this is considered as rich data.

■ **Coding and connecting themes:**
  ■ The data is coded – organized into categories (themes) – based on reading and re-reading of the field notes. Coding could also include content of pictures and video clips.

■ A graphical representation of categories and their connection is created with case or text examples.

■ The analysis is summarized in "memos" so that independent readers can follow how and why the connections between the themes are suggested.

■ The categories (themes) are organized into lower-order and higher-order themes to create an overall picture of the meaning of the data.

■ The researcher interprets the data based on the summary table but it is important to consider alternative interpretations.

■ **Produce an account:** The researcher produces a coherent description of the phenomenon under investigation. This could lead to formulation of new concepts and theory, which has emerged from the data (grounded theory).

A graphical representation of a summary table of emerging themes in an observational study to investigate benefits of a youth mentoring programme.

```
┌─────────────────────┐          ┌─────────────────┐
│ More likely to attend school │ ──────→ │ Educational    │
│ and better performance │        │ benefits       │
└─────────────────────┘          └─────────────────┘
                                          ↕
┌─────────────────────┐                  
│ More self-esteem and │ ──┐       ┌─────────────────┐        ┌─────────────────┐
│ self-efficacy       │    ├──────→│ Personal        │ ──────→│ Multiple benefits│
└─────────────────────┘    │       │ benefits        │        │ of the programme │
                           │       └─────────────────┘        └─────────────────┘
┌─────────────────────┐    │               ↕
│ Belief in the future and │ ──┘                  
│ have goals          │              
└─────────────────────┘          ┌─────────────────┐
                                 │                 │
┌─────────────────────┐          │ Benefits to     │
│ Reduction in criminal │ ──────→ │ community       │
│ activities          │          └─────────────────┘
└─────────────────────┘
```

10.4 Case studies

Evaluate the use of case studies in research

- A case study can be defined as an in-depth investigation of human experience called 'a case'. The aim of the case study is to describe, understand, and often explain a psychological or social phenomenon from the perspective of the participant(s).

- The case study is particularly useful to investigate sensitive topics such as poverty, health issues, and domestic violence but it is also useful to investigate social processes in groups such as team cohesion or conflicts.

Strengths of the case study	Limitations of the case study
■ It is well-suited to investigate sensitive and complex issues in areas that could not be studied otherwise.	■ Researcher bias could potentially be a problem since the researcher's own beliefs and ideas could influence data collection.
■ It is useful for studying group processes within a social group (e.g. beliefs, norms and communication patterns).	■ Generalization of findings from a single case study or a small number of cases is not always possible.
■ The results from a case study may generate entirely new knowledge, which challenges preconceived notions and contradicts established theory.	■ There is a risk of participant expectancy (or researcher bias) since researcher and participants interact with each other for long periods.

Explain how a case study could be used to investigate a problem in an organization or group

The case study method could be used to investigate a problem

- The problem in this case is a school class in the inner city of a capital. There are 20 children in the class and more than half are minority children. Their motivation and academic performance is generally low and the risk that they will drop out of school is a potential problem.
- The school wants to implement new teaching strategies to increase motivation and learning so a group of psychologists will be asked to investigate the problem.

The researcher will have to define the case and the problem to investigate, for example:

- *why* minority children in a school class have motivational problems and a slow learning curve
- *how* social and psychological processes may prevent these children from learning.

Design: Single case study

- The researcher could choose a single case study because the aim is to describe the problem in this particular group but also to suggest possible strategies to change the situation.
- The main research question in this case study could be: "Can specific teaching strategies used by a class teacher promote motivation and learning in minority students in a class?"

Field research and data collection methods

In this case study the researchers could use the following methods to investigate the problem:

- Participant observation to understand the situation from the perspective of the participants, i.e. students and teachers. The researchers might decide to act as co-teachers for a year and carry out observations during classes.
- Focus groups with all students in groups of 5 to discuss how they perceive the situation (e.g. why they are not motivated to learn; what kind of teaching they prefer and why).
- Student writings once a month where students are invited to write freely about their life and expectations. Their accounts could give insight into individual students' perceptions, beliefs, dreams, or other factors that could help understand the problem.

Data analysis and findings

- The researchers will have multiple data for analysis: notes from field observations, transcripts from focus group interviews and free writings. Inductive content analysis could be used to analyse the data.
- The findings from the case study can be used to implement new teaching strategies in the school and perhaps generate new theory about effective teaching methods for less motivated students.

Discuss the extent to which findings can be generalized from a single case study

Normally it is not possible to generalize from a study with few participants. Qualitative researchers would say that generalization from a single case study may be possible if there is:

- Inferential generalization: the findings from a single case study can perhaps be applied in other but similar settings.
- The researchers should provide rich descriptions of the case to allow for this. In the example of the case study above, it would be relevant to suggest that the teaching strategies found to be effective to increase motivation in minority children could be transferred to similar settings to see whether the findings could be corroborated.

- Theoretical generalization: Yin (1984) argues the results of single case studies can be generalized to existing theory (theoretical generalization). If the patterns from one case study can be repeated, the theory derived from this single case study is said to be robust.

See also unit 10.1 for generalization from qualitative research studies.

SAQ (paper 1, section A)

> Reminder: **SL/HL:** There are three SAQs in paper 1, section A – one from each level of analysis – and you have to answer all three. In the exam this part of paper 1 takes one hour. The SAQ tests your knowledge and understanding of research (i.e. theories and studies).

How SAQ is assessed (mark bands)

Mark band	Level descriptor
0	The response does not reach a standard described by the descriptors below
1–2	There is an attempt to answer the question, but knowledge and understanding are limited, often inaccurate, or of marginal relevance to the question.
3–5	The question is partially answered. Knowledge and understanding are accurate but limited. Either the command term is not effectively addressed or the response is not sufficiently explicit in answering the question.
6–8	The question is answered in a focused and effective manner and meets the demands of the command term. The response is supported by appropriate and accurate knowledge and understanding of research.

What is the SAQ?

- The SAQ is a short answer (around 200 words). It does not require an introduction but it is a good idea to start the response with reference to the question. For example:
  - **Question:** Outline one principle that defines the cognitive level of analysis.
  - **SAQ response:** One principle that defines the cognitive level of analysis could be that cognitive processes are influenced by sociocultural factors. An example of this could be that cultural schemas may influence memory processes as demonstrated by Bartlett (1932).........
- There are **three rules** in writing the SAQ in paper 1:
  - **FOCUS** (on the question and the command term)
  - **STRUCTURE** (a clear development from start to end)
  - **ARGUE** (substantiate your claim[s] with relevant psychological knowledge).

The process of writing SAQs

- Read the question carefully and decide what is the most relevant knowledge to include. Focus on the demands of the question, the command term being the most important.
- Make an outline of your line of argument and relevant research (theories and empirical studies) to use in the response.

- Start the response with reference to the question but apart from that no introduction is needed. Make the response short, clear, and precise and use psychological terms and concepts (follow the three rules given here).

Read the question carefully: What is the command term? What could be used as relevant knowledge?	Make an outline to get an overview of the line of argument and how knowledge should be applied (command term and focus of the question).	Check the question again – and write your response using psychological knowledge (theory and/or study) to support the argument.

SAQ 1: A sample answer from the biological level of analysis

Describe one evolutionary explanation of behaviour [8 marks].

One evolutionary explanation of behaviour could be that the hormone oxytocin is important in establishing trust among humans. According to the evolutionary theory, trust is important in forming relationships between people and in the facilitation of social interactions.

Baumgartner et al. (2008) studied people's reactions in a "trust game" where participants played with a partner. The participants received either oxytocin or placebo via a nasal spray and they were told to act as investors in several rounds of the trust game. The results showed that participants who had received placebo were more likely to show less trust to their partner and they invested less. Participants who had received oxytocin in the nasal spray continued to invest at similar rates. The researchers could observe that different brain areas were active in the two groups. Participants in the oxytocin group showed decreased responses in the amygdala, which has many oxytocin receptors.

This could indicate that oxytocin plays a role in decreasing fear reactions as a consequence of betrayal. This could be useful in terms of evolution because it allows people to "forgive" and work it out despite "betrayal".

Examiner's comment

The answer is focused on the question. Relevant knowledge is used effectively and demonstrates an understanding of the research (the theory and its link to the study mentioned). The demands of the command term is met although there is a tendency towards explanation in the last paragraph. The response is in the top end and received full marks.

Mark band	Level descriptor	Comments
6–8	The question is answered in a focused and effective manner and meets the demands of the command term. The response is supported by appropriate and accurate knowledge and understanding of research.	There is a clear focus in the response. The command term is met. The knowledge is appropriate and accurate and there is a clear understanding of the theory and the study used to support the argument.

SAQ 2: A sample answer from the cognitive level of analysis

Explain how one principle that defines the cognitive level of analysis can be demonstrated in research [8 marks].

Cognitive processes are influenced by social and cultural factors. This principle of the cognitive level of analysis can be demonstrated in research most simply through the use of social or cultural factors as the independent variable within an experiment. The dependent variable would be any cognitive process. Hence changes in social or cultural factors could be directly related to changes in cognitive processes. Frederic Bartlett conducted an experiment with this structure. He tested people from different social/cultural backgrounds and their ability to recall information from another culture. What he found was that people had difficulties recalling information from another culture. This experiment demonstrates that cognitive processes are influenced by social and cultural factors.

Examiner's comment

The response is not explicit in answering the question. It shows limited and inaccurate knowledge and understanding of research. The command term is not effectively addressed. The response received a mark in the lower end of the mark band (3/8).

Mark band	Level descriptor	Comments
3–5	The question is partially answered. Knowledge and understanding are accurate, but limited. Either the command term is not effectively addressed or the response is not sufficiently explicit in answering the question.	Only 3 marks were awarded because the question is only partially answered. The command term is not effectively addressed. Knowledge and understanding is limited.

Writing essays – paper 1 section B and paper 2 (options)

Format of the essay
The conventional format of an essay is:

- **Introduction:** This introduces the essay question and your line of argument (e.g. your thesis statement, what your are going to address, and why). This part of the essay is short and focused.

- **Main body:** This is the development and is divided into about five or six paragraphs. The essay question directs you to what psychological knowledge could be relevant and the command term tells you what to do with the knowledge. In this section it is most important to present a clear argument supported by relevant knowledge.

- **Conclusion:** This must relate directly to the essay question and it should follow logically on from your argument in the main body.

The essay is testing three things:

- **Knowledge and comprehension of psychology** (i.e. your knowledge of psychological theories, empirical studies, key concepts, and that you can use it appropriately.

- **Critical thinking skills** (i.e. that you can apply and evaluate the knowledge appropriately and use it in the analysis of psychological phenomena).

- **Organizational skills** (i.e. that you can focus on the question and structure the essay so that it appears coherent and logical and that you can build an argument).

The four rules for writing an essay:

- **FOCUS** (on the question and the command term)

- **STRUCTURE** (a clear development from start to end)

- **ARGUE** (substantiate your claim[s] with relevant psychological knowledge)

- Use **CRITICAL THINKING SKILLS** (e.g. evaluate theories and studies and take a critical look at methodology)

Your essays will be assessed according to the following assessment criteria for essays:

A: Knowledge and comprehension

Mark band	Level descriptor
0	The answer does not reach a standard described by the descriptor below.
1–3	The answer demonstrates limited knowledge and understanding that is of marginal relevance to the question. Little or no psychological research is used in the response.
4–6	The answer demonstrates limited knowledge and understanding relevant to the question or uses relevant psychological research to limited effect in the response.
7–9	The answer demonstrates detailed, accurate knowledge and understanding relevant to the question, and uses relevant psychological research effectively in support of the response.

B: Evidence of critical thinking: Application, analysis, synthesis, evaluation

Mark band	Level of descriptor
0	The answer does not reach a standard described by the descriptors below.
1–3	The answer goes beyond description but evidence of critical thinking is not linked to the requirements of the question.
4–6	The answer offers appropriate but limited evidence of critical thinking or offers evidence of critical thinking that is only implicitly linked to the requirements of the question.
7–9	The answer integrates relevant and explicit evidence of critical thinking in response to the question.

C: Organization

Mark band	Level of descriptor
0	The answer does not reach a standard described by the descriptors below.
1–2	The answer is organized or focused on the question. However, this is not sustained throughout the response.
3–4	The answer is well organized, well developed, and focused on the question.

A step-by-step guide to writing good essays in psychology

1. **Read the essay question carefully:** What is the command term? What exactly does the question ask you to do?

2. **Choose the relevant knowledge:** What knowledge could be relevant to answer the question?

   a. There may be several relevant **research studies** and/or **theories** but make a choice. Don't introduce knowledge which is not directly relevant to the essay question.

   b. You will probably not need more than three studies, and fewer could be appropriate if you are also presenting a theory. For some essay questions theories may be sufficient but it is nearly always a good idea to introduce a study.

3. **Consider your argument:** What are you going to argue? What are your points and how will you support them?

   a. Consider counter argument and conclusion based on evidence.

   b. Try to create a logical flow in your argument by connecting the sentences and paragraphs to each other (e.g. using topic sentences and terms like, "on the other hand", "furthermore", "however", "as a result", and "consequently").

   c. Avoid stating your own personal opinions unless they are supported by psychological evidence.

4. **Consider critical thinking skills:** How are you going to apply critical thinking?

   a. The assessment criteria focus on application, analysis, synthesis and evaluation, so be sure to introduce some of these in your response.

   b. For example, when you have described a study, you could "step back" and take a critical look at it and comment on the methodology used in relation to findings or say what the implications of the results are. You could also come up with a study that questions the findings of the first. Or you could analyse how the findings of the two studies each contribute to an overall understanding of a phenomenon.

5. **Plan:** Before you start writing make an outline following the 8 paragraph model to be sure that there is a clear structure to your essay.

   a. The organization of the essay is assessed on criterion C so try to outline what you will address and in what order. This also has to do with your argument and the knowledge you use to support it.

   b. Outline introduction (must be short).

   c. Outline conclusion.

6. **Write:** Use your outline and proceed in the order you have planned.

   a. Stick to your plan. Something may occur to you while you write but don't just use it. Consider carefully whether it is relevant and would benefit your argument. If not, leave it and focus on what you have planned.

   b. Be aware that extra marks are given for analysis and evaluation (see point 4 above) and that pure description will not give you many marks from criterion B.

   c. Use the third person when you write (e.g. "the researcher found that...").

7. **Check the essay for flaws:** Check that your response addresses the essay question, the command term is met, the argument is clear, there is use of critical thinking skills, and the language is clear.

Essay sample 1 from the biological level of analysis (paper 1, section B)

Discuss how and why particular research methods are used at the biological level of analysis [22 marks].

Psychologists at the biological level of analysis are trying to find specific biological correlates of behaviour. Researchers choose different methods depending on the aim of research but two research methods used at the biological level of analysis could be the experiment and the case study.

Researchers often use the experimental method because it can establish cause-effect relationships between biological variables and behaviour. The researchers deliberately manipulate an independent variable to measure the effect of that on the dependent variable. The experimental method was applied in Newcomer et. al. (1999). The aim of the experiment was to see how different levels of cortisol affected verbal declarative memory when participants recalled parts of a prose text. There were three conditions. Group 1 received a high dose of cortisol (160 mg), which is the same as a person experiencing a major stressor. Group 2 received a low dose of cortisol (40 mg), which is the same as a person experiencing slight stress. Group 3 was the placebo group, which acted as control. After four days the participants were asked to recall the text.

The results showed that the participants on the high cortisol dose performed worst on the verbal declarative memory test. This indicates a relationship between high levels of cortisol and memory. By deliberately manipulating the cortisol levels the researchers could demonstrate its effect on memory.

Some methodological concerns arise, however. The experimental procedure is often said to suffer from low ecological validity due to artificiality. It could therefore be argued that such results do not give insight into how cortisol levels affect memory in real-life situations. However, since biological processes are assumed to be more or less similar in real life and in the laboratory this argument could be refuted. The use of the experimental method indicates a clear cause-effect relationship between levels of cortisol and memory and this is probably why the researchers chose this method.

Another method used at the biological level of analysis is the case study. This is an in-depth study of an individual case (e.g. an individual with brain damage). Case studies are "natural experiments" and researchers can use them to study phenomena that cannot be studied otherwise. In case studies it is only possible to observe what already exists and no cause-effect relationship can be established. One important case study was by Scoville and Milner (1957) of H.M. who suffered from epileptic seizures and eventually underwent experimental surgery to stop them. Scoville removed tissue from the medial temporal lobe, including the hippocampus. The seizures stopped but after some time it became clear that H.M. could not store new explicit memories at all – he suffered from permanent amnesia. H.M. became one of the most extensively studied individuals in the history of cognitive neuroscience. His memory was tested in a number of ways and he was also scanned (Corkin, 2002). This gave a more precise picture of the brain damage and helped researchers to get an even better understanding of H.M.'s memory.

The case study of H.M. was a very important step for cognitive neuroscientists towards understanding the role of the hippocampus in memory and to develop revised theories of memory. Knowledge from this case study was also used to perform experimental surgery on animals to establish the biological correlates of memory more specifically. This shows how case studies can spark off new research and why researchers at the biological level of analysis use them.

On the other hand, there are some ethical and methodological concerns in the use of a case study such as H.M. Ethical concerns are relevant since consent from an individual with amnesia who was not even able to remember what happened 15 minutes ago can be hard to get. However, in the case of H.M. his parents gave consent. It could also be argued that so much knowledge that benefits other humans has been gathered from this case that the extensive use of H.M. in research is justified. A methodological problem is that results from case studies cannot be used to make generalizations about human behaviour because they represent unique individuals. However, similar case studies show that the hippocampus is very important in storage of memory.

In conclusion, researchers within the biological level of analysis use different methods. Case studies such as that of H.M. give invaluable insight into conditions that could not otherwise be studied and the experimental method can establish cause-effect relationships between biological factors and behaviour, so case studies and experiments can complement each other in the study of biological correlates of behaviour.

Examiner's comment

This essay is well focused on the question. The argument is well developed and supported by relevant knowledge throughout. The research studies are highly relevant and they are used effectively to demonstrate how and why two specific research methods are used at the biological level of analysis. Critical thinking skills are demonstrated but a bit mechanical in the evaluation of the methods used although the comments are quite relevant. The response is in the top end and received 20/22 marks.

A: Knowledge and comprehension

Mark band	Level descriptor	Comments
7–9	The answer demonstrates detailed, accurate knowledge and understanding relevant to the question, and uses relevant psychological research effectively in support of the response.	There is accurate and detailed knowledge of the two chosen research methods. This knowledge is integrated with specific studies, which are then used to illustrate the rationale for choice of method at the biological level of analysis. (marks 9/9)

B: Evidence of critical thinking: Application, analysis, synthesis, evaluation

Mark band	Level of descriptor	
7–9	The answer integrates relevant and explicit evidence of critical thinking in response to the question.	The elements of critical thinking in this response are analysis and evaluation. (marks 7/9)

C: Organization

Mark band	Level of descriptor	
3–4	The answer is well organized, well developed, and focused on the question.	There is a clear structure to the essay. The argument is well developed and focused on the question. (marks 4/4)

11.3 Paper 3 SAQ (HL only)

Reminder:
- Paper 3 is a paper on qualitative research methodology. It includes stimulus material (a brief account of a qualitative study or a scenario) and three SAQs.
- All three SAQs. must be answered using your knowledge of qualitative research methods and with reference to the stimulus material.

Paper 3 is testing:
- Your knowledge and understanding of qualitative research methods.
- Your understanding of how to apply that knowledge to the stimulus material (i.e. you should try to place yourself in a researcher's position and reflect on how the questions raised could be applicable to the study in the stimulus material.

All SAQs in paper 3 are marked according to the criteria below. Examiners will use the mark band when marking and try to find the best fit.

Mark band	Level descriptor
0	The answer does not reach a standard described by the descriptors below.
1–3	There is an attempt to answer the question, but knowledge and understanding is limited, often inaccurate, or of marginal relevance to the question. The response makes no direct reference to the stimulus material or relies too heavily on quotations from the text.
4–7	The question is partially answered. Knowledge and understanding is accurate but limited. Either the command term is not effectively addressed or the response is not sufficiently explicit in answering the question. The response makes limited use of the stimulus material.
8–10	The question is answered in a focused and effective manner and meets the demands of the command term. The answer is supported by appropriate and accurate knowledge and understanding of qualitative research methodology. The response demonstrates a critical understanding of qualitative research methodology applied to the stimulus material.

The process of writing an SAQ in paper 3

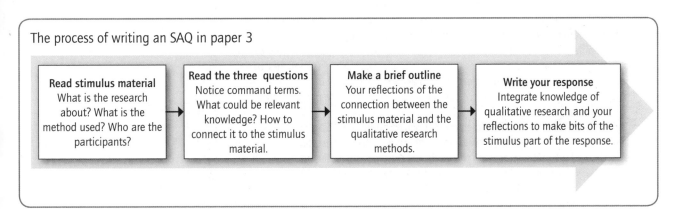

Read stimulus material	**Read the three questions**	**Make a brief outline**	**Write your response**
What is the research about? What is the method used? Who are the participants?	Notice command terms. What could be relevant knowledge? How to connect it to the stimulus material.	Your reflections of the connection between the stimulus material and the qualitative research methods.	Integrate knowledge of qualitative research and your reflections to make bits of the stimulus part of the response.

Example of a paper 3 question with stimulus material

Qualitative research study: Placebo effect in competitive sport

1 The "placebo effect" is defined as an effect of *beliefs* rather than a drug. In research athletes have been made to believe that they received anabolic steroids, carbohydrates, or caffeine and they performed better than baseline or controls. The focus in placebo research in sport is on the role of *beliefs* as a psychological factor in

5 performance. Sport psychologists have argued that many technologies, products, or substances that seem to have an effect on athletes' performance have no clear biological basis but may simply be the result of the placebo effect.

The aim of this qualitative study was to investigate athletes' experience of placebo effects in competition. The researchers were all sport psychologists with a history of

10 being professional in sport.
The snowball sample consisted of seven males and seven females (N = 14) from different sports. Each participant first heard a brief description of the placebo effect. The researchers used semi-structured interviews to collect data. All participants were asked (1) if they believed that performance could be influenced by the placebo effect

15 or by similar false beliefs and (2) if they had ever experienced a moment in sport in which a "false belief'" affected their performance.

The interviews were transcribed and the data was analysed using inductive content analysis to identify themes related to the placebo effect.

A little more than half of the participants believed that the placebo effect had

20 influenced their performance. They could recall an event in which a form of placebo effect or false belief had positively influenced their performance. The inductive content analysis revealed that factors such as *rituals* (e.g. shaving the legs before a swimming competition), *false beliefs based on ingestion of a substance* (e.g. a drug believed to enhance performance) or *false beliefs based on misperception* (e.g. a

25 coach saying, "You have already done this so you can do it again.")

The identified themes were all based on the participants' own statements and these were used as documentation in the report to increase credibility. For example, a weightlifter explained that he was fooling himself into believing that he was lifting less on the bench-press and that this helped him to a better performance. The

30 participants all pointed at the important factor of "expectations" in performance. The belief in the efficacy of a substance, training procedures, coaches' statements, or rituals was seen as important factors in the placebo effect. Many of the participants said they believed that performance could be manipulated by the placebo effect.

The researchers concluded that "the power of belief" ought to be taken into

35 consideration when preparing athletes for competition. They suggest that "the placebo effect" could perhaps interact with the biological system to increase performance in a natural way but that more research is needed to explore this systematically.

Answer all three questions

With reference to the stimulus material
1. Explain how researchers could use inductive content analysis on the interview transcripts in this qualitative study [10 marks].
2. Explain how reflexivity could be applied in the context of this qualitative research [10 marks].
3. Discuss sampling techniques appropriate to this qualitative research study [10 marks].

Sample answers

1. Explain how researchers could use inductive content analysis on the interview transcript in this study

Inductive content analysis is used to organize and categorize themes emerging from the data in the interview transcripts. Through the categorization of themes the researcher can analyse and interpret the data. The researchers wanted to investigate the athletes' subjective perception of the possible influence of the placebo effect (or false beliefs) on sports performances. They conducted semi-structured interviews, which were transcribed. To analyse the data they read and re-read the transcripts in order to code the data and identify categories and themes.

The analysis resulted in different themes emerging and they were organized into lower- and higher-level themes. An example of a lower-level theme could be a routine such as "shaving the legs before a swimming competition improves performance

level". Lower-level themes are organized into higher-level themes (e.g. "false beliefs about routines" or "false beliefs about power of substances") to create a hierarchy of themes. This is often represented in a table to create an overview. Each theme is supported by quotes from the participants to make the final interpretation of the data transparent and to increase credibility. In the study in the stimulus material, the researchers concluded based on the result of the inductive content analysis that "the power of belief" should be taken into consideration in competition preparation.

Examiner's comment
This response is focused on the question and meets the demands of the command term. Knowledge and understanding of inductive content analysis is appropriate but a bit limited, but it is well linked to the study in the stimulus material. This response received 8/10 marks.

2. Explain how reflexivity could be applied in the context of this qualitative research study

In order to achieve a high level of credibility or trustworthiness in qualitative research one important factor is reflexivity — researchers reflect on their own role in the research. A researcher must reflect on why they are studying the particular topic and whether they have any expectations or opinions that might influence collection, analysis, and interpretation of the data.

This could be illustrated in the qualitative study. The researchers were all former professional athletes and it is possible that they have personal experiences with the placebo effect. This could influence the research process unless the researchers account for their reasons for studying the placebo effect in sport and how experiences and beliefs as former athletes could potentially bias the collection and interpretation of the data (e.g. they would try to look for things confirming their own expectations). To be aware of this potential bias means researchers have an opportunity to avoid it.

All factors that could influence the analysis and interpretation of results should be included in order to achieve transparency and credibility – the interpretation should be based upon logical connection of themes from the inductive content analysis and not reflect the researchers' personal views or experiences. Since the study was only based upon interviews it might have increased credibility further if there were several sources of data (e.g. observations). This can be achieved through method triangulation.

Examiner's comment
This response shows appropriate and accurate knowledge of reflexivity in qualitative research and the knowledge is well connected to the stimulus material. There is a tendency to redundant information in the last paragraph and this could affect focus of the response here at the end. On the other hand, there is a clear focus in the first two paragraphs. The command term is met effectively. The response received 8/10 marks.

3. Discuss sampling techniques appropriate to this qualitative research study

The qualitative study deals with sport psychology and the power of beliefs so a sample of athletes would be a natural choice. Since this is a special criterion, the best sampling technique is purposive sampling — sampling to get participants who have specific characteristics. Since the researchers wanted to investigate false beliefs in athletes from various sports, a purposive sample would be fine. A problem with purposive sampling is, that it could be biased if the sample lacks variation (e.g. contains only white male athletes) but it is assumed that if the selection criteria are objective the bias will be limited.

The researchers in this qualitative research study decided to use a snowball sample, which is a kind of purposive sample but the selection criteria are subjective. Snowball sampling here means contacting one or a couple of athletes and making them recruit other athletes that they know. This sampling technique is usually used in cases where it is difficult to get participants

due to the sensitive topic (e.g. drug abuse). One advantage of snowball sampling, which could have influenced the decision, is that it is quite easy to get participants and it is time efficient. One could argue that snowball sampling is similar to purposive sampling because the sample still has to live up to certain criteria — however, unlike purposive sampling, the risk of bias is much higher since participants might be the same type of athletes and know each other. Confidentiality would be a problem with this kind of sampling. On the other hand, the researchers in this study might not have thought it important although the topic could be somewhat controversial.

Examiner's comment
This response is well focused and meets the command term "discuss". It demonstrates knowledge and critical understanding of sampling techniques in qualitative research and effectively discusses two potential sampling methods in the context of the study in the stimulus material. This response received 10/10 marks.

11.4 Command terms in IB psychology and assessment objectives

Command terms in IB psychology and assessment objectives

In the IB psychology course there are three levels of assessment objectives.

- Level 1: Knowledge and comprehension
- Level 2: Application and analysis
- Level 3: Synthesis and evaluation

The command terms indicate the level of study, i.e. in how much depth you should study a particular learning outcome.

The rules are:

- A learning outcome at level 1 and 2 will only be assessed with command terms at these levels. All command terms at level 1 and 2 can be used interchangeably. Level 3 command terms cannot be used in exam questions.

- A learning outcome at level 3 can be assessed at level 3 as well as level 1 and 2. All command terms at level 1, 2, and 3 can be used interchangeably. This means that a level 3 question in the guide can be changed into a level 2 question in an SAQ in paper 1 section A.

In SAQs there can only be level 1 and level 2 questions. In essays there can be level 3 questions.

Command terms level 1: Knowledge and comprehension

Command term	Explanation in the guide	What it means	Example
Define	Give the precise meaning of a word, concept, or phrase.	Say what it means in psychology and use the right concepts to do that.	Define attachment.
Describe	Give a detailed account.	Give a reason for, or a narrative of, something.	Describe the role of situational factors in explaining behaviour.
Outline	Give a brief account or summary of something.	Give a brief summary of whatever is mentioned in the question.	Outline one principle that defines the biological level of analysis.
State	Give a specific name or other brief answer without explanation.	Give a very brief answer but don't explain anything.	State the role of communication in maintaining relationships.

Command terms level 2: Application and analysis

Command term	Explanation	What it means	Example
Analyse	Break down in order to bring out the essential elements.	Analyse means to consider existing evidence in relation to a specific problem; investigate possible explanations of a psychological problem.	Analyse why relationships may change or end.
Apply	Use a theory or an idea in a given problem or issue.	Describe how a theory would explain a given psychological phenomenon.	Apply a relevant theory to explain burnout in sport.
Distinguish	Make clear the differences between two or more ideas or concepts.	Indicate differences between two concepts or theories.	Distinguish between altruism and prosocial behaviour.
Explain	Give a detailed account including reasons and causes.	Give reasons and causes for a psychological phenomenon.	Explain factors related to the development of addictive behaviour.

Command terms level 3: Synthesis and evaluation

Command term	Explanation	What it means	Example
Compare	Give an account of the similarities between two (or more) items or situations, referring to both (all) of them throughout.	Focus only on similarities and refer to these throughout the response.	Compare two theories of cognitive development.
Compare and contrast	Give an account of similarities and differences between two (or more) items or situations, referring to both (all) of them throughout.	Focus on both similarities and differences and refer to these throughout the response.	Compare and contrast two theories of cognitive development.
Contrast	Give an account of the differences between two (or more) items or situations, referring to both (all) of them throughout.	Focus only on differences and refer to these throughout the response.	Contrast two theories explaining altruism in humans.
Discuss	Offer a considered and balanced review that includes a range of arguments, factors, or hypotheses. Conclusions should be presented clearly and supported by appropriate evidence.	Address the question in a balanced way (not biased) where you consider available evidence and choose the most appropriate evidence to support your argument.	Discuss factors related to overeating and the development of obesity.
Evaluate	Make an appraisal by weighing up the strengths and limitations of something.	Assess the value of something (e.g. a theory or study) by looking into the evidence.	Evaluate one sociocultural explanation of violence.
Examine	Consider an argument or concept in a way that uncovers the assumptions and interrelationships of the issue.	Carefully scrutinize an argument (or theory, concept, explanation) to see how it explains something and perhaps why. An examination could also include finding similarities and differences.	Examine models of health promotion.
To what extent	Consider the merits or otherwise of an argument or concept. Conclusions should be presented clearly and supported with appropriate evidence and sound argument.	Assess the value of a theory or concept in explaining a psychological phenomenon (e.g. depression). The conclusion must be clear and supported by relevant evidence (i.e. empirical studies and evaluation of the theory) throughout the argument.	To what extent do biological, cognitive and sociocultural factors influence abnormal behaviour?

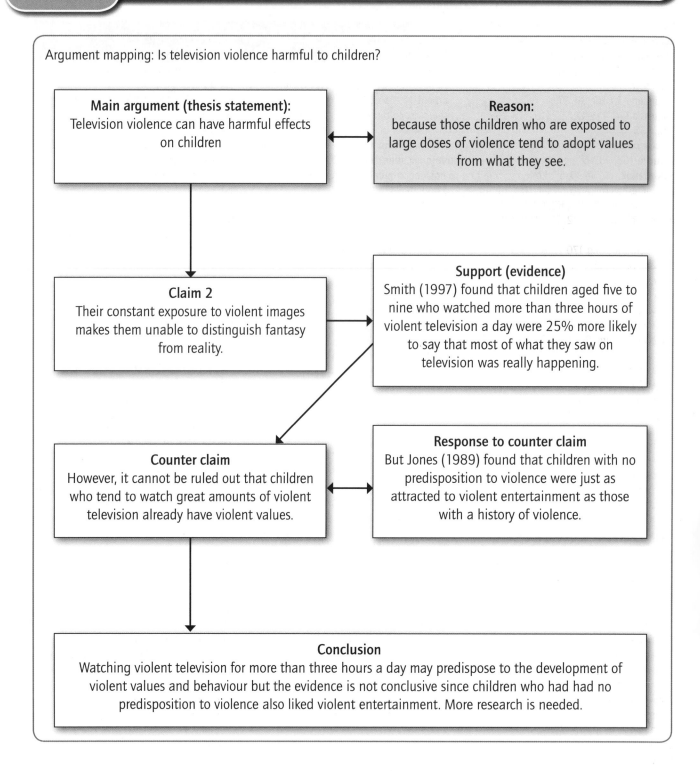

Argument mapping: Is television violence harmful to children?

Main argument (thesis statement):
Television violence can have harmful effects on children

Reason:
because those children who are exposed to large doses of violence tend to adopt values from what they see.

Claim 2
Their constant exposure to violent images makes them unable to distinguish fantasy from reality.

Support (evidence)
Smith (1997) found that children aged five to nine who watched more than three hours of violent television a day were 25% more likely to say that most of what they saw on television was really happening.

Counter claim
However, it cannot be ruled out that children who tend to watch great amounts of violent television already have violent values.

Response to counter claim
But Jones (1989) found that children with no predisposition to violence were just as attracted to violent entertainment as those with a history of violence.

Conclusion
Watching violent television for more than three hours a day may predispose to the development of violent values and behaviour but the evidence is not conclusive since children who had had no predisposition to violence also liked violent entertainment. More research is needed.

Index